PUNCH BEDSIDE BOOK

**Also edited by William Davis,
and available in Coronet Books:**

THE PUNCH GUIDE TO GOOD LIVING

Copyright © Punch Publications Limited
First published by Punch Publications Limited
Coronet edition 1973
Second impression 1973
Third impression 1974

Printed and bound in Great Britain for
Coronet Books,
Hodder Paperbacks Ltd,
St. Paul's House, Warwick Lane,
London, EC4P 4AH
by Compton Printing Ltd
Pembroke Road,
Stocklake,
Aylesbury, Bucks
and bound by Hazell Watson & Viney Ltd
Aylesbury, Bucks

ISBN 0 340 18216 4

Punch
Bedside Book

Edited by

William Davis

CORONET BOOKS
Hodder Paperbacks Ltd., London

CONTENTS

Introduction

EARLY in 1970 Punch ran a cartoon feature by Graham, one of the best-loved cartoonists in Britain, on the theme "A suburban orgy". When I first suggested the idea to him, he was doubtful. "What would readers say?" I told him not to worry. Punch readers could take it. The feature, when it appeared, proved a point which has tended to be forgotten in all the boring fuss about permissiveness —sex is not only fun, but also funny. Graham brilliantly conveyed the awkwardness of middle-class people faced with a situation which they are told is *de rigeur*, but which makes them feel embarrassed rather than erotically stimulated. There was the wife, anxiously asking her husband just before they knocked on the host's door, "Now, did you remember to put on a clean vest?" And there were the two middle-aged businessmen, looking most un-erotic in their striped underpants, watching a colleague chase a fetching female guest across the room. "So the group profits", said one to the other, "were £75,000—interim 5% already paid, of course."

We expected a few protests, but as it turned out there was only one. It came from a doctor's wife who objected to Graham's final quip—a cartoon which showed a couple saying goodbye to the host. The wife was shaking his hand and saying: "And thank you for having me." The doctor's lady thought this was simply too much. Punch, she insisted, had descended to unspeakable levels and henceforth would be banished from her husband's waiting room. I wrote back and said it was all in her mind, and anyhow it seemed cruel to deprive patients of badly needed laughs. I did not mention the Punch line we nearly added in a further cartoon—a caption which had the host replying: "And thank you for coming."

People, of course, have always been ambivalent about sex. They are interested, to be sure, but there is a widespread feeling that—as a reader once put it—"it is not a fit subject for public discussion". The younger generation tends to find this amusing, and I'm not surprised. An Essex headmaster banned the BBC's sex education films, not long ago, because they were "too shocking and sexy for the parents". For the children, he added, they were excellent. So they were: whatever the faults of the young, hypocrisy is not one of them.

One convenient way out, for people who have wanted to discuss sex without actually mentioning the unspeakable, has been to use Latin. It still is. Even Indian terms such as *lingam* and *yoni* are respectable: anything will do as long as you don't actually speak English. It is an attitude which has, understandably, proved an irresistible challenge for writers, artists, and others dedicated to proving that sex *is* a fit subject for public discussion. In the process, they have come to be lumped together with those whose sole interest is financial gain. It was inevitable; puritans are not noted for their sense of discrimination. The end result has been "the puritan backlash"—or at least, so we are told. The backlash, as far as I can make out, has so far consisted mainly of the appointment of a well-meaning committee under the chairmanship of Lord Longford. The committee includes one of my predecessors, Malcolm Muggeridge, whose sense of humour (one hopes) can be relied upon to prevent excesses. Some people fear that, eventually, we shall get back to tying skirts on piano legs, but I doubt it. The young are not that foolish.

Punch has been accused of many things during its 130 years of life, but not even the most dedicated puritan has ever suggested that it is pornographic. We have always believed—and still do— that we should produce a magazine which readers can safely leave around the house and even in doctors' waiting rooms.

Happily, a very large number of people now accept that one can mention sex without being pornographic. Perhaps their children (who leave magazines like Rave, Honey, and Petticoat around the house without worrying about the effect on their parents) have managed to persuade them that the two are not necessarily synonymous. We are grateful, but agree with Raquel Welch that there's been too much talk about sex as such, and not enough about ancillary features such as romance. "Sex", she recently declared with an exquisite feeling for words, "is shoved down our throats and, more and more, it begins to look like a commodity, a product—like Campbell's soup or underarm deodorants. It's become one of the status goodies that people use to convince themselves they're part of the 'now' generation." This Bedside Book, we hope, strikes a reasonable balance. The articles and cartoons have appeared in Punch over many years—proving, if nothing else, that sex is not an invention of the swinging sixties or the frantic seventies. They are light-hearted, witty, and for the most part concerned with the comedy surrounding the subject rather that the act itself. I have also included many articles which have nothing whatever to do with sex; they concern other night-time activities. I hope our efforts give you pleasure. And don't worry: this is our book which you may safely show your children without fearing the wrath of Lord Longford—or theirs.

William Davis

"*No. I'm not in the mood any more . . .*"

AFTER EIGHT By WILLIAM DAVIS

WHATEVER else you might say about Harold Wilson, you've got to admit that he is a splendid story teller. It was, however, a little disingenuous of him to claim that he was dismayed when, at a dinner given by Ian Smith in Salisbury, Lord Graham got up and told a well . . . er . . . questionable joke.

It was not, to my certain knowledge, the first high-level gathering at which a story of this well . . . er . . . doubtful taste had been told in his presence. Don't take my word for it; ask George Brown.

The awful truth is that, when the platitudes are done, even statesmen are wont to sip brandy, nudge each other, and tell the one about the actress and the bishop. I have no doubt it was so at Yalta, Potsdam, and Vienna. And I suspect that the fellows sitting around the conference table in Brussels, or in the United Nations, delight each other with ribald tales after posing, with solemn, statesmanlike mien for the benefit of innocent photographers. Krushchev would not have considered any conference a success unless he had heard at least one new . . . er . . . tasteless joke. President Nasser (so I was reliably informed in Cairo last Christmas) had several full-time spies whose sole function was to keep him in daily touch with the latest trifles. And some of Mr. Wilson's colleagues profess to have been embarrassed, more than once, by African Ministers gleefully repeating half a dozen familiar jokes picked up at an English public school. In short, Lord Graham was following an ancient, thoroughly British tradition.

Any young man intent upon a public career knows—or, if he doesn't, soon learns—that it won't do to be over-sensitive about what we persist in calling well . . . er . . . *dirty* jokes. (The pretence that sex is dirty is, of course, another cherished tradition.) It's not that parliamentary selection committees include this type of entertainment on their syllabus: it's just that men who hold senior positions, at local as well as national and international level, expect juniors to laugh at their jokes and usually remember only those that are well . . . er . . . spicy. One of my more illuminating experiences, over the last twenty years, has been to meet a large number of Mayors, Aldermen, and other dignitaries, including presidents of trade and professional associations. Worthy gentlemen all, and

"Not sex again!"

ever so dignified. But how they love well . . . er . . . daring jokes. I particularly recall one occasion, a few years ago, when I was invited to address 300 accountants in Manchester's Piccadilly Hotel. The violins bid the assembled men of finance to be upstanding and I walked in, feeling rather foolish (why violins? why the self-important little procession?) between his Worship the Mayor and the frightfully senior representatives of the Law and the Church. Over the mock turtle soup the Mayor kept tugging at my sleeve and whispering well . . . er . . . lewd jokes. "Tell them, *tell* them, he urged. "If you don't, you've had it". I nodded and glanced apprehensively at the stern features of the high-ranking Churchman on my right. I might have gone through with it if the Mayor had not pushed his chair back, after the main course, and explained that, sorry he couldn't stay for the speech, but he had another banquet to go to. I have a suspicious nature, and I decided to make some insulting remarks about accountants instead. (If there's one thing audiences like this love almost as much as lewd jokes it is light-hearted abuse of their own profession.) I am grateful to him because, to be honest, I don't personally care for well . . . er . . . libertine jokes.

Mind you, he had a point. I realise, whenever I face a sated after-dinner audience, that they *expect* to hear another boring recital of platitudes, and *long* for some new dirty jokes. They shouldn't, of course (half of them would head the queue of subscribers cancelling Punch if we printed one of their favourites) but they've come to enjoy themselves, dammit, and why on earth didn't the committee get Dick Emery? You sense this as you get up to speak, you know that they'll feel let down, and you wonder whether you should even bother to quote Leacock or mention the balance of payments. And, of course, sometimes you weaken. I have never told a really dirty joke (honest) but there's an excruciatingly silly story I slip in occasionally, when I sense that I am losing a late-night audience of businessmen. It's to do with the confusion some people feel when confronted by pompous forms, and it stars a pretty young girl who applied for a job with a London engineering firm. She dutifully supplied all the various statistics she was asked for: age, height, religion, colour of eyes and so on. When she came to sex she paused and put: "Once, in Scunthorpe". Groan if you like, but it usually gets a laugh.

A few months ago, you may recall, there was an awful row, in a town whose name I forget, because the Mayoress told a joke which actually included the dreaded four letter word at a gathering of several hundred businessmen. It was a very funny tale about two pilots who take a couple of girls up in a plane . . . but no, you wouldn't want to hear this kind of filth. The Mayoress was a nice little old lady, with grey hair and an imposing chain of office, and she was the only woman at the do. Once they had managed to get over their surprise, it seems, the businessmen delightedly competed in the telling of indescribably daring stories. The Bishop, guardian of the town's morals, looked suitably appalled—and, when that proved inadequate, walked out.

This sort of thing happens more often than we like to admit.

The brandy releases inhibitions, and the cigar smoke produces an atmosphere of *camaraderie* in which grown men revert to their schooldays and, amid much giggling, impress each other with their fund of ribaldry. They would be angry if anyone had the bad taste to tell one of these jokes over a business deal, but the evening is supposed to be different, not matter what the occasion. Women are usually embarrassed by these free-for-alls (and understandably so) but occasionally a female speaker does decide that, if risque stories are the way to a male audience's heart, there is no point in holding back.

One reason for this custom is, of course, the generally low standard of public speaking in Britain. A really competent, witty, after-dinner speech takes several hours to prepare and considerable skill to deliver. In America this tends to be much more readily accepted than it is here. U.S. organisations make widespread use of professional speakers, and pay them well. In Britain we assume that any fool can get up and make a speech. He can't. But every night some doctor, solicitor, engineer, accountant, or Mayor rises unsteadily to his feet and addresses his fellow men. If he is wise, he prudently confines himself to platitudes. "Let's get the country moving again . . . releasing the energies of the people . . . meeting the challenge of the seventies . . . " that sort of thing. But wise men are rare: it is much more likely that he will deliver a few, familiar jokes, and emboldened by the laughter, add a few of a well . . . er . . . indelicate nature.

I am sure that, like me, you have seen some carefully-built reputations take a dive after the dangerous hour of eight. There is nothing worse than a dirty joke which happens to be unfunny—and so many of them are.

One solution, I suppose, is either to put public speaking on a more professional basis, or at least to ensure that a professional writes an acceptable speech for them. In New York, a man called Orben makes a handsome living by sitting down at his typewriter each morning, composing twenty or thirty topical (and clean) jokes, and sending them off to grateful subscribers around the country. There is no reason why some of our more skilful comedy writers should not do the same.

One contribution I have long wanted to make to the cause is the creation of a new trade union—the National Association of After-Dinner Speakers. The rules would be simple: no speeches without payment, and if any employer insists on a dirty joke we come out on strike. Fie to actresses, bishops, and travelling salesmen. And, yes, fie to Lord Graham.

THE Saturday night John Smith took all his clothes off in his car; had his bottom slapped by a young woman he was driving home; and heard SOS being sounded out on his car horn, was described to Tottenham magistrates. At this stage, said a detective in evidence, Smith put back his clothes and decided to take his passenger back to her home on the Noel Park Estate.   *Tottenham Weekly Herald*

Ten Cents A Dance

By ALAN COREN

IF there's anything sadder than a man who has to pay a fee to get a girl who'll go to bed with him, it's a man who has to pay a fee to get one who won't. After all, the former can always argue, either to those who sneer and commiserate or to himself, that, despite the tidal wave of permissiveness currently washing away our moral breakwaters, he hasn't yet been able to find a girl who's heard the great news. This doesn't, you understand, necessarily mean that dollies flee shrieking as soon as the light falls on his face, but merely that he mixes with a different class of people or that Dame Fortune has not as yet led a raver to his lobster-pot. Now, bogus as this defence may be of those who lope through Soho in search of a wallet-ful of lust, it's a damned sight more of an excuse than is available to the poor bloke who can't even find anyone to share a plate of ravioli with him or clutch his sleeve during *Dracula's Godfather*. The man who has to pay just for *company*. The man who has done so much to put the escort bureaux on a sound financial footing.

So in order to see just how much pleasure one of these unfortunates could buy for a bedless evening, I decided to call on an agency whose name is a household word wherever the talk runs to brief encounters. It involved considerable disguise on my part, of course, since to the casual eye I am nothing if not a man for whom Raquel Welch would gladly lay down her raincoat, and had I not taken certain precautions, the bureau receptionist would have sneaked one gasping glance at my incomparable lineaments, closed up shop forthwith, and personally followed me to the ends of the earth. I therefore (being able to do little to defuse my sheer good looks) took pains to mask my normal aggressive sexuality beneath a shy virgin smile, a self-conscious shuffle, a nervous cough, and one or two other little tricks which generally built up a vignette that would have passed muster at any Lonelyhearts Club outing in the land.

This dissembling was actually forced on me by the agency itself, who, when I phoned, insisted that I come down in person for interview. A wise move on their part, for two reasons: first, it enabled them to relieve me of the requisite eight guineas before I'd even seen the girl of my dreams, so that even if my date turned out to be the winner of last year's Miss Pig contest, the agency at least would be insured against dissatisfaction; and second, and a little more selfless, it served to reassure them that they were not delivering the goods to the Boston Strangler. If there's one thing that gets you a bad name in the agency business, it's having your pert little blondes sent back to you in a brown paper parcel.

I must say the whole deal was carried out in an atmosphere of total horror, I think the word is. Or, at any rate, tastelessness. It being a bisexual bureau, I sat in a line of three other blokes, facing three terrified girls. It was like the Annual General Meeting of Derelicts Anonymous, seven fragments of life's jetsam bobbling uneasily together, looking for something to wash up against. We all avoided one another's eyes (and you wouldn't have found a dozen eyes more worth avoiding), preferring instead to flip through the pages of glossy magazines filled to the eaves with pictures of svelte, half-clad dollies and virile, iron-chinned blokes in sun-kissed Ferraris. Not the sort of literature, I'd have thought, that you want to shove into the hands of the world's unmatable. One by one, the customers were called away for scrutiny and transaction, until at last, my own name and shouted discreetly down the corridor, drowning the Muzak which was playing (I swear to God) "You Were Meant For Me." Making a mental note to get them to include "If You Were The Only Girl In The World" in their future repertoire, it being somewhat more to the point, I got up, and crept self-effacingly into the indicated cubicle.

The woman behind the utilitarian desk, in a room that smelt of aerosol scent and radiators, smiled at me sympathetically. If there's one thing I can't stand, it's women who smile at me sympathetically. She looked like a policewoman moonlighting.

"Do you want a partner for a particular occasion?" she said.

The opportunities thus presented for sauce and sarcasm were illimitable, but my new persona merely replied, meekly:

"No. I just wanted to go out with someone, that's all."

Next week, don't miss A. Coren in *Little Nell*.

"Ah," said the WPC. She pushed a cyclostyled sheet across. "If you'd care to fill in a few personal details, interests, that sort of thing, I'll start looking through our files."

The space available on the sheet for hobbies and interests was enormous, an insight into the world of the loner. Not having any, I was forced to fabricate a few right-sounding idiocies, such as fretwork, walking, watching cricket, and tropical fish. This done, and having given my profession as "clerical," I allowed the WPC a few moments' musing, after which she took an album from a green metal cabinet, and passed it to me. Page after page of female faces, head and shoulders only; it reminded me of nothing so much as my tailor's, and the impossibility of choosing a suit from two square inches of ragged worsted.

"You can't see much of them," I said.

"I would have thought it was enough to go on," she said, tartly.

The implication being, you'll have guessed, that a fink like me was in no position to be choosy about busts or calves, and ought to think himself lucky if he ended up with Lon Chaney's grandmother. after a couple of quick flips, I selected a neat retroussé nose, worn with a pair of matching blue eyes, trimmed in brunette. Rather more innocent than my normal garb, but more than adequate for a fretworking guppie-fan. The WPC nodded.

"Louise," she said, "yes. A bright girl, with wide interests."

"And a nice pair of lips."

"What?"

I lowered my virgin eyes.

"I mean, I hope she likes me," I said.

She lifted the receiver, and dialled. It was a cold exchange, in which no mention of my striking similarity to Tony Curtis came up; it was arranged that Louise and I should kick off our tryst in the bar of the Mayfair, that same evening.

"We prefer cash," said the WPC, as I opened my cheque book. "The time element, do you see?"

I counted out the eight notes, and the four florins. There is something ridiculous about guineas when they're paid in currency. And oddly sordid. It was like prostitution by proxy.

An association utterly dispelled by Louise herself. She was a neat, well-assembled girl of around twenty-three, and she drank tomato juice, and smiled a lot. I realised, very early on, that I wouldn't be able to maintain my blushing subterfuge; faced with a real girl, human nature and masculine conquest-hunger asserted itself.

"I see Worcester had a bad day," she said, as I looked deep into her eyes.

"What?"

"134 for 6, on a batting wicket," she said. "I don't call that much, do you?"

"I'm not really interested in cricket," I said, with a smile that would have charmed Nelson off his column. "I just put it down."

The baby-blue eyes hardened into granite.

"It may interest you to know," she said, "that I spent two hours this afternoon mugging up matches of the past three weeks."

"Oh. What about some vodka in your next tomato juice?"

She looked at me very closely, very professionally.

"How many eggs does a sunfish lay in an average clutch?" she said.

I sighed.

"I made a toast rack at school," I said. "And I do walk here and there."

After the theatre (at which she was extremely quiet), Louise ordered a very, very expensive dinner, out of all proportion to her wasted research into goldfish and Sobers. She ate long and expertly, and didn't say much, and as she cast aside the last sucked-out lobster claw, she looked cannily up at me.

"You won't get me into bed, you know," she said.

"You could have told me that over the escargots," I said. "I wouldn't have snatched the plate away."

She softened, slightly.

"I'm sorry", she said, glancing at a passing bowl of strawberries. "It's just that I've been escorting for three months, and I've never yet had a genuine case. I suppose you're married, too?"

"Yes, but——"

"Ho, ho," said Louise. "Everyone always says 'yes but.' "

"Boring," I said.

"Depressing," she emphasised. She sank a strawberry sadly. "You see, I'm only doing this to save up for my wedding. My fiance's an escort, too. I mean, it makes one wonder about the whole marriage business, doesn't it?"

"No, it doesn't" I said. "I think I'd better tell you the full story. I'll get the bill."

"What about the full story?"

"We'll talk in the cab going home."

"Oh, God," said Louise. "Not again!"

"So you've got a hangover—you don't have to be so dramatic about it."

Sex
and the Seniors

By OLGA FRANKLIN

WHERE have all the nice Aunt Ednas gone? You may well ask! Now there are so few matinees of the kind they used to weep at.

In sexy Britain today, there are few places where Aunt Edna can find a cosy refuge—only those meaty Swedish films up and down Oxford Street, where everyone is compulsorily Born Free and Naked with it. So our Senior Citizens are, willy-nilly in the late afternoon of their lives, being driven into conformity. And for those who are, say, rising sixty, all this new Permissiveness is so unsettling.

I was quite surprised at first when my best friend rang up to say . . . wasn't it a shame her grandparents were getting divorced. "To *think*," she said, "we always thought them so devoted."

They'd always been a trendy couple though, proud of their smart, up-to-date outlook. So when the critics were blasting away at silly old Aunt Edna misty-eyed in the Dress Circle at the latest Rattigan, my friend's Grandmother switched to Edna O'Brien instead.

First Grandma asked for a separate bedroom. Then Grandfather got trendy with long sideburns tinted faintly ginger and frilly waistcoats from Carnaby Street.

Now the old man who's sixty-eight is to marry the au pair who is barely twenty-two. Grandma goes around saying now she can "lead her own life" and "anyway I'm several years younger than Dietrich, aren't I?"

Of course, we know, Permissiveness generally can do some funny things to people. We know what it has done to Mr. Muggeridge because he told us, often. But on so many of his contemporaries, it's all had the opposite and devastating effect.

Surely the time has come for the whole thing to be exposed, say on *Man Alive*. My friend's grandmother is dying to be interviewed by that nice, fair-haired man who asks very intimate, very serious questions. She's going to say straight out that she's never felt the same towards Grandpa since the Lady Chatterley case, when she read the unexpurgated on her fifty-sixth birthday.

I keep hearing of more and more families where parents or uncles or aunts, stricken with a 27-year itch, are behaving in a most unprecedented way. Should we, then, call on some Mr. Enoch Powell to stop any more sex-freedoms from being admitted into Britain?

Some people blame it on American novelists; others condemn the Common Market influence. Certainly, Britain has always felt a little proper un-ease about the more amorous problems. Unless all dressed up as in the *Forsyte Saga* ("Do you think *that's* why Irene hated Soames?").

You see, in conflict with a lot of the evidence so far, Britons—unlike the French and Italians who are capable of coolness and calculation . . . are a wildly passionate people. Give them their head and they go quite mad. Young Reg insane over Peggy Archer makes a more convincing story than Romeo and Juliet, I feel.

That's why the Victorians sensibly enough, kept their young and their old on a pretty tight rein. They *knew* what hot-blooded Britons are capable of.

But now! . . . What with the Experts, like Dr. Alex Comfort and other eminent Geriatricians and Psychiatrists . . . who keep on nagging that Sex *must* go on till seventy . . . And now the Marriage Guidance Council are at it too, issuing Statements and Advice. Couples are urged not to give up too soon but to persevere into their seventies and eighties. The case-history of one potent lover of ninety-one was triumphantly cited as blessed encouragement to fainter hearts. (Victor Hugo . . . you should be living at this Hour; England has need of thee!)

Gone are the days when a man's marital duties could happily be met by mowing the lawn on Saturday. Ah, for those peaceful nights nodding off in front of Eamonn Andrews and *This-is-your-life*. Now it's . . . "Jack dear, I think you *ought* to watch tonight's *Wednesday Play*. The *Radio Times* says it is an analysis in depth of OUR . . . problem."

It *is* unsettling, to say the least. It's all very well for Dr. Kinsey, but has no one any sympathy for the poor BMA, who will have to get around to the problem one day, and issue their own Report?

Meanwhile, what with the youngsters in our society always complaining their seniors are just jealous of their freedom and all the new Permission, can you blame Aunt Edna for deserting the Dress Circle and trying to get into the act?

Life on the Expense Account

*"In Paris it was Doris, the fairest of the bunch,
But down in his expenses she was petrol, oil and lunch."*

A ND that, roughly, is what the expense account saga is all about.

Changes in the law have naturally brought forth some ingenious counter-moves. Before the war you took your secretary to Paris and called her your wife. (Early symptoms of a mistress have often been revealed by a sudden surge of creativity in an executive's expense account.) Now, in order to wriggle through the tax-gatherer's net, you take your wife to Paris and call her your secretary.

The net had become little more than a series of loopholes tied together with red tape by the time and Chancellor of the Exchequer thought up Sec. 15, ss. 4, of the Finance Act of 1965, the provisions of which you doubtless know by heart.

Mr. Callaghan argued that there were, from time to time, circumstances in which a company's entertainment ought to be paid for out of the firm's profits, and not subsidised by the Exchequer. And he went on to suggest that too many businessmen made a habit of eating themselves daily into a stupor at the tax-payer's expense, and then drove nightly in the company car to the company's flat in preparation for their week-end on the company's salmon river or grouse moor.

I believe the *Daily Herald* did actually succeed in bringing one genuine company trout stream to light, but by and large Mr. Callaghan's picture was not only a travesty of the truth, but also a slander on the Inland Revenue, who are usually down on this sort of thing like a duck on a June bug.

There may have been some abuse, not because the British businessman is basically dishonest, but because he regards the present level of taxation as confiscatory. He feels therefore that he is entitled to retain a bit more of the gravy, and to achieve this he occasionally oversteps the mark, and, alas, fudges his expenses.

Underlying all this, however, is a mis-apprehension of the whole concept of expense accounts, and this Mr. Callaghan and his friends, perhaps deliberately, did little to dispel. To begin with, few executives (by which I mean the sort of people who can take two hours off for lunch without being missed) have expense accounts at all. You have to take along to your company's accountant a record of what you have spent, and he invariably goes through this with a fine-tooth comb. "What's this," he cries, throwing up his hands in horror, "*two* chops for lunch? And after all that rich Spaghetti Bolognese you had with Mr. Turfus at the Coq d'Or on Monday. This will never do." (Incidentally, I believe the waiters in Rio de Janeiro make a fortune out of picking up receipted bills and selling them back at a profit in the appropriate quarter.)

The Act of 1965 produced further complications for our chief accountant; notably in the controversial person of the foreign buyer. His lunch, you will remember, remained chargeable to the Exchequer, while the native buyer's nosh had to be paid for by the company. This produced an awkward position if Mr. Okomoto from Kobe started off his lunch with you as a buyer, but eventually (deuced clever, these Orientals) ended up as a seller. It was more awkward still if you'd invited along some influential English friends to help impress your customer. "Come, Mr. Okomoto," you exclaimed, "a little more of this excellent Mignon de Boeuf en Croute Lutèce? And how do you find the Chateau Pichon-Longueville Baron '45? Just right for drinking, don't you think? But how about, Sir Halford, another sliver of the hake? And you, Hartley, a drop more of the Algerian, perhaps?"

This ludicrous arrangement had to be changed because it inevitably gave birth to the all-purpose notional foreign buyer. A machine tool firm of my acquaintance had a French director on their note paper. He didn't have to do much to earn his keep; he was the chairman's nephew, and only held his job because of some interesting piece of boardroom blackmail. As soon as the 1965 Bill became law his colleagues made him into a private company called Rentafrog,

and then hired him out to any of their friends who wanted a tame foreigner to bring an export air to their luncheons. The scheme worked well enough for a while, but poor Alphonse had soon put on about two stone in weight, and was starting to develop cirrhosis of the liver. He eventually blew up one lunch time at the Ecu de France, and the whole scheme had to be recast.

It's easy, of course, to make fun of the "Who fed whom" announcements in *The Times*. Some business lunches are admittedly over-done, and most after luncheon speeches are grossly over-done. But at others a lot of genuine and important work is done as well.

The Americans call such luncheons eating meetings, but they have the uncomfortable habit of drinking far tee many martoonis before the meal, and only freezing water with it. *Fortune Magazine*, however, recently revealed that a large number of important deals are in fact concluded over the luncheon table. Here at home such information is not so easy to come by. When the head waiter at the Savoy Grill was asked how much business was discussed over lunch in the restaurant he replied coldly that it was not the job of the Savoy waiters to eaves-drop on their guests. My guess is that the situation is the same as in America.

In Japan the expense account has become a cross between a social accolade and a religion. If he gets black-balled for a fashionable expense account golf club the Japanese businessman commits hara-kiri. In Germany they try to get you tight over lunch so that you will tell them more about your p/e ratio than you intended. In Sweden businessmen spend three hours over lunch and tell very unbusinesslike stories. In other countries they have different habits, but few business communities can do without the practice in some form or other.

If Mr. Callaghan's Sec. 15 drove a lot of London restaurants out of business it may also have done a bit of good by stealth. Suppose your bright young executive, having spent his lunch break at Pruniers guzzling Pieds de Mouton Poulette washed down with the Gevrey Chambertin Lavany St. Jacques 1964, had to trot home in the evening to bangers and a bottle of Bass with the little woman in Pinner, he noticed the difference, and he did not like it. So the restrictions of Sec. 15 may have saved a few marriages, although this advantage may have been offset by the rules about company flats. These desirable residences now have to be made available to all the directors of a company, and not just to one, otherwise the tax-gatherer will sting him for it as an emolument. An engineering firm we do business with in the Midlands accepted this point, and made appropriate changes in their company's arrangements. Unfortunately this wider use of the flat led to an outbreak of company wife-swapping, which was understandably mal-vu in Wolverhampton. We must, however, be thankful for small mercies. At least Sec. 15 doesn't make us paint the name of our firm in bold letters down the side of the company car.

I hope that the new Chancellor of the Exchequer will take a long, hard look at the whole business. It's become messy, time consuming and very undignified. I hope also that he will remember the extent to which an expense account has become, perhaps undesirably but nonetheless certainly, one of the perks attached to many responsible positions. Without it a lot of worthwhile people are going to find their jobs less rewarding, as well as more difficult. They will begin to think that the game is perhaps no longer worth the candle. Abolition of expense accounts could be in effect for them a vast increase in taxation. We have heard a lot about the brain drain. Unless the Chancellor gets to grips with this problem both realistically and quickly even the stupid will begin to emigrate. The very brainy, of course, will realise that the best way to remain solvent is to stay behind and live in sin.

"*As a practising phychopathic rapist, what did you think of the love scenes in tonight's play?*"

"Aren't we perhaps being a little premature?"

Nature is a Terribly Interesting Thing

JAMES CAMERON
writes
"Lady Chatterley" in the style of Godfrey Winn

HAVE you ever wondered, as I do whenever I read of some little act of unsung sacrifice in places like the Midlands, how wonderful it is to love *people*—to the *full*, enjoying the simple things of life even in some honest working man's rude hut?

Ours is really a terribly exciting age, and lots of us refuse to be *blasé* about the wonderful things of nature, which is full of great beauty that quite transcends the difference between rich and poor. I pray with all my heart that nobody would cast the first stone at a woman just because she liked gamekeepers.

This was more or less Constance Chatterley's position, or one of them. She had married Sir Clifford, a well-born marvellous young man with a lovely seat. The seat was called Wragby Hall, and you have no idea how lovely it was, there among the sooty, soulless, gruesome workers' cottages, though they were very sweet inside. How marvellous the honest working wife is at making the best of her simple possessions, under such difficulties.

Constance Chatterley, although a very different type, had her difficulties too. The war came (the first war, and I cannot tell you how rough it was; I am sure you have read about it in those wonderful stirring books by Philip Gibbs and people) and Sir Clifford was called to a Destiny at the Front, as indeed were high and low, including his late Majesty King George VI, whom I met when I was a *matelot* in the self-same Royal Navy, though indeed that was not the same war.

The brutalities of war caused a scar on Sir Clifford's soul, indeed I am bound to say worse. He had always been a clean-living young fellow. But he was to become even cleaner, *in a certain sense*. For Sir

Clifford returned from this man's war *very badly wounded*. To be terribly frank, as sometimes we have to be, he had very little of him left below the waterline, nor had that little long.

I wonder if you can imagine how this distressed Constance Chatterley—so young, so wholesome, so ardent, so full of compassion; and of course such a nature-lover. Seeing Sir Clifford there in his wheel-chair, so patient and undemanding of her, it was as though she, too, sensed the pangs of loss.

After all, she was still so fresh and gay. In the world of imagination she reminds me of my mother, except of course in a way she doesn't. There was this sad thing about Sir Clifford. The sight of his stiff upper lip brought tears to Constance's eyes. She was such a pure girl, it almost drove her insane. What a terrible thing is mental illness; I pray with all my heart we never stoop to mocking it.

So one day Constance was walking through the woods of the estate, admiring the poignant affection of the daffodils and the tender impertinence of the primroses and the gentle laughter of the cowslips, and various other aspects of the sweet challenge of spring. And into the mind of Lady Chatterley came a deep sense of the essential *rightness* of Nature, and of her husband, especially of what he had once used to have been.

She arrived at the clearing flushed and semi-conscious. There was the shirt-sleeved gamekeeper; his name was Mellors, no more and no less. He was closing up the chickens for the night. But still one trio of tiny things was pattering about on tiny feet, tiny mites, refusing to be called home by the anxious mother.

"I'd love to touch them!" she panted. Before Constance knew it she was touching them. The little tiny chickens ran around "cheeping" at being ignored.

By and by the gamekeeper gazed at her. Compassion flared in his, well, bowels, and the nettles had evoked a strange stirring in his loins.

"Eeh, but thar't winsome, like," he said in the vernacular, "Happen thar'll coom opp to t'oot." His voice had the simple manly honesty so often corrupted by the veneer of education. Education is of course a marvellous thing, but.

A surge of democracy welled up in Lady Chatterley. As they entered t'oot it grew unaccountably stronger, more urgent, more democratic. I often wonder if everyone understands the real affinity between the landed classes and the simple estate-workers—as our Prime Minister does, though of course rather differently.

This is an age of frankness, and my readers know well that there are times when I am forthright. The ensuing hours in the simple woodland home of Mellors was so tender, so simple, so *real*, so HUMAN, that it has to be described in detail, as tribute to wonderful Mother Nature. These two young people were in *love* . . . They expressed it in a fashion that I *know* is not customary in the grounds of Buckingham Palace. Nevertheless I am confident that they intended no disrespect to the person of Her Majesty our Queen, whom I had the pleasure of meeting in 1961. This hut was something really quite different. This was direct and *elemental*, and if in retrospect it was a bit sick-making, it was somehow *right*.

Under his shirt was his slim smooth body, rippling with the play of muscle under the silken skin. His rough manly breeches lay like an offering on the homely floor. Constance's costume was quite pretty, too; she was wearing a cinnamon two-piece by my friend Norman Hartnell, at least to start with. In wonder she confronted the gamekeeper Mellors; he looked so confident, so cock-sure. Already she was beginning to forget about wheel-chairs . . .

For no one knows how long Constance was aware of nothing but a cleaving consciousness, a rhythmic growing motion like the waves of the sea at Antibes, where I had a marvellous holiday two years ago; a convulsion of deepening whirlpools of ecstacy in his man-smell and his man-touch and the quivering maleness of his man-handling. She could have swooned at the carnal rapture of those slender buttocks.

She felt slightly ashamed of enjoying it so much. For of course Lady Constance was aware that *this* is only a part of love, which is really made of companionship, and *understanding*, and common interests. I know a sweet old couple whose marriage was saved time and again by a shared hobby; in this case fretwork. All this Constance knew well; in her heart of hearts she knew full well that the last moments had been just a phallacy. She thought with gratitude of the tiny defenceless chickens that had brought them together.

But then the wondrous magic took possession again, and all this stuff about wispy lingerie and loins and deep breathing, which I assure you is really *nothing*, though it seems important at the time.

Only when it was all over did she become aware of the oppressive closeness of the hut, the windows closed, country-style, over the airless heat of passion.

"*What* a fug!" she whispered.

"Tha canst say that agen," he breathed, stretching his great male arms behind his great male head: god-like.

"Tha an' me's a sacred rite," he said. "Sex is nowt wi'out shared faith, companionship, bairns. Tha knows t'body's only part, just a private part."

And for a while Mellors the gamekeeper made with the high philosophical phrases, for we all know, do we not, that the one thing the British working man likes is a bit of cant.

Then they talked about the industrial system for a while, and the need for the workers of the smoking valleys to get a square deal and an eight-hour day.

"Tha mun coom one naight to t'oot," he said. "Shall ter? Slaip wi' me? 'Appen Sat'day?"

"As a matter of fact," said Constance, "I do have a sale of work Sat'day. But next time I'll really try to come."

And as she ran home in the twilight, or gloaming, the trees in the park seemed erect and surging as though they were alive, and who is to say that they were not? Nature is a *terribly* interesting thing.

Next week I am going to continue my series on *Passion Without Pain*, with the Love-Life of Doctor Schweitzer. This is a *terribly* ennobling story, and I really *do* hope that . . .

Pursued by Chambermaids

In which HUMPHREY LYTTELTON is woken by the dawn chorus

THE British chambermaid, like the British music hall, is a unique and moribund institution. I bring in the British music hall deliberately, for it has long been clear to me, as a persistent traveller on the one- and two-star hotel circuit, that our chambermaids belong to the same proud tradition. Elsewhere in the world, beds are made, towels replaced and carpets Hoovered with uncanny stealth, irrespective of when you crawl from the room or slink back into it. In America I once collided in the doorway with a vast black lady who appeared to be moving on rubber castors and in whom, judging by the smouldering look she gave me, a Black Panther was snarling to be let out. But this encounter was exceptional. I don't think I ever set eyes on a German chambermaid, except perhaps in Bradford.

By contrast, the British chambermaids' motto is "Stay in front of the public!" This, like many other rules, wrinkles and tricks of the trade, has been handed down by the same oral tradition that instructed Marie Lloyd, Nellie Wallace and Revnell and West. It occurs to me that it might be useful, especially for our visitors from overseas, if we put the spotlight on this previously unexplored area of showbusiness.

As with every other type of theatrical presentation, "venue" is

"Basically, of course, you're afraid to delegate responsibility."

all-important. Nothing is killing the British chambermaid more rapidly than the modern American-style hotel in which the rooms are laid out geometrically in endless, thickly-carpeted corridors and automatic tea-making machines replace the early morning call. The old-fashioned maid's pantry-cum-broom cupboard is essential to a good performance, sited if possible at a junction of corridors where four or more rooms huddle round a landing and the maximum audience can be reached. It is here, at crack of dawn, that the traditional curtain-raiser is performed—a brisk, rousing medley on the musical cups and saucers. Nothing, not even a clanking version of the "Zampa" Overture by massed radiators, has proved more effective at breaking down audience resistance. I have heard some seasoned artists who could lob teaspoons into saucers with deadly accuracy at a range of ten feet while at the same time endeavouring to play a chorus of "Nola" on the rattly lid of a giant teapot. By the end of a virtuoso performance such as this, the whole house if fully roused and ready for the cross-talk act.

Such is the exclusiveness of the modern media—radio, television and the like—that it is not generally known that every well-appointed family hotel in the British Isles has an Elsie and Doris Waters on each landing, performing daily. As a chambermaid connoisseur of many years standing, I must confess that when you've heard one of these double acts, you've heard them all. There's always an aggrieved soprano who does most of the talking, and a sympathetic contralto who intones the responses and acts as a "feed". Most of the material concerns some off-stage "she"—a manageress, perhaps, or a truculent guest—with whom the principal performer has had a row. The script is ridden with clichés like " . . . so I told 'er straight, I said . . ." or ". . . and d'you know what she 'ad the cheek to turn round and tell me ?" In all my travels, I can claim to have heard only one inspired line. This was when I woke in a hotel in Shropshire just in time to hear a shrill voice proclaim "Well, I looked 'er straight in the face and said don't you turn your back on me!!!" I always feel rather sorry for the contralto stooge, who is lumbered with material that would defeat a Vanessa Redgrave or Maggie Smith. "Yes, well, there you are, you see . . ." " . . . ooh, she never!" and sometimes just a repetitive "Mmmm . . . Mmmm . . . Mmmm . . ." like a broody pigeon.

The traditional exit line—"Well, this won't get the baby bathed!"—heralds the intermission. This is a brief moment of respite for the audience, interrupted when the sales staff visit all parts of the house, knocking on doors, rattling keys in locks and purveying trays of tea. Like all good troupers, they rise to the challenge of an unresponsive audience, beating the liveliest tattoo on the doors of those who have expressly written and underlined "NO CALL" on the blackboard downstairs. I should perhaps say here that the subtleties of the British chambermaid can best be appreciated when, through unavoidable circumstances—a late conference, perhaps, or a Rotary Club dinner-dance—one has retired in the small hours and anticipates a lie-in. I have known provincial hacks of no great talent who have become veritable Vesta Tilleys at the sight of a notice saying "PLEASE DO NOT DISTURB."

It is after the interval, when the lull before curtain-up has persuaded the optimistic customer that the show is over, that the musical highspot of the show occurs. It was the late Gerard Hoffnung who first exploited the musical potential of the vacuum cleaner. But with all respect to his efforts to promote it to the orchestral platform, it is, and always will be a folk instrument. Like the bagpipes, to which it is clearly closely related, it is best heard on its native landing accompanied, not by banks of violins and violas and woodwind, but by one solitary, unschooled, ear-splitting female voice. If I were asked to pick a classic, a sort of desert island disc, in the chambermaid-and-Hoover genre, I would go unhesitatingly for "Around the World in Eighty Days." It has everything to keep an audience not only on its toes but curling them in anguish. In any regional accent you choose between Arrroond the Wurrrld to Araaahn the Woald, the opening line with its broad vowels answers to perfection the twin demands of voice production and dramatic interpretation. Timing is essential to putting across a song with Hoover accompaniment. The full potential of the instrument will never be fully explored unless long pauses are left in which the rise and fall if its siren-call and the percussive effects of its blunt nose nudging the wainscoting and bumping into doors can be heard. Thus a star performance will start "Araaaahn the Woald" . . . whirr . . . boomp . . . clonk . . . clonk "in Eyeeetee Dyeees" . . . thud ooowheeeee . . . clugger . . . shroooomph. It's not necessary to know any words beyond the title and it's important to get the words wrong from the outset. It also helps to keep the audience in suspense if wordless syllables like "Da-dara-dee" are put to the ensuing bars of music. Bare print can scarcely do justice to the great British hotel landing performances of our time, but some idea of their subtlety might be gained from this short extract:—

Araaaahn the Woald
whirr . . . boomp . . . clonk, clonk
In Eyeeetee Dyeees
thud . . . oowheeeee . . . clugger . . .
shrooomph
Da-Dara-Dee
clump . . . scraaaaape
Da-Dara-Dee
schveeeeee . . . schvooooo . . . judder judder . . . freeeep . . . crrrurg . . .
boop-a-doop . . . zaieeeeowrrrgh . . . CROOMPH
Da-Dara-Dee Dah Dah

Follow that, as they say—and well they might. The traditional climax to a British chambermaid performance is when the whole cast goes out amongst the audience with the express aim of depriving the customers of their bedclothes. It's a sort of striptease in reverse, really. The routine in this part of the show is kept fairly free, so that each performer can approach it according to her particular talents. Some favour the "cheeky chappie" angle, like the lady who once roused me from five hours' sleep with the words "Come on, be a sport—let's 'ave yer sheets!" Others favour the dramatic climax, bursting into rooms without knocking and reacting, in true R.A.D.A. style, to whatever meets the eye. Since shrieking hysteria worthy of

27

Lady Macbeth is the standard reaction to a bare torso at the shaving mirror, I must leave to your imagination the *coup de theatre* which I was lucky enough to witness not long ago. Just along the corridor from me, two chambermaids—Elsie and Doris, perhaps— walked unannounced and simultaneously into the room of a colleague of mine. Unencumbered by vestments of any kind, he was on all fours with his back to the door, doing his exercises with the aid of one of those patent weight-reducing wheels. I can't begin to describe the duet that rent the air, but it would not have been out of place at Glyndebourne. And it certainly brought the audience to its feet.

"Blast this dawn chorus!"

Doing Your Own Thing And Doing It Sober

By STANLEY REYNOLDS

RICHARD Burton got almost as much publicity the other week when it was learned that he was on the water wagon as he got when he bought Elizabeth Taylor that diamond as big as the Ritz. Burton says the last six months have been the first time in twenty-five years that he is "seeing the world without an alcoholic haze." And almost all the newspapers I saw hymned this marvel. Indeed, I was contemplating his publicity when the editor of this journal telephones me saying, "Have you heard that Richard Burton is on the wagon?" "We've been talking about nothing else," I gasped. "Write something about it," he said, adding, "after all, *you're on the wagon too*."

Hmmm, I said, replacing the receiver, so it seems that in my own little circle the fact that I have been on the wagon has, just like the glamorous Burton, not gone unnoticed. One, of course, expects to get noticed when one saddles up and goes to town, rides one's horse into El Vino's or some such saloon and shoots the place up, but if one does not ride into town shooting off the six guns one feels some how the lack of this *diversio* will not get brought to attention. I should think me and Richard Burton should be a trifle worried this morning that the fact of our being sober is news. Come to think of it, as soon as I pen this essay I am going out to scotch the rumour.

Anyway, the word Drunk carried some pretty nasty social connotations. One thinks of Ray Milland in *The Lost Weekend* watching the bats fly out of the woodwork or of chaps in gutters or fellows waking in the morning with the bottle tied to their wrists. There is, happily, another side to drunkenness.

There is the excuse for youthful high jinks, the bringer of the hazy glow that makes all women look as soulful as Garbo, the mixture that eases the inhibitions and makes the dirty weekend blush-free, the thing that sticks the courage and gets the boss told off; champagne, the symbol of big winnings; whisky, the salve of small defeats. By and large the drink has undoubtedly done more good than evil in a world whose countenance is generally very hard and very sobering.

Richard Burton, in the *Sunday Times* "People" column, was quoted as saying, "Don't make me out to be against alcohol. If you print that I've seen the light I'll get all sorts of letters of congratulations from the temperance people—and I certainly don't want to encourage their cause. One word of support from them and I'll probably be roaring drunk. I owe a lot to booze. A lot of good times and a lot of clear thinking, so I don't want to offend it."

There is, one knows, nothing more likely to set the extrovert drunk off than the idea of "temperance people." From their grim ranks, however, one can exclude the AA, the only really and truly successful booze group which has got its success by making sure that its members are just the opposite of what everyone thinks of when they think of the reformed drunk.

Sparing no expense at researching this piece the editor of this journal sent me a newly published book called *The Drinking Game and How To Beat It* (could the editor of this journal be hinting at something?) by an American woman AA member. This is published by Rapp and Whiting at twenty-five shillings, and it is a thoroughly amusing and sensible book on drinking which should clear up many misconceptions that stupid people have about the AA, which is actually to say it cleared up the stupid idea I had about Alcoholics Anonymous.

Actually I have been reading up on John Barleycorn (Jack to me now) and have discovered so many misconceptions that one does not know where to begin. Enough to kill the latest booze rumour which, is that drink is now strictly a middle-aged problem now that our wonderful hippy kids of today are dreamily boxed out on grass and hash. This rumour came about because beer and whisky sales at universities have dropped to new lows since the kids started smoking the funny cigarettes. Only recently was it noticed (*Time* magazine saw it the week before last) that wine sales have sky-rocketed at pubs and off licences around university campuses. Wine, apparently (like your correspondent doesn't know this), keeps a hash high going and because of this the plonk rate has increased among the teens and twenties.

The thing is that normally a person only gets to realise that he has a pretty dodgy drink pattern after he has been on the sauce for a number of years. A man can eat one punnet of strawberries, break out in hives and know they do not agree with him, but the same fellow can lose overcoats, jobs, wives, door keys, and friends for ten or twenty years of boozing and somehow always manage to fail to put two and two together and get anything faintly resembling four. I personally have never lost any of these things, although I did lose a very nice homburg to a man named Walsh, who took it from my head in a pub and then punched me on the nose and knocked me down when I attempted to snatch it back; somehow I feel the dodgy drink pattern was not mine in this case although stone cold sober I would not have the guts to wear a homburg. And here is a ray of joy I have gleaned from *The Drinking Game and How To Beat It*.

Under the heading PRACTICE DOING IT SOBER the anonymous American lady says:

> Most people I know who have returned to drinking after long periods of being away from it have done so because they wished to do something which liquor alone permitted them to do. For instance: If you have attained a sense of accomplishment by tearing up two tickets to the theatre, hopping on a plane to Nassau, or falling into bed with a stranger—then you must practise doing each of these things sober. If you don't, you will drink again in order to get your kicks.

This came right at the end of the book and I must confess to having read through all the alcoholic symptoms without identifying a hell of a lot until I came upon this item which is, in the parlance of the shyster lawyer, a beautiful loop-hole.

For the dim-witted among you who have not the barrack-room lawyer mentality this simply means that all those things that you did while drunk and felt so remorse-filled about the morning after that you went on the wagon can now be done without any of that phoney remorse; the excuse for the bed behaviour now can be that it keeps you off drink.

Whatever is your thing, Bob is now your uncle. The expensive, time-consuming, liver-poisoning, mind-busting, rather-awful-tasting middle man is now cut-out.

To bring this discussion above the mundane level of beating the wife or telling Tim Brady to go to hell, think of how much better literature would have been served if, say, F. Scot Fitzgerald had known he did not have to ruin his health to get an excuse for driving his brand new car into that river that time or the world of art if Modigliani, another sufferer from alcoholic poisoning, had known he could have stood at the zinc bar of the Dome screaming filthy abuse at the passing philistines on non-allergic ginger beer; poor Brendan Behan, with his love of life that detested the grey everyday, could have spared his body and still turned the pavement of Dublin into a stage for his one man holy show.

These otherwise fine men are only a few of the very very many unfortunate notorious examples of the doing-what-you'd-always-like-to-do-anyway-under-the-cloak-of-booze syndrome. Drunkards unfortunately always seem to be our biggest and grandest dreamers of dreams and the new man on the wagon must steel himself against their bad example and try to dream the impossible dream on milk or soda water. Fitzgerald, Modigliani, Behan and the rest are best forgotten; new examples of doing your own thing without booze must be found.

I have been searching around rather wildly for some teetotal fellow who has without the booze dreamed and done the sort of great excessive things that come normally only in the midnight longings of drunkards. It is, I am afraid to say, rather slim pickings. For what it is worth, the new wagoneer could, perhaps, remember that Hitler managed to march into Poland stone cold sober.

The Cult of Togetherness

By GILLIAN TINDALL

"TOGETHER we chose a Morris" the advertisement sticker runs, and couples who fancy themselves as wits add "But we had to make do with this." We. No one seems to think it even funnier to say "My husband chose this, not me." Basically the advertiser's image of a couple in the full flower of Togetherness is not debunked.

Since Togetherness *is* so fashionable (the sociological phrase is "the male and female roles are becoming less differentiated") it is perhaps useful to make two points about it. The first one is that you can have too much of it. While a number of shared interests ("both are keen speleologists . . .") may well be the secret of a lasting marriage—indeed I can't think how any marriage endures without them: surely it just falls to bits after a while like an out-dated friendship?—a *totally* shared life, on the other hand, must in time, far from promoting even closer communication, render communication itself pointless, since all the joint thoughts are known to both anyway. Unless it is the sort of communication described in an American survey, where a wife lovingly questioned her husband every day on what he'd had for lunch, and on being told she was a bore remonstrated: "But darling, I want us to be One like it says in church . . ."

While few couples actually try to share the same gut, the secret, unfulfilled of many of the heavily married is, I suspect, not extra-marital sex but extra-marital ideas. If you don't invariably read the same books or even see the same people as your partner, you may have more to talk about when you do coincide over the supper-table. I knew a happily unmarried couple, one of them technically the other's lodger, who staunchly and jointly resisted matrimony on the grounds that then she would have to hear too much about his obsessional research and he would be invited obligatorily to dinner by her awful friends. It wasn't the spurious glamour of unmarriage either wanted: husband-like, he changed light-bulbs and complained to the (joint) cat, and she washed his handkerchiefs . . . It was just that they saw no good reason why they should be identified with one another in all respects just because they were in some.

I don't know about identi-

TOGETHER WE CHOSE A MALE

fication, but personally I can never see why couples go on so much for doing the washing-up together, going to the launderette or shopping together. Most of these intrinsically tedious chores can be done as quickly and often quicker by one person alone, so why not? Another sphere where redundant duplication of labour is nearly always a trap is child-minding. It's all right when you're doing something else, like harvesting grapes or visiting Russia, and the children just happen to be there too, but if you both settle down to a solid afternoon's family-rearing the chances are you will end up arguing about the best way to do it, or else having a stimulating adult conversation with each other, shushing the poor children when they try to speak too. The only satisfactory way for all concerned is for one of you to child-rear while the other does something lovely and childless, like buying a new coat or writing an article about Togetherness . . . That will make the minder feel noble and the other feel relieved. You'll admire one another more that way too. No one admires someone who is doing exactly the same thing as themselves.

The other important point about Togetherness is that, like sex—that quintessence of it and occasional substitute for it—however assiduously you practise it, it brings no guarantees whatsoever of permanence. Some couples seem to think that if they demonstrate their devotion to one another often and publically enough (holding hands under the dinner table, regaling the guests with a blow-by-push account of their last "shared" childbirth) this in itself will create a bastion of obtrusive marital intimacy which will warn off all potentially disrupting agents. But—fortunately—lasting marriage is not dependent on such devices. The only evidence obtainable is that there is no evidence: it seems that the husband who breathes participantly down his wife's neck in her labours is just exactly as likely or unlikely to take off for other shores five, ten or fifteen years later, as the one who, each time, has dumped her in hospital and gone off to play poker.

"A man and wife are one person in the eyes of the Law"—but not, let's hope, in their own, for what fearful secret tensions and resentments must flourish within the hybrid flesh of such Siamese twins? "Our friends, our home, our kids, passport, joint-account . . ." The protective phrases build up, obscuring the fact that, after all, it is the *differences* between a husband and wife which make them interesting to one another. The most obtrusively married couple of all time (apart from the Windsors) were the Australians who, in the early 'fifties, claimed telepathic communication with one another and did a radio turn based on this. A journalist, this year, thought of looking them up. He found them—separated. That proves nothing? Nor did their telepathy.

Stop the Bed, Little Lotus Blossom, Your Mikado Wants to Get Off

In which PATRICK RYAN explores the latest achievements of the Japanese sandman.

DISCIPLES of Oblomov who have hitherto avoided Nippon because of the hard lying may soon find it has become their Mecca. Perhaps in sore-hipped backlash against all those spartan centuries of kipping on the unrelenting floor, the Japanese have lately been revolutionising the occidental bed. Dedicated to the proposition that bed was made for more than sleeping, they've applied their electronic ingenuity to developing a range of play-pads called *beddos*. These products have mainly been snapped up by their Western-style hideaway hotels as added attractions for swinging lovers. "What's the fun of hopping into bed for the same eternal routine?" explained a manager in Kobe. "We provide our patrons with something new and exciting in beds to help trigger a greater bliss for them."

The bliss-triggering *beddos* virtually bring all the fun of the fair into the boudoir. A simple start was made with the "Come-come" design—doubtless a less versatile phrase in the Japanese context—which featured equipment permitting unsocially separated twin beds to be shot cosily together at the flick of a switch. And, one supposes, flung hurriedly apart at the entrance of irate husband or early morning geisha with tea and sukiyaki. Next on the market was a "Miracle series" of circular beds which could be spun at will around a perimeter set with record-player, television, refrigerator, cocktail bar and other essentials of slumberfun. In selecting a partner for a weekend on one of these Carousel Couches, it is advisable to try her out on the roundabout at Battersea first to ensure that the escapade will not be ruined by any critical blacking-out under *g* forces. Ballet dancers should be safe bets since they're centrifugally resistant from all that pirouetting.

The merry-go-round mattress has now been joined by the "Pegasus," which, in accordance with its equine title, leaps regularly up and down three feet at a time. This model can be recommended to sporting gentlemen having affairs with horsey ladies for lulling them into a sense of false equestrian security. The "Seesaw" type harks right back to the playground by tipping rhythmically from end to end and has clearly been developed with Lolita-loving patrons in mind. At some extra charge, there is also the "Seesaw Pony", which has the added facility to enliven the simple fluctuation by flipping its middle straight up and down. Before booking any birds for a night-ride on the Scesaw Pony it would be wise to check up on any history of seasickness in the family. Round-the-world yachtswomen, Olympic gymnasts or lady butterfly swimmers would seem the only doxies reliably adapted to this undulatory rapture. And, in any event, it's going to be a hell of a job to keep the bed-clothes on.

The "Apollo" pattern is aimed at cultured lovers and features a built-in stereophonic hi-fi linked to a variable lighting system equip-ped to create "a mesmerising bedroom mood." And the "Fantasia" variant includes a pillow-controlled movie projector and footboard screen for good measure. This provides the extraordinary possibility of bedding down adulterously with someone else's wife and illegally watching blue movies at one and the same time. The "Mirror" series has two notable adaptations of this timeworn titillatory device. One is a king-size bed which moves slowly upwards through eight feet into a mirror-covered alcove in the ceiling; and the other features a vast reflector which drops suddenly to within four feet of the eiderdown and scares any dilly-dallying dollies smartly into their consorts arms and about their amatory business. A suitable trade name for these optical *beddos* when marketed in the West might be "Looky-looky-looky! Here comes us!"

American slumber-furnishers, as befits members of the nation most grievously infected with get-up-and-go, are concerned about the problem of getting people out of bed in the morning once their luxury upholstery has lured them in. The false equation of early rising with right living still persists over there, even though its practical credence really went out with the invention of the candle. Early risers are only neurotic people who make a virtue out of insomnia and few contributors to human improvement have ever made a fetish of being up, washed and shaved before the dawn comes over the gasworks. However, this continuing compulsion must be met on the market and for $384, guilt-ridden American lie-a-beds can now buy an "Ejector Bed." Present like an alarm clock, at the appropriate inhuman hour it snaps up its top half, catapulting the masochistic resident bolt upright, letting chill morning air attack his gravity-exposed torso, and giving his spine the impression that Doomsday will now commence. And finally proving, when the accumulated whiplash of a year or so dislocates his mis-guided neck, that Thurber was once again prophetic when he said that early to bed, early to rise, makes a man healthy, wealthy and dead.

Our furthest British advance thus far in dreamland mechanisation runs out at up to £432 single size and simply provides motorised facilities for the prone sloth to raise or lower the head or foot of the divan to any desired angle. Although it must be admitted that this model cannot rank with the Nipponese spectaculars, we do, as is well known to hardened hotel campaigners, have a fair range of traditional variants on the British Standard bed. Frequently met among these is the "Spavined Hammock," that ancient sleep platform with such metal fatigue in its main tendons that it sags on entry till its underbelly brushes the carpet and its occupant spends the night in the enforced posture of a human whiting. He wakes next morning with incipient curvature of the spine and as living proof of the claim that after a week of such contorted slumber, Gregory Peck would come out looking like Quasimodo's little brother.

Our "Bed of Nails" is almost as common in some seaside resorts as it is in Benares, and visiting fakirs over for a sniff of ozone have frequently been moved to complain about the unbearable penance of time-fractured springs prickling through threadbare palliasses. The "Dartmore" design is found mainly in commercial hotels and its basic specification is that the pebble-bottomed mattress should be stuffed with equal parts of petrified flock, millstone grit and cast-off golf balls. But probably the all-time favourite among boarding-house proprietors is our "Musical Bed," in which the understrung suspension is tuned to play harp sonatas whenever the inhabitants take a rapturous breath or turn over. This facility has caused many a restless toper to take the pledge overnight in the belief that the hard stuff has at last caught up with him and he's being nocturnally haunted by invisible, underbed banjo-players. It is unlikely, however, to be copied by the Japanese for their their fun-promising *beddos* since there are few thoughts that can so swiftly put a sporting virgin off the boil and into a passion-snuffing fit of the giggles as contemplation of the prospect of losing her all on a musical trampoline. Unless, of course, they can find some cunning Oriental method of making the rhythmic jingle-jangle resound to the alluring beat of Simon and Garfunkel.

"Anything with it, Miss Bronston?"

What would your perfect world be like? What kind of people would live there? How would it work?

THE LONG, LONG DAY

By PAUL JENNINGS

THERE'S a paradox at the heart of all Utopia-devising and Eden-inventing. The more absolute your paradise is, the more relative it is; the more it is what *you* would like, the less human the other people (if any) in it become. In most people's Perfect Place it's easy enough to imagine the landscape, the warm and musical breezes moving through feathery trees, over meadows with fabulous and innocent beasts, to symbolic, maternal hills; there are even, with a few white arches, distant but spacious courtyards, remote and elegant towers, suggestions of some vague kind of community—although Eden is really a Garden, not a Garden Suburb, let alone a Town.

But when you come to the figures in the landscape you have to admit, even if you don't agree with Sartre that "hell is other people" and what they insist on doing with their free will, you aren't God, you can't trust them with it in your heaven.

My Perfect Place, therefore, attempts a far smaller miracle than making people do beautiful, reasonable, constructive things (like singing madrigals, and even then there is always someone who thinks we ought to be doing them faster). All I would ask for is a slight alteration in the physical structure of the cosmos. I would like the earth to be more or less as it is, but for it take forty-eight hours to go round on its axis instead of the present twenty-four.

After all, there is a whiff of Planner's Arrogance (the Eighth Deadly Sin, I've always thought) about manipulating a cosmos in which all the people dance to a pattern that has no basis outside the manipulator's imagination. But in my system countless appeals can be made to the everyday experience of people and the lives they actually live. All I am doing is to give them more *time*, but without necessarily turning the world into a gigantic self-improvement evening class, as in *Back to Methuselah*. Nietzsche and Marx and goodness knows who else inspired that, but what inspired my vision was something altogether much more real; the Sunday morning breakfast.

Every one of my beautiful, spacious forty-eight-hour days would begin with a Sunday breakfast. Bear in mind that midday would be twenty-four o'clock. We'll come to the rest of the timetable later; for the moment just think what it would be like to begin every day with a breakfast that lasted from fourteen to seventeen o'clock. Half the troubles of the world are due to the sacrilegious daily skimping of the noble and expansive meal of breakfast—not that miserable roll-and-coffee affair but proper English breakfast; say, really good porridge, or two lots of cereals (and I'm not blindly eighteenth-century about it, I'm quite willing to precede these with modern grapefruit or orange juice), bacon and eggs, toast, marmalade—everything. This whole English counter-tradition of not talking at breakfast springs from a subconscious regret that we can't have one like this every day. People are quite ready to talk at a leisurely *Sunday* breakfast as they sit endlessly there chatting, riffling through increasingly gossipy, trivial but beguiling newspapers, drinking seven cups of tea (yes, *tea*. Coffee is for later, the mid-morning elevenses, or, of course, in my Perfect Place, nineteenses).

Now they could do it every day. As I see it, they would have gone to bed at midnight, forty-eight o'clock (I use the forty-eight-hour timetable). After a refreshing twelve hours sleep they would get up, or rather start to get up, at twelve o'clock. You will have noticed that breakfast does not start until fourteen o'clock. This is because *two hours* are allowed for getting up. There are people who will tell you they "can't stay in bed after six," or "do their best work before the rest of the household is up," but I'm convinced such people are a small minority. For most of us no sleep is so sweet as the kind that comes again when one has already woken up once—after all, the main trouble about sleep is that one cannot actually enjoy it consciously and say to oneself "isn't this marvellous, I'm *asleep*"; but this early-morning state gets pretty close to it. If we had two hours for it no doubt we could work up a technique. If not, think of the leisurely bath we could have, every morning.

Then, on to the three-hour breakfast. Apart from anything else, breakfast would now take its place among the other meals as one to which you invited guests, if you felt like it. The breakfast-party, now wistfully remembered only by those who have been rich undergraduates, would be within everyone's reach.

Lest you begin to suspect that this is an impracticable world I have conjured up, in which no work is done, let me now come to the most beautiful part of the whole thing. *There would be an eight-hour working day*, just as there is at present. Nobody really suggests that the world's work can't be done in that time; in fact the difficulty is more and more how to find enough work for enough people, as automation really gets into its stride. So, relaxed, at peace with the world after their calm and nourishing breakfasts, the people would go to work just as we do, for roughly four hours in the morning—seventeen till twenty-one o'clock, with a break for nineteenses, as we have seen.

Then there would be a nice long lunch break, from twenty-one o'clock till twenty-five o'clock. You will notice this is still only an hour after midday, but see what we have already accomplished without any kind of rushing. It is possible that in hot countries this break, as now, would be longer, to allow for the siesta; but even with four hours there would be plenty of time for a relaxed meal, and no one need be afraid that having wine with it would make him fall asleep, because he *could* fall asleep, there would be time for a nice little zizz before he went back, refreshed, to his afternoon stint of four hours, from twenty-five to twenty-nine o'clock.

Now you see the full splendour of it. We have done our day's work, and there remain to us nineteen hours of the day for the real purpose of life—singing, reading, skating, making love, dancing, carpentry, sailing, the cinema, visiting and receiving friends, painting, tennis, golf, funfairs, circuses, bird-watching, barbecues, gliding, drinking, chess, picnicking, the theatre, motoring, making lino-cuts, flower-arranging, theology, even watching television, although I'm inclined to think it wouldn't loom so large as it does now; even people as drained of nervous energy as we are by the fretful rush of trying to cram work and living into a twenty-four-hour day couldn't watch nineteen hours of the stuff every day—let alone people so happy, simultaneously active and relaxed as these inhabitants of my Perfect Place. That's the wrong phrase really, it's the same place as now, in a Perfect Time.

Even in the depths of winter it wouldn't start to get dark till at least eight hours after midday, that is around thirty-two o'clock, so that there would be three hours of daylight after work for healthy exercise in the open air. In the summer there would be from twenty-nine o'clock to at least forty-four o'clock; fifteen hours—that's more than we have now on all but the longest summer Saturday or Sunday, unless we get up very early, for trips to the seaside or the country.

Dinner would start somewhere round thirty-eight to forty o'clock, so it would be absolutely no trouble for say, Suffolk people to pop up to London to have it with friends, or vice versa. And what a marvellously relaxed meal it would be. Apart from anything else, think of the wonderful appetite you would have. And it isn't only social life that would take on new depth and reality; the entire world of culture would be improved beyond recognition. At present it isn't really physically possible to take your wife out to a really good dinner and a theatre in the same evening. Either you gobble something nervously before the theatre, in what you realise too late is a restaurant with very slow service, or else, having decided not to fidget all through the last act worrying about the last train, you eat afterwards, in a place either too expensive or trying to close down while you eat, waiters whipping cloths off tables and standing chairs upside down on them. There would be an end of *that* in my Perfect Time. You could have a vast meal and go to a play and a concert, if you wanted to. If you trimmed things a bit you could go to the whole of Wagner's *Ring* in one evening (if you wanted to).

I think it is beyond doubt that, without any new-fangled educational or social system seeking to change people, my system, simply acting externally, as it were, by providing a time-continuum more suited to the rhythm of human life, would produce people with a luminous, calm beauty of soul impossible to imagine in our world of angry quarters of an hour; you have to work outwards from man to society, and if individuals were like this, war and hatred would wither away.

Moreover, it is just possible that it need not for ever be a mere fantasy. Rockets and atomic power are as yet in their infancy: it is not beyond imagination that enormous earth-retro-rockets, placed equatorially in the Congo, Brazil and Borneo, should act against the earth's rotation to give us a forty-eight-hour day. Of course it might alter the weather a bit with the huge blast. But perhaps it would make Britain semi-tropical. Then it would be a Perfect Place as well.

The Commie Sutra

Mr. Stewart-Smith, MP for Belper, thinks that a
Communist plot is using pornography to undermine
the West. R. G. G. PRICE has managed to get a glimpse
of a Soviet-inspired novel.

WHEN Maggie joined Universal Herbs she was innocent, as
she had grown up among the clean-living Workers in the
foetid slums of Hampstead. So when the Managing Director,
Jasper Clench, asked her to stay behind to take some letters, she had
no suspicions. She simply hoped they might contain details of
interest to the Comrade Secretary.

The office was redolent of evil-scented luxury, from the depraved
abstracts on the walls to the four-poster casting-couch with its silken
hangings. There was a cabinet filled with expensive and subtly
poisonous drinks, very different from the adulterated meths which
was all slum dwellers could get in the foul rookeries of London.

She sat down, her knees firmly clasped together, as she had been
taught in her People's Etiquette Classes. She did not know why she
was so disturbed by the apelike Clench's heavy breathing. His
Fascist-Imperial leer grew beyond his control as he gazed lascivi-
ously at her workmanlike five-piece and 100 denier stockings.

"Come, we must be better acquainted," he smirked. "Capital
and Labour have common interests." Suddenly he put his hand on
her knee. She felt it through all the layers of her clothing. She could
not help drawing back.

Then she remembered that her cell had instructed her to flatter
the capitalist into disclosing his secrets for the benefit of the Soviet
Fatherland. He poured her a glass of champagne and she managed
to make herself say, "Cheers!" and to submit with an alluring smile
to refills. As she drank her third glass Clench gave a vulture's smile
and very slowly began taking off his Old Etonian tie.

II

The comrades groaned in horror at Maggie's detailed report of
the treatment she had suffered from this Wall Street lackey. But
after long socialist analysis, it was democratically decided that the
Comrade Secretary's strategy was correct and Maggie must submit
to further demands, so that the Party would have a hold on Clench
when Universal Herbs was found to have secret contracts with the
Pentagon.

III

When her boss asked Maggie to act as his hostess that evening
and be served to his guests in a pie, she was astonished at this new
evidence of capitalist corruption. What was her increased horror
when she learnt that she was not to wear her bathing costume?
There was even worse to come: the Workers in Clench's costly
Mayfair kitchen were ready to serve his degraded appetite by
making the pastry.

As she blushingly emerged from the crust, she tried to hold some button mushrooms where they contributed most to decency; but Clench and his wine-bibbing cronies insisted that she should display herself ungarnished.

"She's all yours," hiccupped the host. "Who'll start?" Maggie submitted herself to the lust of fourteen guests, humming the *Internationale* under her breath to encourage herself in the sacrifice she was making for the Cause. Finally Clench himself, inflamed by the scenes he had watched, flung himself on her, not once but frequently, uttering loud invocations to capitalist heroes like the Barnato Brothers, Lord Cowdray and Sir Keith Joseph.

No sooner had he slaked his foul passions than an overseas customer from the Federal German Republic, so called, drew on a tablecloth a tableau which reminded Maggie of some pages in her *Khama Sutra* (Workers' Issue). Brushing aside objections on grounds of anatomical impossibility, he began organising the company.

However, just at the delicate moment when the keystone was to be fitted in—Lord Wimpole of Tyburn—a cable was delivered to Clench. The bottom had fallen out of the market! Scarcely waiting to say good night, the guests disentangled themselves, adjusted their dress and left.

As Maggie was scraping off the gravy, now jellied, the chef appeared, wearing only his white hat. He revealed that the was an Assistant Cultural Attaché on Intelligence-liaison at the Soviet Embassy and was keeping a watchful eye on her. "You wouldn't think of defecting, would you?" he asked with fatherly concern. Then he warned her that, if she wanted to discover Clench's secrets, she must become expert in arousing his jaded taste.

Under his tuition, Maggie soon mastered a wide range of new amorous skills. She was quite looking forward to Clench's return from his office, when suddenly the room filled with nude reactionaries, carrying counter-revolutionary whips . . .

"It's comforting to know Elizabeth Arden's working on it all the time."

The Way of All Flesh

TONY PALMER on the current Smut Boom

"MY name is Solo B. Cupcake," the voice whispered over the telephone. "I'm in celluloid and I think you could be very big. Indeed, I'd go so far as to say that you could be huge. Come over to my place and see my posters. I think you'll be impressed. This whole thing could be a big teaser." The film union, of which I am officially described as "a good boy", tells me that I'm seventy-five per cent out of work, so beggars can't be choosers unless they want to finish up as fully practical garden gnomes. I don't feel particularly out of work but every time a film producer rings me up and offers me a job which pays well and requires little effort, it's always sensible to investigate. Anyway, in the film business it's always good to have several balls in the air, as my lady agent keeps telling me.

Mr. Cupcake lives in Wardour Street—indeed, who does not?—in one of those strange little nowhere rooms that have changed hands as fast as production companies have gone bankrupt. This is the heart of film land, I keep telling myself. The big break that will put me into the chauffeured limousine and a dolly for every finger class. "Be there prompt at 9.56 am," the voice had croaked. At 10.40, having downed my fourteenth cup of Nescafé and been spied upon by the glamorous secretary, aged forty-four, spinster, of no fixed abode who doesn't know why she bothers, I ask if there's any chance that Mr. Cupcake may have forgotten about my appointment. "Mr. Who?" she cackles. "Cupcake" I reply apologetically. "Cuttcake" she says I mean. I say I mean Cuttcake. Yes, she says, I know you meant to say you meant Cuttcake. No, he never forgets.

"My name's Christie," says a young man of forty with a flowery tie and shirt. Different flowers, of course, but I suppose that this is what people are seen wearing in Wardour Street these days. "I do publicity. Do you know, it was fantastic. I actually got twenty seconds of full frontal nudity on to Mike Parkinson's show the other night. I mean, it was so bent, it was fantastic. Good old Mike, knew he'd see me through. Old chum of mine. Know him? Real old Mucker, Mike. You should have seen the queues outside the Cameo Poly and the Polio Victoria next day. Unbelievable. I mean it was so unbelievable, it was fantastic. Here to see Cutter are yer?" I notice two dyed blondes sitting in the waiting room, knees together, chests out, and lipsticked to the eyebrows. I *knew* it was going to be the bigtime. Cupcake was right about the posters which cover the office walls. "The greatest sexcess in town" one reads. "We dare not print the title. We dare you to see it," reads another. Front, back and sides; upside down, couples, trebles—almost any combination. I'm convinced it's always the same girl with a different squint, and why must she always be Swedish? Maybe nipples are bigger in Sweden.

"My boys, my boys, forgive me," says a white-haired face stuffed

"I've never known real kindness— except, of course, from soap powders."

with a cigar. "Come in, come in. Take your coat off. Have some coffee. Feel at home. Be relaxed. Put your feet up. Don't worry. Have a drink? A smoke? Charlie? How are you Charlie? You're looking good. Let me look at you Charlie. Let me have a look at you. You're looking good. You're looking good Charlie." The blondes blush. I stand up, sit down, smile, stand up and go into his private office which is damp. "You see," says Charlie, "our problem is that we've made enough money. Money? That's irrelevant. What we want is a real class job. Bit of class. I mean, sex and class. It's a knockout. It's got to be vast. And we wanna do you a real favour. We are prepared to give you anything you want, anything you want if you can bring it off." I knew it was the big time. I just knew it. I ask about the script, the story-line, the stars, the budget. "That's all taken care of," says Cupcake, rolling his cigar from side to side of his mouth with his pockmarked tongue. "We had, and I hesitate to tell you this, Tony boy, we had the most sensational idea." He hesitates. I hesitate. It *is* the big time. "Gritte is a German au pair girl who comes to live in Landsdowne Road with a young jeweller and his wife. Gritte seduces the young jeweller who turns out to be in love with his wife's brother. But his wife has already had her brother which the wife's husband discovers. In anguish—and this is where the class comes in—in anguish, the husband chains his wife to the television set and forces Gritte to have it off with his wife. I mean, that is so sensational, it's got to be huge." "Huge," repeats Charlie.

"We envisage," says Cuttcake, "a three-week shooting schedule and a maximum budget of £30,000. I mean, that's my absolute top. We'll pay you £2,000 and we want to go now otherwise we'll miss the Christmas trade. You'll never look back Tony my boy." As a matter of fact, I'm looking at his cigar-smoked moustache gone yellow with slobbering; the greased, silver-tinted hair, the off-white shirt and the gold stud in his tie. Sixty years in the business and doesn't look a day over ninety. The pouchy eyes and the horn-rimmed glasses. He looks like a caricature but he's real. Very real. He and about six men like him control the lucrative end of the film business in England. They make not quite blue movies which they distribute throughout Britain at enormous profit to themselves. They care nothing about the content of films except that the tit and bum quotient is high. Every cinema that they occupy is keeping out of circulation films like *Kes*. Of the sixty films listed each week as showing in the West End of London, one-third come from Cupcake or his associates. Although great films have been made for less than £30,000, that is a laughable budget for a full length feature film. Such money would not even pay for a film crew plus its raw materials, quite apart from actors, director, producer and so on. If there is a demand for such films, and clearly there is since Cupcake's films gross more per week than most of the rest put together, then there will always by a Wardour Street know-all to supply them. And I don't quarrel with his right to do so. Except, it seems to me, that the expense of everything else. While Cupcake prospers, seventy-five per cent of the film people are out of work at the moment and most of those could probably put Cupcake's money to better use.

Anyway, back at Cupcake House I was still faced with the problem of do I or don't I. Charlie was very insistent. Gritte could be a truly human story and Germany would be all sewn up. A little Deutschling in Landsdowne Road! Wow! I mean, just think of the action. Close up of nipple. Pan across to worried chin and up into those sad little eyes." Cuttcake cut in "If you can't do it for £30,000, I've got twenty outside who can." I couldn't, I told him, and left feeling sick. Is this what my University Appointments Board had told me was the good life?

Wardour Street is always full of gay young things rushing purposively hither and thither, clutching cans of film each of which, they will tell you, contains a masterpiece. About thirty years ago, the film industry discovered a new type of celluloid that was not inflammable when breathed upon. Previous to that, films had been made with what is called nitrate stock which was liable to explode in the projector unless handled with care. Most archive film has now been transferred from the old nitrate to modern safety film. Perhaps my only contribution to Cuttcake's millions was to suggest to him that in future he made his movies with nitrate negative. It would give his products, I said, a distinctive quality, a style all their own, works of art that he would remember for ever. "My boy," he said, "if I can ever do you any favours in return, the name is Cupcake, Solo B. Cupcake and I'm your friend."

By the way, I suppose I should have admitted to you earlier that being an opportunist, I've changed all the names for the purposes of this article. You never know when Cuttcake might come in useful.

THERE was a postscript to that censoring of risque art by Belgian police: I see that students are retaliating by putting pants on nude statues. Fine. But how?

My Husbands, Come What May . . .

By PIPPA PHEMISTER

PROBABLY no woman living has any very clear idea why she married one particular man; let alone, as in my case, why she married four. There was a time when I used to wake in the night and ponder this baffling fact: does it mean that I adore men? Or that I can't stand them? In recent years I've given up such heart searching and I spend far more time tending my garden; what's more, I've taken to relishing the basic benison that emerges from all this marital chaos: over long years, and from a suitably safe distance, it becomes increasingly easy to feel a very affectionate loyalty for *all* one's Exes, whatever their race, colour or creed.

Society gets very bolshie and carps about this lack of post-marital venom; this was brought home to me just after my very first divorce; immediately a veritable Greek Chorus of dear friends rose up and told me just what a bounder my brand-new Ex must have been. "Ah," hissed a charming young man who had always been at pains to assure me what an attractive couple Johnny and I made, "but *we* knew all the time—he was a hopeless alcoholic. And he even stole cars!" "I know all about that!" To my amazement I find myself flying to Johnny's defence, "but he's been a long-trip bomber pilot for three years now! He's the only survivor of a whole squadron! *And* he's been married to me!"

That silenced people for the time being; but after my second divorce this verbal treason started up all over again. This time I was at least braced up and ready to find people who had basked in Paddy's wit turn on him like snakes: "But we knew—he was an absolute neurotic, wasn't he?" In hard fact he was a writer, much given to swanning off on other people's military campaigns and on his own private, literary pilgrimages. Apart from that, as I told them angrily, he was a man of outstanding virtue. Which was why, come to think of it, the marriage failed.

My third Ex redressed this balance; maritally speaking he was an absolute demon. Yet he was, au fond, a warmly hospitable man. Indeed I used often to mourn in my misery "If only I were his guest —not his wife! What a marvellous life I should have!" Yet the moment the decree absolute plopped through the letterbox, buddies who had over years downed his wine, food, music, coalfires and culture ratted on him with verve. "But he was a monster!" raved an elderly man who should surely have known better. "You Judas!" I countered bitterly, "Even you! And he never forgot to put a hot water bottle in your bed—not once, in seven years!" None of our friends, I notice, compliments either of us on my current marriage. We both feel this is a very good omen.

Of course I'm loyal to my Exes; why shouldn't I be? Clearly there was nothing really wrong with them; otherwise I would never have married them in the first place! What's more each of them—in his own peculiar way—has made me a more tolerant, informed, resilient and (wonderful, wonderful let-out, this!) dottier woman! And I have such happy, well-treasured memories of all of them. Working backwards, over the years, I remember Ricky (No. three) playing rosily with our baby sons and becoming hysterical when he thought he had mislaid one! Or Paddy teaching me, just me, Old French with such passion that he triggered off my lifelong mania for Troubadours and Chansons de Geste . . . And Johnny; a distant, urgent, towering powder-blue ghost, dancing with me over polished floors or sandy beaches to Tir Nanoc, that first, that very first paradise: where neither of us, for one uncorrupted instant, suspected that the waiting world had fangs!

What's very fascinating—but here you must have a strong heart—if you look closely at your Exes' subsequent lives, (subsequent to you, that is)—you can learn a great deal about yourself. That ghostly Johnny—he too must have remembered Tir Nanoc; because he married four other women trying to find it again. Perversely perhaps, I believe this proves an absolute loyalty to me! But the literate, ever-vocal Paddy—he married a beautiful, very silent Frenchwoman, a superb cook who bottles fruit, is always elegant and leaves all forms of culture to men! If that isn't a smack on the jaw for me, what is? Ricky is; his attitude to post-marital existence is as sock-it-to-me uncomplimentary as anything I could imagine: he goes about publicly boasting that now he knows he's survived me he's cured of marriage, forever!

Is my present husband uneasy that these three revenants haunt our lives? Of course not; bitter women who can't stomach their own pasts are harder to live with than fantasists like me; because, of course, I *am* in fantasy, even though what I am dreaming is the truth; it's all too easy to be loyal to past husbands' virtues when you're safely out of reach of the betrayals that drove you away! Would I, given the chance, go back with any one of them to where the in-chum, closed-shop, murderous karate really gives? Never. I've *done* that! I too am cured, after my fashion. And my Exes have another, entirely masculine function in our married life; their very sequence, by sheer force of numbers, proves that I am a Very Bad Marriage Risk. I can relax and agree with this. In a way, although I am not past caring, I have given up trying. I know, because there they all are, I must be quite dreadful to be married to (dreadful, not lethal; they are all alive and well). Morally speaking my pile-up of past husbands cannot be explained away; they make me a perennially Guilty Party. This absolutely delights my present husband; a hard-headed, unswerving Lowland Scot, not given to doubt as I am, his very life-blood pulses at the dictum: "A Woman's place is in the Wrong!" (Translated, he assures me, from the Celt-Iberian.) I have been there so long now that I have become comfortably adapted to this ambiance. Spiritually, at any rate, I no longer try to keep up with the Joneses!

Politically speaking it's only expedient to remain loyal to Exes. For you are never, in this life, going to get rid of them. They crop up, by chance or design, in quite extraordinary contexts. Never indulge yourself and say nostalgically "There, now he's really gone out of my life!" He'll be back. Sometimes it's just a phone call: he wants a good doctor, one of his children has mumps; or he's going abroad, can I fiddle the currency drag? Even that romantically treasured Johnny suddenly asked me to his fourth wedding (in a redbrick synagogue at Esher) because he knew I would "make things tick!" I've even been summoned to Westminster Palace to disprove the ecclesiastical legality of my second marriage so that Paddy could go over to Rome! Once again the loyalty syndrome set in; I found myself assuring my inquisitors (who thought to confound me with Church Latin): "Patricius vir forsitan optimus est!" The union was, after much impertinent needling on their part, finally dissolved. So I am back where I started: Paddy will surely go straight to Heaven; and I shall be banished to that Other Place, reserved, with such forethought, for the purely generic Wrong!

And there is nothing like a procession of highly articulate husbands to give you insight into your basic, unvarying faults. Over the years I know *why* I cannot be married, from a man's point of view. To begin with, men have to work in the day time. I was born a nocturnal animal; the mornings find me palsied with sloth, unable to concentrate, or to identify individuals; midnight finds me whooping it up with every device known to man. Although I prefer to do this with people, any music, lights or gin will suffice. What I can *not* do is to go to sleep; and I am only now at nearly fifty, beginning to forgive husbands who want to do just this. And then I worry, day and night, without humour or remission, about *children*. I sweat for their pleasure, fret for their safety, starve for their amusement and never leave them alone. Since I have ended up with six children of my

own, and other people's children can be even more of a worry, this anxiety is a full-time job. I was once told (and by the late Brendan Behan at that) that husbands are all the children women need! Once again I am back in the wrong!

Do I enjoy seeing my Exes when they career back into my life? Of course I do; because now, after all these years when they dished out to me an excruciating mixture of exquisite pleasure and unbearable pain they all make me *laugh* until the tears run down my cheeks. Men, as they age, grow pompous in a way that no woman would dare! All three Exes, well past forty, have become right husbands, right bachelors or right sods. They are filled with a righteous forgetfulness; their misspent youth seems to have gone clean out of their minds; but it hasn't gone out of *mine!* There's that wildly carousing Johnny telling me soberly: "The trouble with youth nowadays is simple—it hasn't got a purpose!" I long to ask him what his purpose was, when he set light to that hangar at Manston? And there's the ever-vocal Paddy openly praying for me, to my face, hoping that I too will find peace and fulfilment in the eternal values. I long to ask him just what eternal values allowed him to keep that stunningly beautiful Italian girl, all to himself, in highly competitive Marrakesh! And the morally paternal Ricky absolutely fells me: he folds his hands over his tum and arraigns me: "The trouble with youngsters these days is—they're all obsessed with sex!" How I long to remind him—once, when we were very broke, he blowed fifty pounds in Soho on a very disappointing Blue Cine Film! I have forgotten which poet said:

"We cannot compose a vacuum

"As we compose a memory,

"Minute by minute, year by year, painstakingly . . . "

All I can say is—if my Exes don't do just that it isn't for want of trying!

But then, I console myself; they're all remarkable men now, with a hell of a lot to live down. Me, for example. Although I *do* nearly burst when I hear them telling their life-stories; their voices take on a loving, sonorous ring; I marvel as they get under way; never were there such pillars of society, such towering monuments of rectitude! There certainly never were—I know; I was there! But I don't interrupt them; I don't say a word; if I did they wouldn't come again and should be said. It's all very well for me, a mere woman, in the Wrong and enjoying it, my past doesn't have to be deleted. Theirs does; men get very restive, in the Wrong; I've noticed that with all my husbands. So I keep my outrageous, crystal-clear memories of each of them tightly to myself. Each day, since I adore all of them, I can muse over a hotch-potch of cherished mental pictures and wonder that one love, alas, never cancels out another. They, of course, have to pretend it does. So the last loyalty I can offer them is that the knife-sharp, image-busting recollections I harbour of all of them will remain where they belong: locked up in my obstinate, wrong-headed tape-recorder skull.

Is anything ever as good as it was ?
HENRY CECIL
recalls a case of seduction versus better judgment

It was fun while it lasted

SOME seventeen years ago I was sitting in my flat when the telephone rang. I was just over fifty and a widower, and I had been a County Court judge for several years. I picked up the receiver.

"Hello, *va bene?*" said a most attractive feminine voice, which I felt sure that I did not know.

"I beg your pardon?" I said.

"It is Angela, the little Italian girl."

"Who did you say?"

"Just Angela, the little Italian girl."

I knew no little Italian girl. No big one either for that matter. And I could not think of any girl with such an attractive voice. I thought hard to see if I could remember an Angela. I could think only of a maiden aunt long since dead and I soon knew for certain that the caller must have the wrong number.

I was about to say so and end the conversation when many thoughts began to race through my mind at an alarming rate. In their order of priority they went something like this. I should like to meet this Italian girl. If her face and figure were anything up to her voice she must be something quite exceptional. But County Court judges, even widowers, should not pick up little Italian girls, even if quite exceptional in voice, face and figure. And taking advantage of a wrong number would certainly be equivalent to picking up. On the other hand, there are not so many adventures round the corner for men over fifty. And, while pain is ready enough to strike, you must take your pleasures when they appear, or you must forgo them.

The mind works with incredible rapidity and these first thoughts only took a split second to materialise. Soon I was beginning to visualise Angela with dark hair and glowing, inviting eyes. Next I thought of a retired County Court judge who would be only too pleased to do my day's work for me. "If I can get the day off, will you have lunch with me?"

"That will be lovely."

"It's silly of me, but I've forgotten your address. Oh yes, of course. I'll be with you at half past twelve. Could you be looking out for me because parking is a little difficult around there and I shall be in my car. Bye-bye for the present."

I had begun the adventure. The next step was easy.

"Hullo, can I speak to Judge Dean, please? Oh, it's you, George. I wonder if you'd do me a favour? Are you doing anything special today? Good. Could you take my Court for me? Thanks ever so much. It is good of you. No, I'm perfectly well. It's just that I'm—I'm—I've just had rather an attractive invitation which I don't want to miss. Thanks ever so much. Bye."

This was very wrong, but at any rate I should have to pay the deputy judge's fee myself. And was there any real harm in it? After all, if a judge is supposed to understand the permissive way of life shouldn't he indulge in a little bit of it himself? People were always complaining that judges were too remote. Perhaps after an outing with Angela I should be a little less remote.

She was waiting on the doorstep and was everything which I imagined her to be. I got out of the car and went up to her.

"Good morning," I said.

"Good morning," she replied in a not unfriendly voice, though with the right amount of surprise in it.

"Angela," I said, "please forgive me but I couldn't resist your voice. You rang me this morning."

"But—" she began. Then she laughed. "Oh I see," she said, "but you don't know me."

"I'd like to," I said. "Will you come to lunch?"

"I've never done such a thing before," she said.

"Nor have I", I said. "Where would you like to go?"

To my surprise and pleasure I found that she knew something about food. She chose the only restaurant in London which is worth a visit if you're interested in food. We had a really splended lunch and, when we weren't actually eating or drinking, we talked very happily. I learned that she was twenty-seven, unmarried and on holiday in England. She was having a gay time. After all one can only be young once.

"But, with men it is different," she said. "*Young* men are always young."

I'm afraid she learned nothing about me. I told her that my name was George Meadows and that I was a stockbroker. I added that I was a widower and that I thought she was one of the most gorgeous girls I had ever seen.

"But," she said, "how could you be sure? The telephone is an awful liar."

"Not on this occasion," I said.

Eventually we finished lunch and went for a stroll in Hyde Park. It was a lovely day and I certainly felt young. We talked of many things, music, pictures, mountains, and, finally, of love.

"I am in love," she said.

"Lucky man."

"Oh, it's no one in particular. I am in love with life, with everything in life. That includes you."

I took her hand. I did not care to imagine what the Registrar of my Court or the clerks or the usher would think of me, wandering hand in hand along the Serpentine with a girl whom I had never met before. But I had better things to consider.

"Will you have dinner with me this evening?"

"I should love it," said said.

I called for her at eight o'clock, and we went to a big hotel. Her conversation over dinner sparkled. But it was her eyes that really did it. I wondered for a moment what a judge would do if a witness looked at him with those eyes. How could he disbelieve her?

It was over a glass of brandy that I made my approach shot.

"I've brought a suitcase," I said.

"Good", she replied. "They like one to have some luggage."

I was glad she required no persuasion. This could hardly be called seduction. After all she was twenty-seven and obviously capable of looking after herself.

After dinner I went to the reception desk to book a room. Just as I was about to give my name I heard a voice behind me.

"Hullo, sir. It is the judge, isn't it?"

I turned round. I haven't a good memory for faces and could not recognise the man who had spoken. But obviously he knew me.

"Good evening," I said. "I'm terribly sorry but for the moment I can't remember your name."

"I don't see why you should," said the man. "You appeared for me once when you were at the Bar, and I've never forgotten it. An enticement case. You got me off. I nearly wrote to you on your appointment but then I thought that you'd have forgotten me, as of course you have."

"How d'you do?" I said. "No, I do remember the case, but I've a shocking memory for names." At that moment Angela arrived. She came right up to me and I had to do something about it. One of the few things I had learned as a County Court judge was to be able to make a noise that sounded like a name but which couldn't be recognised as any particular name.

"This is Mr.—." I looked at him.

"Crowthorne," he said.

"This is Mr. Crowthorne," I said. "Miss —" and then I made my sound. Two or three consonants and a couple of vowels, part of it in the nose and part in the throat. If Angela hadn't come up at the time she did, I think I should have fled, but, when I saw her, she looked so radiant that I felt I would risk anything rather than forgo my adventure. So somehow I got rid of Mr. Crowthorne.

I then booked a room and we went up to it. As we shut the door behind us, with the thought of a glorious night in front of us, I realised that I did not even know her name. I asked her.

"Just Angela, the little Italian girl," she said.

"I'm sorry", I said. "I'm afraid you've got the wrong number," and I replaced the receiver.

But it was fun while it lasted.

No, But I Saw The Movie

NOTED outside the Jacey Cinema, Trafalgar Square, on a hoarding rife with nudes: "*She Lost Her You Know What* (X) from the masterpiece by Alexander Dumas." We rang to find out which particular masterpiece (*Elle A Perdu Sa Wossname*, perhaps?), but no one could tell us. Information please, to . . .

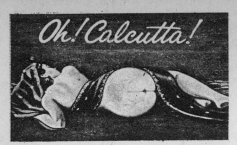

A GUIDE TO THE BLACK HOLE

By ALAN COREN

IF you think it takes guts to stand up in public and strip to the gooseflesh, then I have an item of news without which you should not embark on the long trek to Chalk Farm: the guts involved are mere offal compared with those required of citizens prepared to sit down in public, clothed to the collar, and watch the stripped perform. It takes courage, determination, practice, daring, and acting talent of a very high order indeed to be a member of an *Oh! Calcutta!* audience, and many an overnight star will rise to shine unseen in the first few rows of stalls when Ken Tynan's pimply oeuvre hits the Round House boards.

Having been tried out in New York for a walk-on-sit-down-enjoy-enjoy part, I shall not be appearing in the London production. I won't even let me know. My appearance at the Eden Theatre on Second Avenue last November was a fiasco fit to prick a critic's tear-ducts: despite his long theatrical experience, his intelligent and sensitive interpretations of Pinter, Brecht, Shakespeare, Rix and Strindberg, Mr. Coren proved totally inadequate when faced with the demands of nude theatre. It was beyond his apparently eclectic range. It was embarrassing to see so experienced a figure so totally out of his depth. We cannot think why he should have attempted so patently unsuitable a role. His training at Stratford and the Old Vic appeared to stand him in no stead whatever.

And so, for those of you lucky enough to have got a part in the Round House audience, allow me to jot a few pointers, a few tips which may enable you to carry off the performance better than I. To all intents and purposes (and, believe me, the evening is fraught with both, if with nothing else), New York and London may be taken to be similar enough: the lessons learned in the one ought to be applicable to the other. Immeasurably the most important thing to get over, right at the start, is, of course, first night nerves. Most of you will never have tackled a naked play before, and whatever rehearsals you may have undergone, such as getting your loved ones to dance nudely through the bedroom reciting *Sonnets From The Portuguese*, will count for nothing when the house lights fade: this is the real thing, a thousand people are watching, and whatever organs may subsequently be pressed into service, it is that initial beating of the heart that you will have to conquer.

As a curtain-raiser and nerve-breaker, your performance in the cab is invaluable. In New York, I failed this abysmally: my face buffed to an odoriferous post-electric sheen, my suit new-pressed, my shirt and accessories irreproachable, I leapt into the taxi with all the controlled poise of a sophisticated homme du monde and, licking dry lips, cried: "Eden Theatre!" I might as well have been wearing an old fawn raincoat and a stubbly leer. "That's where they got that dirty show, ain't it?" said the cabby, winking me into a conspiracy of which I wanted no part. I avoided looking in his mirror. "Pretty horny evening they got down there, right?" Now, at this cue, your line ought to be: "Yeah, heh-heh-heh, jist can't wait to git down thar and scope all that nekked flesh!" or, in your case, the Cockney equivalent. My line—"Oh, it's rather more than that, you know, I mean, well, what I'm hoping to see is something in the nature of an avant-garde theatrical experience . . ."—will immediately classify you as a lying pervert and call for a mollifying tip likely to break resources already severely strained by the cost of the most expensive tickets in the world.

When you get to the foyer, all the other performers will be walking around, very nervous, very taut, buying chocolates in a high voice of shrieking unconcern and nonchalantly dropping them all over the stairs. Don't let this communal stagefright infect you, don't attempt to appear cool, and above all don't try to give the impression that nothing could be further from your thoughts than smut: those groups talking about Wittgenstein or the Trade Gap are the most jittery of all. Take a leaf out of Alan Brien's book, and overbid in spades: he, I'll just bet, will be standing in the centre of the floor, discussing the activities of dogs on Primrose Hill or his own physical landmarks.

And check your coat. I know you don't normally do this in theatres, what with the crush afterwards and so on, but you would be ill-advised to sit through the performance with a raincoat folded on your lap. You know how people talk.

When the show itself begins on stage, acting ability of an almost illimitable order is required: most of you will have feigned burning interest, at one time or another, in Polish plays at the Aldwych or monosyllabic crypto-Irish works at the Court, many of you will have contrived to laugh heartily at resurrected nineteenth century farces at the National, or wept practically real tears when a bereaved dustbin grunts a requiem for a fallen sink at the Open Space Theatre, but such responses are mere Christmas charades compared with what you will have to fake at *Oh! Calcutta!* You will, for example, have to counterfeit shock, just so that those around you don't think you're trying to suppress it. There is, I promise, nothing shocking at the presentation of genitalia to a spotlight, but you must pretend there is: unconcern will be interpreted as puritanism infibulating itself to death. Boredom, an equal threat, is even more dangerously suspect: nod off for the merest millisecond, and you will be pointed out forever after as a person who could not bear to watch a nipple pass and exit, left. And don't laugh too uproariously; everyone else has heard the jokes before, too, and if you're too hearty this will be taken to indicate (a) a sheltered life, or (b) nervousness, but, mainly (c) both. Smile broadly, to show you recognise the public acknowledgement of what people of *ton* have known/said/done for years.

And don't on any account move. At almost any other performance, fidgeting is permissible: during *Oh! Calcutta!*, an involuntary move to loosen a tie-knot, the shifting from one buttock to its neighbour, the bending to remove a pinching shoe will be taken as incontrovertible evidence that the whole thing is making you uncomfortable.

Intervals will almost certainly be the most testing time of all. After the battering your motionless body will have taken for an hour, after enduring an inflexible rictus welded across your teeth for the same period, after keeping your cool when all around you are losing theirs (or, worse, keeping it), and after having worked so hard at gay spontaneity of response to things you haven't even had time to watch, so intent have you been on your own performance, you will be grasping for a few resuscitating belts. Tough luck. Anyone rushing to the bar, tearing at his collar and spilling florins will be sneered to death; you're supposed to appear utterly relaxed by what you've seen, so the first one into the bar's a cissy. (Unless, of course, you're really a cissy, in which case the first one into the bar's a butch: because if you're homosexual, you'll have to appear even more nonchalant about the Full Frontal histrionics than the rest of us.)

Once in the bar/aisle/foyer, or wherever it is you're planning to stand looking unconcerned and relaxed, don't on any account fall into the usual audience-acting trap of interpretation. Those who've acted in Pinter or Beckett intervals will get short shrift here if they start running off at the mouth with such phrases as: "Of course, what he's *really* saying is . . ." or "Well, one hardly needs to say, does one, that the bare bum represents the essential division running through Western society today . . ." The coolest, most hang-up-free comments, delivered with a light, emancipated chuckle, should compare the actors' and actresses' various talents with those of one's enormous circle of nude friends. If you're standing in a large mixed group, be sure to touch one another a lot; but not, naturally, too much. It mustn't appear to be the first time you've done it.

And when, at last, the time comes for you to leave, the importance of the correct exit-line cannot be stressed too strongly. In the press struggling down the Round House steps, loud comment will obviously be called for. "Shocking!" should, it goes without saying, go without saying. But don't be misled into thinking that the cool alternative is a loud "Disappointing!" Not only is that obvious and crass and predictable, but it will be taken to mean that you were looking for something you didn't get, and your life is supposed to be so full, so satisfactory, that you do not seek surrogate thrills in the theatre. I haven't a sure-fire winner of my own to offer, and I myself walked out into the New York midnight mumbling. But, as I did so, I heard a remark that you may like to use, and which seemed to me at the time to be invulnerable to attack or speculation. Two well-dressed night folk elbowed past me through the doors, and as they went by the man turned to the girl and said: "You know, I think my parents would like it a lot."

KEN ALLSOP RISKS HIS LIFE AMONG THE TEENAGE MAGAZINES

DEAR Mr. Punch,—Please help me. I am a teenage girls' magazine, big and well developed for my age. I am not a stick in the mud. I circulate a lot and seem quite a rave with the crowd, but I get suspicious about how loyal they really are. Honestly, I don't know where I fit in, and I get terrible hang-ups about sex. I know some people think I'm promiscuous because I'm willing to try anything that might make me a bit more popular, to make me *wanted*. But then there are others who think I'm really priggish and puritanical, and I've even been called a pixie-teaser, or something like that, because I don't always "deliver" what I seem to be promising. You see, I used to be rather prim and reserved, and for a long time wouldn't hear a word said about sex before marriage. But I've sort of changed my mind about that now, although I'm still not sure how far I should go. In fact, I'm not sure about anything. I am very confused and I badly need some advice because I don't want to become a drop-out. What should I do?

Yours desperately,
"Teeny,"
Fleet Street, EC4.

An edgy neutrality, a candour just a mite too strident, pervades those bright energetic publications which compete for the twenty-and-under female market. They hover to the right of Germaine Greer and Women's Lib and to the left of Mrs. Whitehouse. They'd like to keep one or two readers so they can't ignore that in their adolescents' dreamland, fantasy cannot now be entirely divorced from flesh. Scrambling along the slide-area between, they pursue their quarry: the child of the Pill Age. Pillage, indeed: how best to seize the spoils of the age group's £500 million annual spending power, there up for grabs? How to stay cool about the new permissiveness without quite condoning it?

The techniques vary. The customer is not a single stereotype, and the wares are prepared by some of the best minds in Britain outside Wardour Street. Never has boloney been sliced so diaphanously into fine degrees of sophistication, from minimal to moderate: pre-fifteen or post-seventeen, grammar school or secondary-mod, London or provincial, typing pool or factory hand.

There is, however, an overall ambiance common to all. As I Rip Van Winkled about in this excitable, introspective, flimsy nether world of trannies and discos and knickerbockers and fellas—so fizzy and yet so oddly inert, so decorative but so constricted—I began to get my bearings by certain landmarks. One is the amazing female absorption in the female body, in its excrescences and

55

excretions, in the garments which most intimately swaddle it, in the devices which fit into it. In male orientated publications, of course, there's a proportion of ads for aftershave and shirts—but not for jockstraps and condoms and penis-stretchers. Girls' papers are unabashedly crammed with the equivalents. Apart from fashions and cosmetics, there is a gruesome obsession with armpits and crotches: page after page of vaginal sprays and tampons and Niknax with cover-up gussets and hair-removing pastes and throwaway panties. Apart from the problems of bad breath and nail biting and fat legs, the letters agitate with gynaecological anxiety. "I am very worried about the size of my nipples, as they are very tiny. In fact I've hardly any at all"—18-year-old in *Petticoat*. Another enquirer: "Has it ever been known for the outer part of a woman's vagina not to be normal? If so what can be done about it?" A *Loving* correspondent: "My problem is driving me mad. Don't laugh, but one of my breasts is bigger than the other."

These genuine agonies are soothed by frank, factual answers. It is when moral issues press in that the bluffness falters into foot shuffling. Although their fiction and picture strips still have mandatory happy endings, the romance rags have taken a few steps out of their timeless fantasy toward acknowledging the existence of real-life inconveniences, like pregnancy, illegitimate babies, abortions and VD, which may not be entirely unconnected with the obsessional harping on groovy guys and how to hog-tie them. The policy of the Miss Lonelyhearts and lovelorn columns is to tell girls: "No, don't," whereas most of the surrounding material is based on the acceptance that girls do. "Look," says Marsha in *Loving* to a girl who is "courting a fab boy" and wants to go on the Pill, "this is a difficult situation and I refuse to take sides," and she thereupon relays the right pill-furnishing addresses. Within the same covers is an interview with a groupie: "Being a groupie gives your status a boost. It gives you satisfaction. I got fed up with home and work and wanted some excitement and glamour . . . I used to go with boys in the backs of their vans. Nowadays, I go back to their flats with them." This is "balanced" by a mature view: "Groupies are self-destructive, lonely and miserable"—but that may not be the more dominant impression left on groupie age-group readers.

There are matter of fact references to unmarried liaisons: "Peter Frampton of Humble Pie and his lovely model girlfriend Mary Lovett live in a flat at Hampstead" (*Fabulous*). A *Loving* interview with Harry Simmonds, Chicken Shack's manager, "a fast moving executive on the pop scene," mentions that "although Harry is living with his girlfriend he has his doubts about some people's motives." To a bird who, when the car stops in a country lane, realises "I've got meself landed with a wolf," a *Mirabelle* feature-writer points out: "Obviously it all depends on how much you fancy him. If that's what you've been working hard for all evening, then you've got what you wanted." There is a noticeable sag in exaltation of chastity, an irreverence—even flippancy—unthinkable or anyway unprintable five years ago. To the question "Virginity: Who Cares About It?" in *19* appears the answer: "I don't. Virginity is a pretty useless qualification for a wife, when you think about it"—countered, as is the custom, by a following piece warning against the monotonous drudgery of sleeping around. In the *Rave* containing the drill on contraception is also the cautionary "Your Holiday: Sun, Sea or Sex!" which advises the Majorca-bound to spurn swarthy seducers. *Honey* has a frivolous story about Elf, a scrawny sixth former who has been trying, vainly, to lose her virginity since she was fifteen. (When she does, was it worth the effort? No: "Terribly boring really.")

More often the treatment is less blasé. Usually the blunder over the brink has the tipsy-mishap explanation: "I thought cider was pretty harmless, but it made me go all soft and floaty. I hardly knew what was happening in the back of the car, and then Bill was so very gentle and tender that I didn't want to stop him" (*Loving*).

Other stark *Man Alive*-ish matters are now broached in these hitherto cosy corners. "Is He Queer?" heads a letter in *Petticoat*. *Rave* carries a two-page spread: "26 Selfish Reasons For Not Taking Drugs," showing a frowsty blonde, syringe in hand, who obviously has lost interest in fellas and probably also in underarm freshness. A *Romeo* strip serial features the Skulls, a menacing Hell's Angels horde wearing Nazi helmets on motorcycles with Easy Rider handlebars. "Plenty of crumpet about in Oxford Street," writes *Fab*'s young man about town, Ross. "Diana Ross does things to me that couldn't be printed even in randy old *19*," writes that paper's record reviewer (male), and under the headline "Me and My Boobs" Anne Batt confesses: "Flat as two queen buns without bicarb, that's me." Yet despite this abreast jauntiness, and venturing gingerly into social-realism, the teenage mags finally play safe with the tested formulae. Beneath their back-combed touselled hairstyles and under their harlequin bellbottoms, are the same decent lads of yesteryear who once wore brass-buttoned blazers and smoked pipes. Out of the pale, mournful faces of the dolly girls, dark-rimmed eyes seek the same old security.

The recurrent homily is of the flibbertigibbet who goes off the rails, pretty little noddle temporarily turned by the dazzle of alien jack-o'-lanterns—often, at the moment, the debauched hippy. Corinne, in a *Loving* strip, rebels against her parents' "semi-detached smugness" and Kenny, the bank clerk next door, and runs off to Pete ("I've rejected the values of present society") in his neighbourhood Spahn Ranch. Then, sickened by "the greasy, broken lino and the pile of unwashed clothes"—and a she-hippie in shortie nightie—in Pete's pad, she realises that "she'd been happy in her little world till he'd come along." She rushes back, back to "safe, dependable Kenny, not good looking, not particularly intelligent, but devoted to the end." Often the discontent with culture-crazed local worthies (Jill in *Mirabelle* "That drip Jake rabbiting on about the Drama Group. How droopy can you get?") throws them into the arms of ageing playboys: The rotters are instantly identifiable. Jacquie's defiler in a *Rave* serial wears a lambswool-lined suede jacket and jeers about faithful Terry: "Wrong class for you. Leg of lamb for Sunday lunch and Saturday night sex with lights out." Terry's substance is displayed when he suspects that Jacquie has been inside that lambswool lining again: "Ee, lass, I may look a fool but I'm not daft." There is a similar contrast in a *Loving* novelette. Married smoothy Eric comes between Jane and teacher Leo, who in his "shabby, funny little room" has "lots of books with titles I didn't understand." It is when Eric lures her to a pub and she sees him approaching ("hair curling over his collar, trying to be something he wasn't any more—a long-haired young man") that she suddenly knows him for what he is, even if she can't read close print. And he is bringing her "a pinkish drink, I think it was a Campari": he is clearly degenerate to his zip-sided Hush Puppies.

What batter as pitilessly as the drama are the hammerstrokes driving in more nails to uphold the wormy beams of Britain's trad class structure. Demolished it may theoretically be in our modern meritocracy, but it remains an emotional straitjacket around the husband-hunting magazine heroines. Here (and presumably the editorial strategists are acutely tuned in to the market research soundings) the sensible girl doesn't get ideas above her station. She doesn't yearn for the flash and filigree of the beau monde—or for education, independence, career or much of an identity. She prizes the stable, if dullish, reliability of the young chap in the same street. "My Boyfriend's Great, But Am I Good Enough For Him?" is the title of a *Valentine* story about a girl from a "comfy working class home" uneasy in Robin's "beautiful house at Richmond" where she meets female cousins, "debutante sorts, with about three languages and a Cordon Bleu".

In a *Romeo* strip Sandie works at Star Records for Mike, the sound engineer—boringly sound, Sandie feels, when glam pop singer Paul Delaney arrives to cut a disc. "The old routine was suddenly—well, dreary," says the caption, and Sandie reflects in a thinks-balloon: "I dunno why I go around with you, Mike. Nothing turns you on, just nothing. A steady guy is just a drag." Undraggy Paul makes a track of a new chart-bound sound which goes: "Sandie, I love you! Sandie, be mine." He takes her out ("Paul—well, he made a girl feel special") and in a candle-lit club says he wants to introduce the writer of the song. Who shambles up but Mike. "Wanted to surprise you," he mumbles diffidently. "I've been a blind fool," Sandie thinks as she pulls down his familiar homely mug within kissing range, and the legend over the last drawing is: "Because any fool knows that there are times when the old routine is just great!"

And the teenage mags hope that, made just a weenie bit racier, the old routine stays just great.

MRS. Joan Fox, on holiday at Shoenmakersdop, awoke to find a young baboon in bed with her, gently stroking her hair. Her husband had let him in when he heard a rattle at the door and he made for the bedroom in a couple of bounds. The couple ejected him into the garden where a man from the local snake park caught him in a net. *East Anglian Times*

LOVE SONG

by A. P. H.

ON May Day, after oysters,
  They say that monk and nun
Run madly from their cloisters
  In search of love and fun:
They say some stuff called celery
Is good for wedding-bellery:
    These aids may do
    For one or two,
      But I need none.

I need no oyster
  To be in love with you,
Nor, when I roister,
  Raw roots to chew;
I need not suffer hard-boiled eggs
To see that you have lovely lègs.
  I need no rations
    Of Danish Blue,
  To improve my passions,
    And, as for you,
  To see you walk,
  To hear you talk,
    Gives me my cue.
  I need no oysters
    To be in love with you.

They recommend red pepper
  With quantities of stout:
It may get hep men hepper,
  But I can do without.
They say that frangipanni
Can make a man more manny,
    But who requires
    Such borrowed fires
      When you're about?

I need no oysters
  To be in love with you
Nor at my roisters
  Mussels for two:
No radishes, I beg, and please
No curried prawns or Persian cheese!
  I need no shell-fish,
   No hellebore,
  To make me elfish
    Or even more;
  If you but blow
  A kiss or so
    I'm on the floor.
  I need no oysters
    To be in love with you.

MONDAY I TOUCHED HER ON THE ANKLE

NICHOLAS TOMALIN on the end of Prudery

A MAN I know was asked to a dinner party which, his hostess warned him with a slight nervous pause, would be "very high-powered." Not entirely certain what this meant, he dressed with care in white tie, tails and medals and was embarrassed to discover after he had offered his opera cloak to the butler that he was in the middle of an orgy—nakedness mandatory.

The next occasion his hostess asked him to dine, she made the situation very clear by pointing out that this time the dinner party would be "very casual," and he must not make such an effort.

Therefore, on arrival he handed the butler his cloak and hat, his jacket, trousers, underpants and string vest. Light-heartedly skipping into the dining-room in a properly naked state he was faced by a startled group of six elderly married couples, seated round a candle-lit table. They were all in evening dress.

The first sad point to be made about these incidents is that they reveal the awful anarchy now prevalent amongst our social conventions. How much easier things used to be when hostesses wrote in precise instructions about party dress!

The second point is that the dual humiliation poses a useful prudery test. Which would you rather be? Bemedalled at an orgy? Or naked at a dinner-party? If you would rather be over-dressed than under-dressed, you are a prude.

In general I am a passionate under-dresser. The social trends encourage it. To be caught less formally dressed, or less dressed, than one's fellow guests is no real humiliation in these egalitarian permissive times. It tends to imply moral superiority. You can explain it away, or brazen it out, and no one is likely to object. But to be caught with too many clothes on! That is pretentious; that is egotistical; that is stuffy. It is indefensible.

Disregarding—for the moment—sex, the conventional moral response nowadays always favours under-dressing. Heroes and heroines, archetypally, always wear fewer and humbler clothes than villains.

Think of the great historical, or literary set-pieces. The noble slave, dressed only in chains, at the be-toga'd court of the dissolute Roman emperor. The when-did-you-last-see-your-father child, being interrogated by filthy Puritans in leathern armour. Little Black Sambo, stripped of his purple shoes with crimson soles and crimson linings, surrounded by ravening over-dressed tigers. Mahatma Ghandi in his loin-cloth, passively resisting phalanxes of be-feathered pro-Consuls. Aneurin Bevan in a lounge suit at a city banquet where tail coats are obligatory. Christ, even, surrounded by money-changers or Pharisees all dressed to the nines.

Whenever we see a group in which one figure is manifestly less well-dressed, or less dressed, than his companions we assume that he is the good guy, the others are bad guys.

Most modern advertising urges us to come alive, or join the swingers, or take off, or dream something in our maiden-form bras. Every time this is illustrated with the image of grey, over-dressed prudes being left in the background by a highly technicoloured new us, leaping into emancipation in a bathing suit, or less.

Every Sunday we read yards and yards of print urging greater informality, less stuffiness, and an end to censorship, restrictions, kill-joys, Lord Chamberlains and Mrs. Grundies. How right, and how high-minded they are! At times their zeal can lead to a kind of intellectual prudery-in-reverse, as if they were compensating for their public openness.

I recall seeking to write a story about that fiery theatrical crusader, Lindsay Anderson. Mr. Anderson had, after submitting a translated

script to the Lord Chamberlain, been ordered to cut some dialogue. He had agreed, and then covertly, a week or so after the play's premiere, reinserted the censored words. They were, he felt, artistically central to the play, and no prudish philistine ignorant censor had the right to delete them.

I wanted to strike a blow for freedom by publicising all this in my newspaper. But Mr. Anderson objected. How dare I set back the cause of freedom in the theatre by such a revelation? If I printed my story the Lord Chamberlain's men would return to the theatre, notice the reinsertion, and enforce the censorship once cain. Frankness would suffer.

For half-an-hour we argued over the telephone. I tried to tell Mr. Anderson that by forcing me to suppress the story he too was acting as a censor.

He could not understand this point so, ultimately, I agreed to keep silent.

And what were those sacred, precious artistic words for which his play had been endangered and the freedom of the press sacrificed? I remembered them clearly. They were: "Piss off."

The case against prudery is so obvious it scarcely needs stating. Obviously, in an ideal society we would always be totally naked and totally frank. Such a state is more than ideal, it is—quite literally—Paradise. After the apple of knowledge came the fig-leaf of prudery, satorial symbol of our lost innocence.

The amazing thing, really, is that any prudery still survives. When you consider the force of opinion, the ferocity of campaign, that has been waged against it for the past two decades, it is incredible that people preserve any modesty.

What human instinct does prudery represent? Why should we hesitate to disrobe? Why is morality somehow so involved with sexual privacy? There is, after all, no logical connection between sin and nakedness or sensuality. None whatsoever. Other moral conventions have a basic rational cause; this has none.

The thought came to me very recently why this particular arbitrary morality survives. It is, no doubt, well-known to biologists, but to me it is a new and fascinating revelation.

I realised that the association of sex and privacy is a mechanical, animal thing. That is to say, it is clearly an irrational instinct built into the race for biological reasons which civilisation made irrelevant aeons ago.

Consider the animal, human or otherwise, before progress removed the constant danger of attack by predators. Obviously while actually engaged in the act of love any such animal is vulnerable to attack. He—or she—will be concentrating too keenly to be able to keep watch for the approach of enemies.

Any animal that loves too frankly and publicly is clearly putting himself in danger. Thus any animal which by evolutionary mutation was imbued with the inhibitory urge to feel, and display, erotic activity only in private—immune from attack—was at an advantage.

We must still have this instinct, even though the dangers no longer exist. Modesty is the result of a very primitive desire for survival.

This thought explains more than the apparently inexplicable survival of prudish inhibitions. It also explains many other strange social phenomena. Why is it that nudist colonies, for instance, are always so unbearably high-minded? Obviously they consider themselves not more animal than the rest of us, but less. By disrobing they are being supremely unnatural. They are moving further from our primitive animal state than the rest of us.

It also explains the extraordinary prurience of highly clothed souls like Judges, Members of Parliament, or Chairmen of Boards of

Directors, once they find themselves in protected, private circumstances, in their clubs, their Turkish baths, their smoking rooms, or lolling swinishly over their port wine. They are only responsing to animal impulses: once assuredly amongst friends, in private, they cut loose. The smoking-room joke is a primitive evolutionary phenomenon.

Having—I hope—demonstrated that prudery is both reactionary and snobbish *and* primitive and animal, I have only to demolish one final argument sometimes advanced in its favour.

This is the "aiming off" argument. A public convention or law, it states, should always be some degrees to the right of the actually permitted human behaviour. If you want drivers to go no faster than thirty-five miles in built-up areas you impose a thirty mile-an-hour official limit. Policemen's discretion, and the universal desire to go just that little bit beyond the law will take care of the rest.

Similarly, although marijuana smoking is transparently harmless, you do not make it legal. If this were done the daring, avantgarde, and rebellious would move on to some more heinous narcotic, in order to defy authority. You do not, by a similar token, reform divorce or abortion laws as much as logically you should.

By analogy, the same argument implies that although, of course, there is no moral harm in nakedness or sexuality, it is necessary to keep them tabu in public while tacitly allowing them in semi-public and private. By this means you permit a healthy amount of nonprudery in practice, and give the advanced that small, therapeutic thrill they so enjoy. To abandon such token prudery would allow the floodgates to open (incidentally, has anyone who has used that puritan's cliche ever realised that floodgates are opened to *drain away* floods, not to create them?).

But the analogy is wrong. For in this particular case there is a limiting factor which is totally lacking elsewhere There is no limit to speed; you can go faster and faster with only the hindrance of law to hold you back. There is no limit to drug addiction, you can turn on harder and harder drugs until death intervenes.

But with nakedness and frankness there is only one destination to arrive at. Beyond that there is nowhere to go. Furthermore there is this limiting corrective, this counter-force, which will always prevent all the wraps falling off.

This corrective is very sad, and ever present. It is human ugliness.

Boy Rode Nude Through Park
A FIFTH former has been suspended from Poole Grammar School, Dorset, after admitting that he rode naked on a motor-cycle in a local park a week ago . . . His father said: "We are not trying to whitewash our boy but . . ."   *Daily Telegraph*
Might be better than nothing.

Farewell, My Ugly

In which STANLEY REYNOLDS takes on the assembled might of the male cosmetics industry.

STAYING overnight in London the other week with a redheaded actress who is one of my oldest and dearest of just good friends, I awoke in the morning, clamped a black Burma cheroot between my yellowed teeth and walked around her flat scratching the hair on my chest and looking for some place to spit. Handsome is, as they say, as handsome does. Anyway, the wandering brought me past the flat's bedroom where, after falling to my knees and peering through the keyhole, I could not help but see upon the beige satin pillow slip there lay two tousled heads.

"By Sister George", I muttered, "*Les Biches*." But then I noticed that one of the little faces under flowing locks was badly in need of a shave. "Nancy boy," I chuckled before being reminded by the ache in the region of my fourth lumbar, just who it was who had spent the night on a Victorian chaise longue obviously designed for a Victorian midget. Chaise it might have been, but longue it wasn't.

But that is neither here nor there. The point is, had it not been for the tell-tale shadow on his delicately etched jowls the young punk in there looked just like a girl; in fact, of the two heads floating on the downy billows, his curls were the tousleder. This, of course, is hardly news. The Beatles have even written a new song about it with the terrifying line, *Have you seen Polythene Pam, She's so good looking she looks like a man*.

From looking like girls, the boys now have managed somehow to get better looking than them. Ordinarily, I must stress, it does not bother me. Ordinarily one merely passes these Aubrey Beardsley-looking youths, puffing out one's tremendous chest, squaring the shoulders, jutting the jaw, narrowing the killer-male eyes, and one giggles over their ridiculously girlish waspy waists.

"Eeee by gum," one thinks (at least I always start thinking in a coal mining area accent when my manliness is in question), "if yon lass got shut of Wee Willie Winkie there and got in t' front parlour wi' me she'd know summat."

Actually what she'd know was that, when that bulging chest is standing at ease, it is a waist line and that I wear choo choo train print underwear given to me every birthday by a wife who knows what she's doing. As Malcolm Muggeridge, or was it the actress talking to the bishop, once said, "Some are born to chastity and some have it thrust upon them."

Be that as it may, one of the sad by-products of living in an age of youth and pretty young boys is that we men begin to court our own ugliness as a defence mechanism. Frightened by the pretty young things the imaginative man snarls back and tries to get himself looking like Lon Chaney Junior under a full moon.

I hasten to add here that I am not really ugly. Not the sort at least that you have to make an excuse and leave the room in the face of, like a *People* reporter fleeing from sin. No, if the truth were known, I am devilishly handsome, especially in the dusk with the light behind me and could at one time pull my eyebrows up into an inverted V like Peter Lawford.

But just like everybody else, I am walking around these days growing and shaving and growing and shaving again, all manner of beards, sideburns, mutton chops, and natty little or big droopy moustaches. It is a time of extraordinary looks. People would rather look extraordinarily ugly than just plain. Normal looking people have taken to disguising themselves, so much so that it is a wonder anyone recognises anyone else any more.

This is, I think, what this whole skinhead business is about. It is an appearance backlash. A desperate fight against the uncommon number of girlishly pretty boys. In this backlash I am merely a sort of thirty-four-year-old skinhead who has grown a lot of hair in order to look ugly just as the real teenage skinheads have their heads cropped in order to look pugnacious and plug ugly. But being ugly is a difficult job. One is fighting the whole damned new and expanding male cosmetics industry and barbers who think of themselves as artists. "Listen," I told my man when I went into the barber shop asking him to give me an old-fashioned short back and sides, "I want this haircut to be a Tribute to Burt Lancaster. I'm an old movie fan, watch them all the time on TV." "On you," he said, "it'll come out like Jerry Lewis."

And it is not merely a question of appearance. Added to appearance is the role the appearance forces you to play. You have to do things like smoke stogies first thing in the morning and relish nasty dishes to go with your nasty looks. One shoves into the background the New England upbringing, the private schools, the cameos of tortured sensibility that one pens in the early hours. At a dinner party where you have been placed next to the lady novelist whose soul you have appreciated for years and whose every dear little semi-colon and comma has stirred your heart, you suddenly start explaining to her how to butt people with your head and how you sure miss not being able to get rattlesnake fritters here in England. One wonders, did Frank Harris—who was invited to all the best houses but only, as Oscar Wilde said, once—did he feel the same? Was he a tortured aesthete who could not reconcile himself to his hairy jug ears and turned himself into a hairy ape at every possible occasion just to spite those ears?

It is a mystery and one despairs over the psychological implications involved in twisting one's personality around to fit the ugly look, and quite rightly. But rising in the morning there before you is the redhead's other non-paying guest, the dolly dolly boy who has obviously *not* been sleeping on the chaise longue. Pride . . . indeed, one's very tap root of manhood demands that you puff on that damned stogie and ask if there is such a thing as a piece of thick seamed tripe in the house, all the time praying that there is nothing more hearty than raspberry flavoured yogurt.

"No, mate," the kid said in the whinnying tones of a gamin of a cockney gutter, "but we got gorgeous kippers, haven't we?"

Right away I could tell I was going to have trouble. This kid had a natural crude streak that would make Rasputin baulk. I gave him my meanest I've-knocked-all-over-the-world-kid look but he just sat there sucking his teeth, And talk about table manners. This kid would make Charles Laughton in Henry VIII look like your Aunt Bertha wrestling with a cream cake at Brown's Hotel. I could have rubbed down with yak grease and he wouldn't have batted one of those long girlish eye lashes. I was afraid of tossing in a few remarks about putting in the head and boot in street fights because I knew in my bones that this kid had cut his teeth snatching old ladies' handbags. Still, I was going actually to get sick to my stomach and give the whole ugly tough guy game away if I sat there any longer listening to him eat kippers.

"Say, Lorna," I said to the redheaded actress, looking at my watch, "I've got to get to work" and just then out of the corner of my eye I saw a hint of chartreuse discolouring the kid's otherwise unblemished cheek. "Well," I said, loading my voice with doom, "you know how it is. Married with a *wife* and *kids*, a man has got to get out to *work*" and then I piled it on, throwing in a few extra kids and some horrible stuff about pensions and mortgages, watching the kid get sadder and sadder looking until he finally pushed his plate away and mumbled something about having to lie down. I got up then and threw him the old nine to five commuter's wave and strolled out.

Of course now I had the whole morning to kill but I popped into a real barber-shop, one of those old time places with a bad tempered grouchy old barber shuffling around in a stained apron, and I got the beaver removed and one of those real wage slave nondescript haircuts. Then I put on the old tortoiseshell eyeglasses, the kind people used to wear when they only wanted to see better and I passed the time until lunch looking purposeful and scaring the hell out of two hippies in Piccadilly Circus just by walking fast.

The new fascia is an improvement, certainly, but the village still considers it blatant and distasteful."

The ting-a-ling in Spring

Young love strikes KEITH WATERHOUSE

THE *Oxford Companion to English Literature* did not have space to record that, between the dissolution of the Northern School and the evolution of the Satirical Period, I was for a time consultant psychiatrist to a knitting magazine. If they want to make a note of it for the revised edition, the unvarnished truth is that I was only the back legs of a consultant psychiatrist. My job was to wring the juice out of a genuine head-shrinker, ghosting his more saleable thoughts on phobias, complexes, the adrenal, thymus and pre-pituitary glands and, on lean weeks, the meaning of dreams. All this was in dramatic contrast to the elevation and plan of toddlers' cable-knit romper suits that was the journal's staple fare, and my readers were legion.

It was in spring, though, that I really left the knitting patterns at the starting post. Any student wanting to write a thesis on the Freud/Jung/Kraft-Ebbing influences on my work should pay close attention to my three-part essay, WHAT PUTS THE TING-A-LING IN SPRING, written under the pseudonym, "A Leading Harley Street Doctor." Its central meta-physical argument—that at the time of the vernal equinox Western man is subject to powerful Ur-forces impelling him towards the ritual act of self-renewal—is nowhere better stated than in the opening paragraph: "*Pow! Suddenly it's spring—and you've got that ting-a-ling feeling. Buds blossom, birds spring . . . and like it or not, lady, you're in love.*" The author wishes to express his gratitude to Dr. X, without whose valuable advice and professional encouragement this work could not have been completed.

Dr. X, I now want to explain, was not the regular front legs of the outfit but a stand-in for Dr. Y, sometime lecturer in abnormal psychology at one of our teaching hospitals, a fashionable psychiatrist and author of the authoritative "Sunday Surgery" feature in a now-defunct national newspaper. At the time my readers were being promised THE TRUTH about the ting-a-ling ingredient in the period March-June, Dr. Y was called abroad—either to an international health conference in Zurich or to meet his literary agent in New York, I forget which. He recommended as locum this Dr. X, research assistant in psychopathology, who while ethically opposed to working for the yellow press was looking for a fast buck to finance a paper on flexor rigidity in the male frog. I arranged to meet Dr. X over expense-accounts in the Mirabelle restaurant.

One has seen it happen in all those *Doctor in the House* films. We are expecting, are we not, some bearded character in a pepper-and-salt suit, as personalised by James Robertson Justice—and lo and behold, who should roll up but Julie Christie, with the announcement—I hope I'm not doing the scriptwriters a disservice here—"But weren't you expecting me? I am Dr. X."

So we got down straight away to mixing business with pleasure. It was a gorgeous spring day, the sun poured in through the open roof, the whole place stank of jasmine or some such bloom, the martinis were perfect. Dr. X rattled on as required about the ting-a-ling factor as it relates to this happy season—why we fall in love as illustrated by the case of Mary A, the nesting instinct as illustrated by the case of Jane B, an astonishing example of human similarity to the birds and the bees as singularised in the case of Patricia C. Dr. X was determined to give value for money—if spring as the time of sexual excesses was what I wanted to write about, that was what she would give me copious medical proof of. The very crocus bulbs, I was given to understand over the duck à l'orange, were nothing but so many phallic symbols. She was vivacious, provocative, indiscreet—all that one finds delightful in a woman. I looked up from my notebook, basked in the late March sunshine, sipped a heady glass of wine and realised that I was violently, passionately, hopelessly and irrevocably in love with Dr. X.

How the BMA looks at a guilty relationship between a doctor who looks like a goddess and her unworthy literary ghost was something I wasn't very clear about. I didn't want to get her struck off, and in any case she was so admirably brisk and professional, refusing brandy and obviously dying to get back to the male frog which she'd got strapped down on the dissecting table. I abandoned spring-like thoughts of a trot round Green Park, feed the birds and all back to my place on the excuse of taking coffee.

But at the office next morning, discovering that instalment one of WHAT PUTS THE TING-A-LING IN SPRING was coming off the typewriter in rhymed couplets, I knew that I could not put Dr. X out of my mind. Somehow, some day, she would come back into my life, and not only in the form of a rejected expense sheet endorsed: "This is more than the editor spends on lunch for six people." The birds sang in Fleet Street. The sun bounced off the yellow newspaper vans. There was a rainbow, I think, over the *Daily Express* building. I did two mad things on that mad day. First, between my ghosted fables of how spring love struck Mary A, Jane B and Patricia C, I inserted the entirely unauthorised story of Jack D, who over a duck lunch one March day had discovered himself to be in love with a lady psychiatrist. Secondly, I telephoned Dr. X and, not liking to come straight out with it and ask her to join me on the next train to Gretna Green, invited her collaboration on a new series we were running, to be provisionally entitled YOUR SECRET FEARS. She agreed, subject to the usual fee, and my cup was full.

Time doubling with its role of great healer, is also the great louser-up of romantic plots. After the ting-a-ling orgy, the Angora wool lobby on the knitting magazine were all for settling back to a routine of matinee coats and bed-jackets, and it took me some weeks to sell the editor on the idea of YOUR SECRET FEARS. Then Dr. X, presumably having made some important breakthrough on flexor rigidity in the male frog, was away spreading the good news in Helsinki. So it was towards the end of May before we met again, this time—at the suggestion of the knitting magazine's accountant—in a Soho kebab house.

I had counted the minutes—86,438 of them, subject to audit—since we had said good-bye to each other all those weeks ago.

What would she look like? What would she be wearing? What erotic anecdotes concerning Gladys E and her fear of snakes would enliven her thoughts on YOUR SECRET FEARS?

"I liked your articles," she murmured, as the waiter poured rough Greek wine, "but I don't remember telling you anything about a Jack D—the one who loved his psychiatrist."

So far I had not dared to look at her. I took a deep breath and said: "I am Jack D." Our fingers touched across the plastic tablecloth, and I noticed for the first time the warts on her hand. Outside, a fine May drizzle had begun to turn into heavy rain. The shashlik was bad. The wine tasted like a cleaning agent. I looked up and

found myself in the tender gaze of possibly the most unattractive woman, certainly the ugliest psychiatrist, I had ever seen in my life.

YOUR SECRET FEARS contains the curious story of George F who could not bear to be touched or to receive telephone messages, an obsessive phobia arising from his dread of the medical profession. Spring gave way to an indifferent summer, and I never saw Dr. X again.

"Quick! Out the back way. My husband is coming."

Love, the hard way

"IT'S about time you and I had a serious talk about the facts of life," said my father, trying to bite through his pipe. "I want to talk to you about women, sex and life insurance."

We sat in silence for a bit.

"How do you mean, Dad?" I said.

"It's like this," he said. "You know the crysanthemums down by the sundial? Well, have you ever thought how they come again next year?"

"Cutting or pruning or something, isn't it?"

"Something like that. Trouble is, I haven't seen my pruning knife for about three months and it's a bit late now."

He sat worrying his pipe, and broke it into three pieces.

"What was that about sex, Dad?"

"Oh, nothing much. It's just . . . have you ever wondered where your mother and I came from originally?"

"I've always believed you when you said we were a Wiltshire family."

"You could say that."

He clenched his fists in agony.

"Dad, have I told you about Julia?"

"Julia!" he said, brightening up. "I had a girl-friend once called Julia. She was hot stuff. Took her out on my new motor-bike in 1928 to the pictures. She wasn't there when we arrived. I often wonder what happened to her."

"Julia and I are going to be married."

"I hardly think that's likely, son. She'd be pushing sixty-five by now. Not that she won't still be worth looking at."

"In fact, we *have* to get married."

"Everything turned out for the best, as it happened. Met a lovely girl in the cinema queue called Helen. I'd appreciate it if you didn't mention her name to your mother."

"Actually, we are married."

My father smiled and crossed his knees several times.

"Helen never fell off my motor-bike," he said.

Love, the easy way

ONE day I was a simple, pleasure-loving model on the outskirts of *Vogue*. The next day I lifted my head and found myself looking into the deep brown limpid light-meter of Ralph Nugget, the famous photographer and seducer.

"Good Lord!" I cried.

"Exactly," he said softly. "Shall we dance?"

"I must be mad," I told his lapel. "My father warned me against men like you."

"I hope he mentioned me by name," he smiled.

"This is hopeless," I groaned. "How can I fight this thing which is bigger than both of us and equally suitable for daytime and evening wear?"

The next time I met him I was engaged to model a top grey-green coat against the tough hard-wearing Cotswold Hills and Ralph was to take the photographs. We met at Paddington station.

"Ralph, my darling!" I cried. "To think that for the next two and a half hours we shall be all alone in a fast non-smoker!"

"I didn't quite catch your name," breathed Ralph. "Shall we dance?"

Hopelessly locked in a tight-fitting mazurka, we roamed all day over the lonely platform while the porters wheeled and screeched overhead—deep into the afternoon we danced and back again in time for tea.

"How soon can we be married, Ralph?"

At the mention of nuptials his handsome face darkened, a straw boater appeared in his hand and he started an Al Jolson song. He had gone too far.

"Ralph, I must tell you that my father has nothing against white men who imitate negroes, but he would never let me pretend to marry one."

I next bumped into Ralph on platform three at Islington registry office. He was dressed in a dark suit and a small photograph of a red carnation. He smiled reassuringly at me and put a large photograph of his arm round my shoulder.

"Penny Fairweather," said the registrar, "do you take this life-sized reproduction of Ralph Nugget to be your husband?"

"Yes, yes, yes, yes."

"Ralph Nugget," said the registrar, "shall we dance?"

The sub-registrar leapt to open the door, the registrar drummed his heels imperiously on the floor and the last I saw of my husband-to-have-been was a pair of husky ankles.

"Ralph!" I cried. "You promised me the first dance!"

Bumper to bumper and cheek to cheek, Ralph and I found ourselves waltzing across the English countryside. The scent of the late flowering saxophone hung heavy in the air and old man's beard knitted quietly to itself in the hedgerow. I turned round to drink Ralph in. He was nowhere to be seen. It did not matter. I knew that nothing could part us now.

SHE said that sex was even getting into the television hospitals—men in hospital never wore pyjamas. "They have someone in hospital and he must always be absolutely in the nude. And who likes to see a man in the nude?" she asked. The meeting, chaired by the B and P Club president Mrs. Betty Ford, ended with a vote being taken.

Morecambe Guardian

The Egerias of Westminster

By MAURICE EDELMAN

"I WAS in bed with Mrs. Armistead," said Charles James Fox, MP, when he was accused of taking part in a riot against Pitt. "And she's ready to substantiate the fact on oath."

Looking up the form-book of political popsies, I can find no one to equal Mrs. Armistead in frankness, loyalty and self-sacrifice. It's true that she's left standing at the post if you compare her, say, with Mme. Caillaux, who shot and killed an editor for writing nasty things about her husband, the Prime Minister. But Frenchwomen are notoriously quicker on the draw than Englishwomen, and it's a pity that we don't know more about Mrs. Armistead, that prototypal aide-de-camp, than that she married the Leader of the Opposition some years later. In secret, of course.

In France, the political mistress thumping her fist on the Cabinet table—think of Mme. de Portes—is a familiar figure in public life. Lacking the vote till only a few years ago, Frenchwomen in the past have made and unmade politicians through private rather than

Quentin Blake

public interventions. The *Egeria*—the confidante who takes the name from the goddess of the grove and adviser to King Numa—is a stock figure of the Palais Bourbon. In the Palace of Westminster, she is more shadowy. The Family Room of the House of Commons, expressing the admirable tradition that an MP's best adviser is his wife, stems not from Fox but from Gladstone. "Fortunately," said one of Mrs. Gladstone's guests before dining at No. 10 when they'd reached stalemate in a theological discussion, "Fortunately"—with a finger pointing heavenwards—"there's One above who knows all the answers!" "Yes," said Mrs. Gladstone, "Mr. Gladstone will be down in a few minutes."

That's the sort of wifey piety which has become a model for political wives ever since. When a constituency party take a look at their prospective candidate's wife, they want discretion, amiability, and the shining reverence for his qualities that they expect the electorate to show as well. When Mrs. Disraeli overheard someone say at a party that her husband was ugly, she said angrily, "He isn't. You should see him in the bath." The electorate likes such total commitment. Happy families are still, I'm glad to say, vote-winners, and the bigger the family group in the election photograph, the more reassured the voters are likely to be.

Well, we know what the constituency party is looking for. But what does the young political wife hope to find? Leaving aside the image of her husband as a tribune of the people—secretary of the local party, candidate, MP—glorious day—Under-Secretary, Secretary of State and Prime Minister (why not?)—her thoughts turn to all those routs at Lancaster House, those dinners at Carlton Gardens, those premières at Leicester Square, those annals of William Hickey. Ascot, Cowes, Montego Bay, Deauville—all those places where her husband's new title will be a letter of introduction. The prospect is exciting, and makes the hard slog of electioneering all the more worthwhile. Goodbye the provincial suburbs; London, we're on our way.

But the problem, she soon finds, is to harmonise her domestic obligations and her ambitions. As her husband climbs upwards with her advice and help, and the calls on him, both social and political, accumulate, so she finds it more and more difficult to keep pace. If she relies on an MP's salary to run her household, she will find herself tied to her growing family. No more those exciting demos and rallies; gone the social dreams; just the hard grind at home, relieved by the babysitter or the unreliable au pair. When her husband goes off to Bogota or Lesotho, she only has time to wave him goodbye. When they're both invited to a Gala at Covent Garden, the baby-sitter is ill and the au pair girl is off. With the baby crying in the morning, there's hardly time to read the *Mirror*, let alone *The Times*. And when her husband comes home after a late night sitting and she wants to talk about his exciting day, all he can say is, "Didn't you see it on *News at Ten*?" before falling into an agitated sleep.

But there are compensations for the dedicated wife. She can go to the constituency at week-ends and stand and sit by his side, and occasionally get a bouquet. Sometimes, it is true, her facial muscles will get cramped through smiling at one of his standard jokes. Sometimes she may feel a hysterical desire to join in his speech like a chorus when he repeats it for the fiftieth time. And sometimes, listening to his sermons, she may wonder why he doesn't practise at home what he preaches outside. On the whole, though, the political wife learns to adapt. She'll learn the pleasures of being loved by strangers who'll call her by her first name. She'll learn a lot about the way people live who never want to be MPs or MP's wives.

As for her husband, moving with the passage of time into more and more sophisticated circles, his problem may well be to cope with the more sophisticated women advisers now at his disposal. Unlike his wife, they won't be tired from the uphill battle. Unlike her, they'll come to him without the heat of the kitchen still glowing in their faces. Now, he has to have all his wits in choosing between the guidance of Mark I, his wife, and Mark II, the new and exciting model that has so much to be desired.

In 1964, a Tory hostess said, "Such interesting men, these new Labour Ministers. But do I have to have their dreary wives?" The new Labour Establishment soon made her complaint out of date, because office has its own—if you'll forgive me—charisma. The "dreary" wives soon flowered in the new states they'd helped their husbands to win. And strikingly enough, the vast majority of marriages in the new political order survived the strains and the deprivations that went before.

As with soldiers and sailors, it's separation that puts the greatest stress on the wives of politicians, and although divorce has increased and become less damaging to an MP's career than in the past, the surprising thing is not that there are so many divorces but that there are so few. Despite the Whips, an MP can dispose of his time at his own will. Indeed, there was an MP, now dead, who gained a national reputation for his busyness in the House. He gained it by regularly asking questions till 3.30, before disappearing in search of advice till late in the night from his Egeria. His wife was eventually obliged to move to Victoria in order to keep an eye on the light in the clock tower that tells whether the House is still sitting.

TV and radio have changed all that. MPs nowadays have to stand and prepare to be counted in the late night news. And the women-advisers in their entourage are under a closer scrutiny than ever before. With over six hundred keen observers on constant watch, the corridors of Westminster hum with as many "*on dit's*" as the Court of Versailles ever did.

And inevitably so. MPs, by the nature of their profession, are thrusting, ambitious, exhibitionistic and benevolent men. But they are subjected to more or less the same stresses as all other men. The only difference is that, like other public performers, they have the added strain of keeping up a public face when privately they're coping with their personal problems. That, of course, is the moment when they need the reassurance, the comfort of the women behind them. That's when the competition starts. Wife? Secretary? That very pretty and intelligent girl at last night's Embassy party? Egeria herself—undemanding, sympathetic, wise and always available?

It's all a matter of taste and judgment. But the wise MP in this situation is the one who, with his hand poised to reach for the telephone, decides to go home instead.

My Love Lies Bleeding

By RICHARD GORDON

I WAS a final-year medical student, passing my days in the
exclusive company of doctors, nurses, patients and corpses,
which rather restricted my choice of sexual chums. We anyway
preferred our affections not to stray far from our own doorstep, our
handmaidens in healing at least seeing our point if view. This was
brought home to me at a hospital party, when I overheard myself
described by a pretty girl from RADA as "A typical medical student,
darling—just like the life of prehistoric man, nasty, brutish and
short."

Unhappily the hospital romances you see on the telly resemble the
the real thing much less than all those highly entertaining operations.
Any affection between student and nurse is an eternal triangle, with
the hospital holding the third corner. You can't lose the atmosphere
of the place, no more than our shiniest NHS institutions lose the
traditional hospital smell of antiseptic, floor polish and distant
frying fish.

The acute frustration arising from this can be illustrated with
four clinical cases.

1. *Transferred Hypochondria*

Sally was a delightful little blonde. She'd just taken up nursing
and attracted every eye in the medical school, despite being put
through the de-sexing machine they seemed to keep down in the
Matron's office. Like most first-year nurses she brought to her work
the enthusiasm she had shown only a month before towards tennis,
horses and the pops. I made a date under the pretence of asking for
a specimen jar, and met her outside the mortuary gate anticipating
a pretty larky evening in the Mecca.

"Perhaps you'd care for a quick dance and then for a bit of a
stroll along the Embankment?" I suggest, buying her a small cider
in the local.

"Gosh, that case of shingles in bed number six is jolly interesting,"
she returned, glowing rather. "I never knew you could get such
terrible scabs. Shingles is related to chicken-pox somehow, isn't it?"

"The same virus," I nodded. "As I said, a quick dance and then a stroll——"

"The same virus!" She looked up with eager eyes. "But do tell me—how does it happen?"

"The Embankment," I continued, after a brief digression on the epidemiology of shingles. "The lights on the water are particularly attractive——"

"And bed number ten! Did you see his X-rays? I never realised you got an ulcer crater looking like that. It was just like the photographs Mummy took of Vesuvious. What sort of treatment does he have?"

I delivered a short lecture on the surgical pathology, treatment and prognosis of peptic ulceration and got back to the lights on the Embankment.

"Number three is an absolutely terrific case, isn't he? Haematoporphyrinuria. Tell me all about it, do."

The patients recovered but romance died. She was soon getting to know more than I did.

2. *Father Figure and Undernutrition*

"Sorry I'm late," apologised Greta, appearing hurriedly at the mortuary gate. "But Sister kept us on cleaning up the theatre after the list. Where shall we go!?"

"I rather thought the Mecca, and then a quiet stroll along the ——"

"I'm afraid I didn't have a moment to eat."

"Perhaps we can find some modest restaurant," I returned considerately. "Good plain food is much better than mucked-up dishes and waiters, don't you think?"

"Mr. Cutmore," she began, settling with her fish-and-chips, "did an absolutely marvellous nephrectomy this morning."

"Oh, yes?"

"The kidney came clean away from the renal artery," she nodded, springling on the vinegar. "There was blood absolutely everywhere. Poor Mr. Cutmore! It quite ruined his trousers."

"Bread and butter?"

"You see, he wasn't wearing his proper operating trousers. It was all my fault. As soon as the kidney came off in his hand, I felt awful. You can imagine."

"Cup of tea? Glass of Tizer?"

"I always warm Mr. Cutmore's operating trousers over the steriliser before the list, and this morning I singed them. I don't think I'll ever forgive myself."

"May I have one of your chips?"

"Mr. Cutmore's a marvellous surgeon, isn't he? He did a gastrectomy in twenty-two minutes. I was standing behind him all the time, dabbing the sweat from his brow."

"When you've finished your fish, perhaps the lights on the——"

"You know what Mr. Cutmore said to me today? 'Nurse,' he said, 'Don't you ever leave the theatre even for meals?' 'No, sir,' I said, 'I'd much rather stay here and watch you operate.' He gave me a wonderfully sympathetic look over his mask."

"I think I'll treat myself to a couple of those pickled onions."

Greta sighed. "Mr. Cutmore does so need a haircut. You know, those little grey bits at the side, which stick out under his cap."

"They've some pickled eggs, too, if you'd like one to finish with."

"Poor Mr. Cutmore! He really wants someone to look after him." She screwed up the fish-bones in the newspaper. "He has such a terrible time at home. I hear his wife is no end of a bitch."

A couple more evenings of this and the better-qualified, if not the better man, won.

3. *The Curative Type*

"You shouldn't smoke cigarettes," began Hilda, meeting at the usual place. "You know they're bad for you."

"I only smoke when I've nothing else to do. Care to go dancing? I expect you've eaten in the Nurses' Home?"

"But have *you*?" She was a dark, solemn girl, and threw me a dark, solemn look. "I'm sure you don't have an adequate diet at all. You'll get an avitaminosis."

"I had a beer and a sandwich, thanks."

"You must be careful, you know. It would be terrible if you developed cirrhosis of the liver. Have you got a cold

"No, just the old sinus." I put away my handkerchief. "Always comes on this time of the year."

"If *I* had a sinus I wouldn't hesitate going to the Throat Department and asking them to do an operation to drain it.

"You wouldn't if you'd actually seen the Throat Department cracking away."

"Are you getting enough exercise?"

I gave a little laugh. "I wind up my wrist-watch every night."

"Really, your health isn't a matter for joking. How are the bowels?"

That romance taught me the danger of trying to prolong your life was ruining what happened to be left of it.

4. *Angela*

What attracted me in Angela was her health.

I met her at a rugger club dance, where she radiated health like the girls in the breakfast cereal advertisements. Her very teeth glittered with it. She had never been to a doctor in her life, and talked only about the inside of her little sports car.

Our romance grew as quickly and firmly as a prize marrow. In a couple of weeks I was asked down to Guildford to meet the family. After dinner her father arranged for he and I to be alone in the conservatory.

"Well, m'boy," he started, filling his pipe. "I'm very glad to make your acquaintance."

"Thank you, sir. You understand, Angela and I——"

"Because this old knee of mine is troubling me again. Fell off my bicycle, you know, in the blackout. I've been meaning to see the old quack, but with the queue in the waiting-room, where you never know what you're likely to pick up . . ."

I had hardly completed my examination of the knee before mother appeared through the chrysanthemums.

"I'm so glad you're still here," she gushed, "because I was hoping you'd tell me what I ought to do about my anaemia. Our doctor's terribly nice, of course, but recently they say he's become a bit doddery. He put me on the green tablets, but do I take them *before* or *after* meals?"

Mother was followed by a visiting uncle with allergies and the man next door, who was invited in for a whisky and advice on his hernia.

As she was driving me home Angela asked "Did you say anything to Daddy?"

"Didn't have much of a chance I'm afraid, running that surgery."

She gave a laugh. "I was going to wait till we were officially engaged, but I won't—I must tell you about My Thing."

"Your Thing?"

She nodded. "Yes, it's a great black bird—rather, sort of half bird and half monkey—with fierce red eyes. It comes into my bedroom at night and tells me what to do the next day. I often hear it, actually, though I can't see it. As a matter of fact, My Thing is talking quite clearly to me now."

After that I stick to my studies and spent my evenings alone in pubs. It was more healthy.

*"Having read this truly appalling book,
I give as my considered opinion that it
is definitely calculated to deprave
and corrupt."*

A View
from the
Bandstand

HUMPHREY LYTTELTON'S report on English
partner-swapping parties

"A GOOD man is hard to find—I always get the other kind . . ."
The erstwhile torch-singer's lament could well be my theme-tune if, for "man," you read "orgy". Other musicians seem ready, at the drop of a paper hat, to recall festive occasions at which, by the end of the first cha-cha, the dance-floor has become an uncensored dramatisation of the correspondence columns of *Penthouse* magazine. I always get the other kind.

There was, it is true, this society ball in Surrey some years ago, at which fair-ground swings and nightwatchman's braziers had been set up in the grounds as a diversion. Rumour reached the bandstand via our car driver—a notoriously unreliable source whose career in the car-hire business seemed to be spent exclusively in driving high-ranking public figures to clandestine and kinky assignations—that from the highest point of the swings, unmentionable scenes could be observed taking place in the roseate glow of distant fires. I am always slow off the mark on these occasions and never even made the queue. But circumstantial evidence did support his story, since for the rest of the night the swings were monopolised by men, all heaving away at the ropes like bellringers of Hades.

I have to report that the Playboy culture, with its bacchanalian office parties and carefree partner-swapping, is still several million light-years away from the average firm's dance in Chelmsford or Stoke-on-Trent. Sexologists may be able to read some deep erotic significance into the Hokey Cokey. From my viewpoint on the bandstand, all that putting your left leg in, your left leg out, your left leg in and shaking it all about resembles nothing more than one of those sublimating activities, like cricket, which public schools invent to keep the boys from base and debilitating habits.

My trouble with the Hokey Cokey is that I never know when to stop. When I'm in charge of the music the revellers soon run out of arms and legs and are compelled, as verse succeeds verse interminably, to put in, put out and shake about quite unaccustomed parts of their anatomy. But even with this encouragement nothing very exciting ever happens.

At first sight there seems more of a hint of Eastern promise in the Conga. For one thing, its movements—three slithery, hip-wiggling steps and then a coy sideways kick like an indolent dog cocking its leg—have a certain sensuousness. But whatever hot-blooded and abandoned Latin-American ways were imported with the dance, you can rest assured that the traditional puritanism of the English ballroom long since put paid to them. While not quite so crudely sadistic as the Paul Jones, which was surely designed by some committee of Mrs. Grundys to nip burgeoning relationships in the bud, the Conga, English-style, has enough built-in precautions to frustrate any hanky-panky. If, despite the counter-aphrodisiac properties of bottled beer and cold sausage rolls, a participant should become so inflamed by the sight of the undulating hips in front of him as to try and steer their owner off in the direction of the bedrooms, there in tow behind him are two hundred perspiring chaperones, one-and-two-and-three-hopping along in pursuit and checking his ardour with passion-deadening slogans like "Ay ay, Fred's at it again!" "Put it down, you don't know where it's been!" and "Ow's the wife?" It's little wonder that, like some great thwarted serpent, the Conga-line so often turns violent and heads for the bandstand, vengefully knocking over the music and treading on the instruments.

If the music at the traditional English "hop" is often indescribably bad, it's unfair to put all the blame on the musicians. I'd just like to see Johann Strauss having to cope with a Spot Dance, for instance, and being called upon to arrest the "Blue Danube" in full flood whenever some retired sergeant-major of an MC wants to offload a few prizes. I doubt if it ever came within the musical experience of the Waltz King to save up "Tales from a Vienna Wood" for the climax of the evening, only to have some twit unleash a netful of balloons from the ceiling right in the middle of it.

You may say—and knowing you, you probably will—that attacking balloons like wild beasts falling on sacrificial prey has profound Freudian undertones—frustrated bosom-complex, perhaps, or birthre-enactment. You might even add fasionably ". . . that's what it's all about," which brings us right back to the Hokey Cokey and not a moment too soon. I have a simpler explanation. Bursting balloons, like putting your right arm in and shaking it all about or weaving in and out of the gents cloakroom in a crocodile, is just another excuse devised by the English to get out of dancing. We hate it, and it's about time we faced the fact. Look at that couple prancing past the bandstand, faces set in concentration, bristling like a hat-stand with elbows and teeth, doing the "Come Dancing" bit for all they're worth. Oh, they're having fun all right, but it's the sort of fun that people get from running round the park before breakfast or swimming in the sea on Boxing Day. It's good exercise and it makes you feel jolly fit afterwards. Or observe that amorphous mass of hair over in the corner, twitching and shuddering with African rhythms. Their "Top of the Pops" gyrations reflect a communal approach to life and the break-up of enclosed relationships in that nobody seems to be actually dancing *with* anyone. You just get out there and do your thing in the direction of anyone who happens to be looking. But it's more demo than dancing.

As for the rest, they're just walking round or leaning against each other, idly passing the time until some specific word of command galvanises them into action. Playing at political get-togethers, I am always relieved to see the local MP or prospective candidate hurry away to more urgent business before the dancing has really got under way. It might put altogether unhealthy ideas into his head to see how easily an English crowd, softened up and tortured into submission by dancing, can be driven into violent, uniform action by "The March of the Mods" or "Knees up Mother Brown." It doesn't take an advanced course in demagogy to realise that, if you can get a man to put his right leg in and shake it all about, you can get him to do anything.

"*Hey Dad! I got a girl into trouble!*"

Keith Waterhouse Goes Looking for an Orgy...

I, Charles Septimus Parkin if 23A Jubilee Mansions, Norwood, make this statement voluntarily in the presence of Detective-Sergeant William Cooney and PC Throstle of "E" Division. I am forty-three years old and a clerk in the employ of British Fat Products Ltd. I am married in name only. I do not wish to add to that.

I first became aware of the permissive society on or about September 5 1969. I remember the date because it is the birthday of my niece Avril, and I had bought her a Kooky-doll as a present. I do not know why the Kooky-doll is still in my possession, or why she was in the cistern cupboard. I cannot explain why she is wearing fish-net tights, see-through bra and a PVC mackintosh instead of the après-ski outfit depicted on her box. The Action Man produced by Det.-Sgt. Cooney from the cistern cupboard in my presence does not belong to me. I do not know why Action Man is wearing only his boots. The Polaroid camera is for the purpose of taking holiday snaps. The photograph which I ate before being cautioned by Det.-Sgt. Cooney was a holiday snap.

On or about September 5 1969 I read in a Sunday newspaper about a wife-swapping ring in Mauncey Road, Birmingham, together with an exposé of certain magazines "for swingers only," also photographs allegedly taken at a drag party in Leeds before the reporter made an excuse and left. It is not true that from that day on I became obsessed by the permissive society, although what I read was certainly an eye-opener. I did not suggest to my wife Noreen that we should engage in similar activities. The phrase, "Let's get some fun out of life while we're still young, or are you too frigid?" is not one that I would normally use. I did not place an advertisement in the *Swapper's Digest*. I have never heard of the *Swapper's Digest*.

I now recall that I did place an advertisement in the *Swapper's Digest*. The fifteen back numbers of this publication under the towels in the airing cupboard are for my own use. The advertisement was a joke. It has been put to me that "Virile husband-and-wife duo wish to meet AC-DC couples, no prudes" does not sound like a joke, but I do not agree. It was an exercise in parody. I know nothing about an accommodation address in Soho. I received no replies to my advertisement.

I have never been in Mauncey Road, Birmingham.

I now recollect that I went to Mauncey Road, Birmingham, on September 9 and spoke to a woman now known to me as WPC Hawkins. My purpose in journeying to Birmingham was to visit an old army friend, 586 Cadger McNally, whose address I cannot at present remember. I asked WPC Hawkins to direct me to New Street Station. I did not employ any words such as "Are you a swinger?" I recall employing the phrase, "Where is the action?" This is an idiomatic expression indicating that I was looking for New Street Station.

I did not deposit a suitcase in the left-luggage office at New Street Station. I identify a suitcase produced by Det.-Sgt. Cooney as my property. I confirm that it did not fly to Birmingham of its own volition. The mask, riding-crop and length of rope are all my property. I purchased the mask at a novelty shop in Paddington in case my friend 586 Cadger McNally was giving his annual fancy-dress party. The riding-crop was a present for my married niece June, who is a keen horsewoman. I have no recollection whatsoever of proposing to my married niece June that I should be her gee-gee and that she should ride me around her living room. The length of rope was in case of fire. I have always carried a length of rope in case of fire ever since reading that Hans Christian Andersen did likewise. It has been put to me that Hans Christian Andersen is the same "Fancy-pants" Andersen who is now doing bird at the Scrubs for thieving lingerie off of clothes lines. To the best of my knowledge Hans Christian Andersen was a writer of fairy tales. I have been informed what the expression "fairy" means in common parlance. I have never been that way inclined. I have never been to Hampstead Heath.

It is not true that I was wandering about Leeds in a polka-dot dress and steel-blue nylon stockings on the night of September 9-10. The polka-dot dress produced by Det.-Sgt. Cooney was purchased at Selfridge's for my friend 586 Cadger McNally's fancy-dress party. I regard flushing clothes down the lavatory as a normal method of disposing of unwanted property.

Having been shown certain photographs, I now wish to correct any suggestion I may have made that I was not wandering about Leeds on the night of September 9-10, but I deny that I was looking for a so-called drag party. I was in Leeds for the simple reason that I got on the wrong train at Birmingham New Street Station. I was suffering from flu and had taken some tablets shortly before drinking a glass of beer. This must have made me light-headed. I was definitely not wearing the polka-dot dress, except for a short period.

I admit to having knocked at a door in Victoria Hospital Avenue, Leeds, between 12.30 and 12.45 am. I deny asking the lady now known to me as Mrs. Jeanette Henderson if there was room for one more. I deny suggesting to Mrs. Henderson that nobody would take her for a sailor. My purpose in knocking at the door was to ask for a glass of water. I was not wearing the polka-dot dress. I had recently drunk a carton of milk which must have splashed over my overcoat, giving it a polka-dot effect. I did not raise my overcoat to thigh level while in conversation with Mrs. Henderson.

Having been given an opportunity to reconsider that portion of my statement relating the the *Swapper's Digest*, I now believe that there may have been one or two replies to my advertisement. There may have been 1,753 replies. Certain parcels which Det.-Sgt. Cooney removed from under the floorboards in my presence may contain replies to my advertisement. I have not read any of them. I do not recognise a typewritten manuscript entitled *Kitty's Awaken-*

ing. I do not know of any invitation to attend a party in Tulse Hill for sex fun.

I am familiar with Tulse Hill. I may have been there on the evening of December 18. An important invoice had blown out of my office window on that day and I thought it might have landed in Tulse Hill. I may have been wearing a shortie nightdress under my raincoat. I often wear a shortie nightdress in the privacy of my own home as I understand there is no law against it. I wear it because it is convenient. At approximately 10 pm, on the evening of December 18, I remembered that I had not taken the dog for his usual walk. I put on a raincoat over my shortie nightdress and took him as far as the pillar box. The dog having slipped his lead and been run over by a coal-lorry I thought that rather than waste my outing I would proceed to Tulse Hill and look for the invoice.

I may have approached several house-holders in the Tulse Hill district with the words, "Have you a French kitten for sale?" I was not aware that this was a password. Owing to the accident to my dog I was anxious to obtain a new pet as quickly as possible. I do not know why I asked for a French kitten. I now think that I may have asked for a *fresh* kitten, meaning one that was only a few days old.

After a conversation with my wife Noreen I now recall that I have never owned a dog. I have been taking pills for a severe migraine and these, swallowed in conjunction with beer or wine, sometimes induce a sensation of owning a dog.

I deny hailing a taxi at Tulse Hill Station at 1.43 on the morning of December 19.

Having been assured that nobody is going to get their collar felt for taking a cab, I now remember hailing a taxi at Tulse Hill Station, but deny asking the driver if he knew anything about blue movies.

The taxi took me to my home. I deny saying, "Well, here we are at Iceberg Manor." I deny offering the driver double fare to take me to Hampstead Heath.

Certain evidence having been shown to me, I admit to being on Hampstead Heath at 3.16 on the morning of December 19 and approaching the gentleman I now recognise as Detective-Sergeant Cooney. I regret having prevaricated about this matter, but I was of the impression that wearing false moustaches went out with Sexton Blake. I concur that if I had stuck to false moustaches instead of polka-dot dresses I would not be in the situation in which I now find myself.

I confirm that I mistook Det.-Sgt. Cooney for a sex maniac, and that I asked him for information about any lewd, filthy, degrading and obscene parties that might be going on in the vicinity. I agree that I falsely represented my wife Noreen as being available for sex fun in the event of Det.-Sgt. Cooney being able to assist me in my depraved endeavours. I now understand that my use of the words "sizzling," "versatile" and "hot pants" in respect of my wife Noreen was an offence under the Trades Descriptions Act, and I wish to express my regret for any embarrassment, distress and disappointment caused both to my wife and to Det. Sgt. Cooney.

Between the Sheets, Beneath the Worsted . . .

COMES time for bye-byes and today's dandy still needs must choose between pyjamas, nightshirt, or kipping in the raw. Pyjamas are still the most popular gear for well-dressed bedfellows and have held this paramount place ever since they were brought over in the eighteen-eighties from India where the thoughtless natives wore them only by day.

In the time of my casanovitiate, black Cossack-style pyjamas with eagles on the pockets and dragons on the chest were *à la mode* and highly recommended for dazzling Brighton weekend belles out of all memory of mother's warning. I think Noel Coward had something to do with it. One of my most memorable sleep-suits was so richly caparisoned with appliqué epaulettes and pectoral frogging that it was all I could do to keep my mind on the job and refrain from breaking out into midnight excerpts from "The Student Prince". It had four buttons on the brocaded collar and once or twice when passion unhinged the fingerjoints, I wondered whether I'd have to send for the fire-brigade to get me out.

Such straitjacket ambitions still lurk in the modern nocturnal two-piece although its colours may have gone psychedelic and the neckline crevassic to give a better view of the chest-wig. All but those whom sleep petrifies will have fought those night-long battles with pyjama trousers bent on snaking up the legs and cutting their wearer off in his actual prime. The *Tailor and Cutter* advises that the modish method of countering such discomfiture is to wear bicycle-clips in bed.

As to jacket-etiquette, Freud held vociferously that psychologists could always tell an introvert from an extrovert because the former tucks his pyjama-jacket into his trousers, while the latter just lets it all hang out to wind and high weather. Jung riposted that he had never heard such a load of bedtime cobblers in all his natural.

The nightshirt made a bit of a comeback a few years ago but its unfortunate shape foredoomed it to failure. Its two main disabilities are that a man can never feel trendy when dressed in a small bell-tent, and such apparel renders him pitifully vulnerable to family ribaldry. Anxious as ever to maintain my Brummell reputation I once bought a nightshirt undetected and donned it at bedtime for the satorial surprise of all resident. I passed my daughter on the landing as she finished her four-hour garrison of the bathroom.

"Lock your door, Mrs. Bardell," she said. "Mr. Pickwick rides again."

I gave her one of my withering looks and would have drawn myself up in full patriarchal dignity only it's difficult to do that sort of thing in knee-length wigwam. When I came into the master bedroom my wife was already dozing with the light on. I took position beside the bed to show my white samite to best advantage and coughed gently to bring her round. She shot up with such velocity that I feared for the chandelier.

"Dear God!" she said. "I thought you were Lazarus risen from the dead. Don't you ever go larking about in that shroud again. You look like Spike Milligan's understudy forgot to put his boots on."

Chilled by her graveyard symbolism, I went back to my closet, took off the burnous and donned my pyjamas with the new long Judo jacket, tapered legs and quick-release waist-cord.

The male underwear scene is currently somewhat tricky for those expecting definitive advice about what they should wear to cheer up Diana Dors under their grey flannel suits. A spokesman for the *Body Linen Manufacturers Gazette* said that the industry hasn't felt so dodgy since that black day in the 'thirties when Clark Gable took off his shirt in *It Happened One Night*. He revealed that he wasn't wearing a vest and thus sending the shares of all male-chemise makers in America plummeting down through the chartroom floor. With all this central heating and shirts unbuttoned to the waist, our sharp lads aren't generally wearing vests any more. Underpants, however, of advancing brevity and increasing strangulation, are still in favour with all but those whose puppy-fat has gone to their hips and precludes the intervention of even a sunbeam between them and their levis.

White underthings are fashionably one with the dodo and if you hope to get anywhere with the nurses who undress you after you've been run over, it is essential to wear your boxer shorts, Y-fronts, jockey briefs or hipster bikinis in polka dots, floral fantasies, union jacks, or all the colours of the rainbow. Conventional gentlemen shy of covering their rumps in scarlet underpants can take reassurance from Desmond Morris that they're only doing what comes naturally, since our hairier brother-apes have always aimed to attract their females by the brilliance of their buttocks.

Among the many sadnesses of being masculine is the strange cross that the removal of the outer garments automatically attracts risibility. A woman in her underwear has ever been considered glamorous, seductive and a suitable subject for expensive phototraphy. A man in his underwear is universally regarded as a figure of fun. The aphorism that no man is a hero to his valet had its origin in the frequency with which that worthy saw him in his pants, woollen, long. Laughing at the exposure of gentlemen's lingerie has become a comedian's mainstay and Arthur Askey, Robertson Hare and Brian Rix have a lot to answer for.

Perhaps things will change for the more respectful when the unisex trend really takes over. Women have lately allowed their underwear the become progressively utilitarian. Where once layers of frou-frou mysteriously obscured all targets there is now but a bleakness of austere tights, puritanical pants and ungarnished girdle. Perhaps the ornamental pendulum will swing back towards the peacock and men's underwear will soon become in counter-balance as frilly as their shirts, delectably lacey round the legs, dotted erogenously with ribbons and rosebuds, and foam-padded in promise of vast virility. And, as one among the high fancy of snoring-suits and unmentionables, I look forward to the sighs of female admiration which must surely echo through the household when I take delivery from Rudy Gernreich, the topless king, of my latest order for see-through pyjamas with posterior portholes, leopard-skin vest, with premoulded muscles, and gold lamé long-johns with three-way stretch and luminous codpiece.

By PATRICK RYAN

Love Song for a Bleak Spring
by PETER DICKINSON

DEAREST, *after bouts of ardour*
Oft I think of Early Man
Carrying cavewards to the larder
  Moose or goose or ptarmigan;
Then relaxing from the tussle,
  Skin all rough with wind and soil,
Every nerve and every muscle
  Weary with accustomed toil.
He loved his squat cavewoman, I'm
Sure, dear, but not all the time

Strange to think how few the fleeting
  Generations in between
Him and me. I've central heating
  But remain the same machine,
Skin designed to feel the weather,
  Muscles built to stand the strain.
Take the strain off altogether—
  Millions of machines complain
Then seek some other satisfaction.
(The jargon is "displacement action.")

Progress leaves us one sensation
  (Or, if you count cooking, two).
Hence the curious relation,
  Dearest, between me and you.
Also hence, extrapolating,
  All the nations' cultures seem
Devoted to the act of mating
  Or variations on the theme.
Kiss me, dear, before I weep.
Damn the girl! She's gone to sleep.

My next Husband

By MARGARET DRABBLE

M Y next husband will be selected upon the principle that underlies the old rhyme:

> *"Jack Sprat could eat no fat*
> *His wife could eat no lean,*
> *And so between them both, you see,*
> *They licked the platter clean."*

For it is clearly a good idea for any marriage to be based upon a nice and convenient balance of tastes, though these tastes need not necessarily be directly opposed, as in the case of the fat and the lean; there are in fact few foods of a sufficiently heterogeneous nature to make such an equal division practicable. Few people, for instance, would be prepared to eat egg white and never egg yolk, or the dark battered leaves of lettuces and never the hearts. On most culinary matters it is really as well to agree; I have always thought that the domestic happiness described in the song *Little Brown Jug* must have involved a great deal of work in the way of tea pots and tea cups, coffee pots and coffee cups. Moreover, there are certain things about which my present husband and I cannot even agree to differ, work or no work: he dislikes the smell of celery so much that he will not even have it in the house, and I for my part am filled with such horror by the sight of peanut butter that I can never bring myself to buy it for him, though I know he likes it. So on these points it is better to agree. However, there is one point of difference upon which I shall insist. My next husband will prefer hard chocolates to soft ones: he will be addicted to cracknel, nougat, toffee, coconut, praline, brazil nuts, and all those other nasty lumps that lie neglected in the bottom layers of old chocolate boxes. Somebody must like them after all, or they would not have been invented, so next time I shall marry one of these hard nut lovers, and enjoy myself guiltlessly with the peppermint creams.

There are departments of life, far more important than the food department, in which the Jack Sprat principle would be of real value— the department of household jobs, for one, where a division of talent is clearly desirable. There are certain things (not very many of them, I admit) that I do not really mind doing, such as washing, washing up, painting walls and digging the garden. There are other things which defeat me entirely, such as getting other people to come in and do things—plumbers, builders, electricians— and, having got them, seeing that they do what they came to do, and not something quite different in some other part of the house. Unfortunately, my present husband's attitude to this subject coincides almost exactly with mine; I sometimes think it must be a bond of sympathetic inefficiency that first united us. So similar are we on this score that we cannot even reproach each other; helplessly we let the electricians herd us round the house, ripping the floorboards from beneath our feet, and once, when the roof was leaking, my husband was heard to express anxiety about the health of the man who had come to mend the roof. He was getting wet up there, said my husband. Of course he was getting wet. It was raining. That was why the roof was leaking. I knew all about that; I did not need to be reminded. What I needed was a husband who would be completely oblivious of such finer human details. My next husband will have to take a firmer line about such matters, and pay more attention to the work than to the workmen. He will send chilly-looking shivering plumbers out into the cold to unfreeze drains, and he will snap at me scornfully when I suggest that people get wet on roofs in the rain. He will keep me under control, instead of encouraging me, or I shall end up like that woman in whose house the plumber negligently left his newly-washed socks drying on the heated bathroom towel rail.

It is on the financial side, however, that my own deficiencies most need supplementing. I do not mean by this that my next husband will have to be a very rich man: merely that he will have to understand figures. He will look pleased and happy when presented with his income tax forms, for they will be a challenge to his ingenuity. He will add my grocery bills up for me in a trice, compare the advantages of various brands of this and that like a kind of private Consumer Adviser, and he will know off hand whether it is cheaper to buy disposable nappies or wash at home. (Hard labour is always cheapest, I suspect, but it would be comforting to be sure.) He will guide me through the financial labyrinths of daily life with a truly masculine authority: he will work out my royalty statements for me, and perhaps he will even be able to tell me what royalties are. He will keep a check on things; he will save me from my fear that money leaks and oozes away without actually being spent. Even in my own more literary world his assistance will be invaluable, because he will be able to explain to me all the financial transactions in Victorian novels, all the credit-debit imagery in Shakespeare and Ben Johnson, and he will know what really went on in the South Sea Bubble. I have never quite understood exactly how Darcy persuaded Wickham to marry Lydia Bennet, nor what happened to the Mill on the Floss and Emma Bovary, though debt was I believe at the root of all their troubles—and as for that line in *Antony and Cleopatra* about boys who pawn their experience to the present pleasure— for many years now I have been trying to decide what that image means: I lie awake at night or stand dazed over the washing up bowl trying to work out the principle of pawning, and who does it to whom, for what, but I have never managed to work out what Shakespeare meant. I also have a whole string of words waiting for him to elucidate for me, words probably quite simple in themselves, like remittance, invoice, assurance, insurance, mortgage and so forth. And then there are all those useful phrases like "blank cheque" and "in the red," which I have never dared to use, being unsure of their implications: the only time I ever embarked on a sentence using a term from gambling (something about odds, if I remember rightly) I got the whole thing the wrong way round, and had it neatly inverted by an editor. It will be handy to have someone on the spot to ask: it will open up whole new fields of reference for me.

My next husband's gift for quick mathematical calculation will be particularly useful abroad. I have over the years worked out my peculiarly primitive and indescribable methods of dealing with pounds, shillings and pence, but I doubt if I shall ever master any kind of decimal coinage. People tell me that all decimal coinage systems are the same, but this is not true. My next husband, however, will have them all well under control, and he will be able to work out what twelve and a half per cent of the price of a meal is, and thus enable us to avoid those twin hazards of travel, the sullen fury or the profuse embarrassing, infuriating (because unintended) gratitude of foreign waiters. It will not matter whether he can understand the languages or not: like Jack Sprat's wife, I will look after the languages, if he will look after the currency. My present husband and I, on our last trip to France, spent many, many hours puzzling over that strange mystery, the rate of exchange: we had endless bitter conversations over the unsolved restaurant bills, beginning with remarks like "Well, if one gets thirteen francs to the pound instead of fourteen, that must mean that each franc is *bigger* . . ." There were fallacies lurking around somewhere, but we could never quite catch them: we had a sense that they were just round the corner, just out of range, but we never managed to pin them down.

It isn't only a question of currency, either. All numbers are difficult abroad. Take kilometres, for instance. My next husband will be able to convert kilometres into miles by some accurate mathematical method; I myself, unable to decide whether to multiply by five and divide by eight, or whether to divide by five and miltiply by eight, have hit upon a system whereby I divide the number of kilometres on the signpost by two, and then add a few miles on, but I must admit that it is not wholly reliable. Litres are confusing, too; I always wonder at the large pints of milk they have in France. I see my next husband and myself embarking on long journeys across Europe (perhaps, on second thoughts, he had better be rather rich), taking in nine or ten different countries, dozens of mysterious hotel bills, untold mileage of kilometres, and all sorts of complicated calculations about litres of petrol, while I sit back in quiet confidence and enjoy all those lovely foreign drinks and posters, and read him little cultural bits from my guides to Ancient Monuments.

There is one thing that worries me. So far I seem to have defined my next husband only by his attributes, and although I ought to be able to fit some dashing and desirable physical image to these attributes, I am not at all sure that I can. Even the wildest flight of fancy could hardly make this cracknel-chewing, workman-driving, income-tax-specialising prodigy look much like George Harrison or Steve McQueen. In fact, I do not think I like this ideal husband very much. He rises irresistibly before my imagination: flinty, peeble-eyed, bad-tempered, critical. I don't think he will be very fond of me, either. Perhaps I expect too much in expecting mutual fondness: I bet the sight of Mrs. Sprat chewing away virtuously at all that fat used to get on poor Jack's nerves. Perhaps what I really want is not a husband, but a cross between an accountant and a Domestic Agent and a chauffeur. It might be better to separate my interests, for after all I have never thought much of men who marry to acquire cheap cooks and washer-women. Perhaps it might be better not to have another husband: perhaps I should stick to the one I've got. Perhaps I should put some peanut butter on my next grocery order. After all, he can mend fuses and change car wheels: things really might get a great deal worse. And it really is too much to expect any one person, in pure disinterest, to like mental arithmetic, hard centres, the Inland Revenue, and me.

"First of all, we'll discontinue the pills."

My next Wife

By LORD MANCROFT

MY Uncle Charlie was happily married to Auntie Maud for nearly fifty-three years. Seeing that he used to smoke a strong Burma cheroot in bed every night and then relight it again in the morning I think this reflects well on the patience and forbearance of my Aunt. Indeed, on the occasion of their golden wedding, I ventured to ask her if, in the course of what must have been fifty exacting years, she had ever contemplated divorcing the old buzzard. She thought this over carefully and then replied, "Divorce? No, never; of course not. Murder, yes, several times. But never divorce."

When I add that he used to refer to her in public as "My first wife" in order, as he explained, to keep her on her toes, you will be able to assess the measure of her forbearance.

The fact that my Uncle Charlie's father had been shot in the ear by his mistress in a tram in Valparaiso must have warned her (if she had any belief in the laws of Genetics) that her married life was unlikely to be humdrum; and it wasn't. It was nevertheless happy, very happy, and if you'd asked my Uncle Charlie to give his opinion about *his* next wife, you'd have got the rough edge of the most abrasive tongue in the county of Norfolk.

I only mention this in order to establish the fact that any speculations about my own next wife are purely hypothetical and are not to be taken as criticism of the situation presently obtaining in our corner of North West Pimlico.

When a man marries for the first time he is venturing into the dark. When he marries for the second time, he remembers where he stubbed his toe. I am sure, therefore, that I wouldn't want just another wife. One wife alone could not, in the future, fulfil all my requirements.

I'd want about twelve wives to do the job properly and what's wrong with polygamy anyhow? Wouldn't a move in that direction be in keeping with the times?

Lord Arran and Mr. Leo Abse have at long and dreary last got their way with homosexuality. Parliament has set the seal of its approval on sexual relations between consenting male adults and this in spite of the fact that the man in the street seems dead against it and has been for a thousand years. Not, of course, that the opinion of the man in the street matters any longer at Westminster.

Abortion is now apparently In and the House of Lords was thought to be squeamish for having given voice to such old-fashioned disquiet. Pot and Pop go hand in hand and in next to no time it'll be Hurrah for Incest. So what, I ask, is wrong with a little polygamy?

It's already practised with genteel approval in many of the African communities that now share with us the burdens of civilisation. It is also well thought of in Malaya and Polynesia and, in a way, it is also popular in the United States of America, though under slightly different rules. Americans don't have all their wives at the same time. The French have lots of mistresses but only one wife because they don't believe in divorce. The Americans think well of divorce but that's because their mistresses insist on becoming their wives, if not for very long. Since America is a Matriarchy and the girls have all the money, this can be important. American gentlemen accordingly accept the implication of alimony more calmly than the British. For my part it has always seemed that paying alimony is like buying carrots for a dead donkey.

Signing on twelve wives will, of course, permit of some margin of error. I was always a devoted admirer of Miss Marilyn Monroe. What, when drunk, one saw in other women, one saw in Marilyn Monroe when sober. She could hardly, however, have been regarded as the perfectly domesticated wife, the sort who can always find in a bottom drawer the sock that isn't there.

In each of my twelve wives, therefore, I shall look for one of the assets that go to make up the dodecahedronal woman who, mercifully, does not exist. If she did, the Prime Minister, not himself wishing to vacate 10 Downing Street, would presumably appoint her to the Woolsack tomorrow. The right of a woman to become Lord Chancellor has now been soundly established as has also her right to train racehorses. A woman can not yet, however, become a member of the London Stock Exchange nor, I think, Archbishop of Canterbury. Much more important, a woman cannot propose marriage. A proposal of marriage still has to come from the man and the woman still has to make it look as if that was the way it happened. Too many women, in retaliation, regard a marriage licence as a licence to drive a man, and that's one of the reasons why I am in favour of polygamy. By that process you can divide and, given a modicum of luck, you can also rule.

At least fifty per cent of my team must have both Beauty and Charm. (The Beauties are the ones that I notice and the Charmers the ones that notice me.) I shall also, of course, want an expert pianist, a blue ribbon cook, a petit-pointiste of genius, a tolerably competent political dialectician and a girl who can mend a fuse.

A few level heads will be needed too. We're an unreasonable lot, we husbands. We point out rudely that Mother Nature decorated the humming-bird, the kingfisher and the dragon-fly in vivid and dazzling hues, but the rhinoceros, the hippopotamus and the elephant are all turned out in a plain and decent grey. We accordingly beg our wives not to overdo it. Neat, we suggest, but not gaudy. We applaud when they accompany us to a rout or soirée in quiet attire. We then spend the evening gawping goggle-eyed at some little piece of nonsense clad in three bits of eau-de-nil Elastoplast and wearing an Israeli melon on her head.

We must therefore, I repeat, have some sobersides in our team. I accept that a woman who will listen to reason is probably thinking of something else but I shall want at least one wife who will take her time, who will make up her mind slowly and whose final decision will not necessarily be the one she will eventually take. I admire a woman who can suffer in silence though I realise she may have a lot to say later on. If she is inquisitive, she must be intelligently inquisitive; in other words, she must learn to ask the sort of questions I can answer.

And all twelve of them have got to be healthy. This, I realise, is an uncouth request and I'm ashamed of it but I simply cannot put up with other people's ailments. If I myself am smitten with the gout or toothache or Webster's disease or what have you, then all my twelve wives must display sympathy and understanding. For my part, I shall not be able to tolerate any one of them suffering so much as a chilblain. Sultan Abdul the Damned had about two hundred and thirty-four wives (etc.) but so sensitive was he to infirmity that it took him less than twenty minutes to discover if any one of them was suffering from lumbago. Some people can tell the moment a cat or a baronet enters the room. Suffers from ill-health have the same effect on me.

I realise, of course, that polygamy is a counsel of perfection. Monogamy is more chancy. You marry one woman in particular and the next morning you wake up to discover you have married somebody else. And you will soon learn from her own lips the sort of man she would have preferred to marry. Not, of course, that a man should ever express a counter-opinion on such a delicate matter as this. A woman who is sensible enough to ask her husband's advice is seldom stupid enough to take it.

I have visited Malaya on several occasions and Polynesia once. I forgot, I'm afraid, to raise the question of polygamy. I discussed, at length, such burning issues as the future of Containerisation in the Pacific Freight Trade and even, if I remember aright, the relevance of the miniskirt in swinging Wolverhampton, but not, alas, the niceties of polygamy as they affect the run-of-the-mill Briton who might be thinking of taking a second wife.

The men I know who get on well with women are usually those who know how to get on without them. I should like, in this context, to have consulted the Texan millionaire whose Will was recently challenged by his next-of-kin in the Probate Court of Dallas. The Will, which was correctly signed and witnessed, consisted of only one sentence. "Give Mabel the works". Mabel got the works and bully for Mabel. Her Gentleman evidently knew when he was well off. If he had been given the chance, he would obviously have married Mabel again, assuming that he had actually married her in the first place.

Some people tut-tut when a widower remarries quickly. I don't. I think it's a great compliment to his first wife for having made him realise that two is company and widowerhood is none.

There's a lot to be said for polygamy, but there's more to be said for Mabel. And what's more, with Mabel, you don't get twelve mothers-in-law.

Killing Time

"MANY women have babies because they can't think of anything better to do," said Lord Beaumont last week. Might have been on surer ground if he hadn't chosen to say it in the House of Lords.

When the rest of the world beds down, who stays up, and why? To find out, Alan Coren has seen in several dawns.

AND A STAR TO STEER HER BY

MUCH of my early life was occupied in reading the backs of Penguins. It was the only place to go for career advice. We had a careers master at school who also took woodwork, personal hygiene, and small boys to France, and doubled on Old Testament for a sad man with a throat spray who kept having to go to Eastbourne on account of his phlegm. So the careers master, who was short and bitter and undeniably in the wrong job, didn't have too much time left over to discuss careers, unless you wanted to go into Barclays Bank, for which he happened to have brochures; if the goal you had set yourself in life hadn't managed to get printed on high-gloss paper along with a detailed breakdown of pension schemes and use of sports facilities, chances were you didn't get steered towards it. We had a strange, surreal life together, the careers master and I; once a month, at the age of fifteen, I'd go and tell him I wanted to be a writer, and he'd give me a Barclays Bank brochure and we'd stare at one another for a bit, and then he'd blow his nose and say "Had I considered the Fleet Air Arm?"

So the only way to find out how to become a writer was by reading the backs of Penguins, which told you how they'd all started and how many kids they had, which was also relevant, since a secondary source of anxiety at this time was whether I ought to marry or not: at a pubescent guess, marriage was likely to do at least two things that were inimical to the burgeoning talent—it interfered with the requisite suffering and loneliness, and it wiped out the prospect of mistresses, without which no writer could be complete. You had to have someone coming round in the afternoon and taking her clothes off, or you might as well go into Barclays and settle in Tring.

Anyway (*lest we deviate from this in-depth report of lorry-driving at night*), it turned out that writers fell roughly into two camps: you either had consumption, and walked about in a herringbone overcoat in somewhere like Prague or Venice, and then, just before you pegged out, you quickly got it all down on paper and were an immediate best-seller, just in time for the funeral; or else you were brawny and cheery and had forty-three other jobs first, during which time you wrote your book on the back of old bus-tickets, and then you sold the film rights and went to live in Antigua Bay. These forty-three other jobs were always whaling, stoking, nightclub-bouncing, pearl-diving, wine-waiting, mining, booth-boxing, lumber-jacking . . . and lorry-driving. (*There we are. And only four hundred words to get there. Maybe I should have gone into Barclays Bank, at that.*)

It was curious the way so many authors could be found in trucks. It's a dead era now, of course, with so much literature currently being turned out by teenage hairdressers and TV personalities, and very few ex-gunrunners with MSS under their belts, but there must have been a period, around the late 'forties, when the chances were extremely high of your being overtaken on the A1 by a man wondering how he could get the juvenile lead back on stage in time for the second act curtain. Most of the transport cafés between London and Glasgow would probably have put the Café Royal to shame, knee deep as they must have been in men discussing iambic pentameters over their double egg and chips. Had the telly and the Colour Supplement not come along to sinecure the struggling author, it's quite possible that we would have had a situation today whereby the only way that a kid could have become a truck driver would have been by writing a novel first. In any event, for me personally, by about 1955, the attractions of lorries were at least equal with the attractions of writing; especially, the lure of the overnight haul. There seemed to be no more available romance than that of pulling oneself aboard a giant ten-wheeler as the moon came up to silhouette the load of pig-iron or boilers; an oily cap set at a rakish angle, a wind-cheater with the collar turned nattily up, genuine boots, a luminous watch (it's one of the few jobs where you actually *need* a luminous watch), a tattoo discreetly setting off the left wrist, the thunder of sixteen cylinders against your thigh, and, above all, the Fellowship Of The Road; which I believe I envisaged as a sort of muscular Bloomsbury Set.

But it's not that way at all. As you'll no doubt have guessed, I didn't actually go into the profession, because I started writing first, which was the wrong order, and when that happened I never seemed to have any time to get away. It wasn't until last week that I finally made my first night run, and if that was anything to go by, the blokes who eventually got into paperback deserved every royalty they received.

My rendezvous with Len lay outside Tiverton, at ten pm on the hottest night of the year, with the bugs whanging off his headlamps and the sweat draining into his moustache. Fury sat on his every wrinkle.

"You wun't think I'd have to load bleeding lettuces," he said, "would you? You oughter put that down," poking a finger at me, "you oughter put that down about where I turn up in the middle of the effing night and have to load the bleeding lettuces myself on account of someone's got a bilious attack. I wun't mind," and his voice rose, and he glared terribly towards the lights of the market gardeners' office which lay within shouting range, "I wun't mind if I was a bleeding lettuce-loader by profession, would I? INSTEAD OF BEING A BLEEDING LORRY DRIVER WHICH IS WHAT I AM!"

The offending lettuces towered above us, edged with starlight, eight tons of them, pressing against their netted sacks, thirty thousand salads trussed helplessly and bound for Covent Garden and destruction. Len, breathing through his nose, turned and swung himself aboard. He slammed the door, and the window dropped with the impact, and disappeared. I got in beside him. The cab smelt of old vegetables and fuel and was furnished mainly with projecting steel edges.

"It's no good looking for a radio," said Len. There was a terrible triumph in his voice, seeking an ally in his fight against wirelessness. "'What do you want a radio for,' they said, didn't they? 'Only fall asleep with all that music.' Look at the state I'm in," he shouted, "bloody lettuce muck all over me. Bloody maggots in my hair, I shun't wonder. You can catch things off maggots, mate."

He punched the starter, and the huge engine whirred a few times, and caught. The clutch crunched, and we jolted on to the A373, and something tin drove into my skull, and my knee hit the window-winder. The truck groaned up to forty mph, lurching. Within ten minutes, the engine, most of which lay in the cab between us, was pulsing heat out like a convector heater, waves of the stuff, which didn't seem to disappear but just eddied around us. Len rolled a cigarette one-handed, lit it, and ignored the sparks dying on his cheeks. The engine-noise was tremendous.

"What do you think about?" I shrieked.

"What?" he screamed, bouncing.

"What do you think about all night?"

We covered about three miles. His cigarette went out.

"Nothing," he said, at last.

"All night?" I yelled.

"Come again?"

"ALL NIGHT?"

"Where?" he shouted, peering out of his window.

I fell back, exhausted, and cracked my ear against a bolt. I felt it begin to swell, gently. We had travelled fifteen miles. There were a hundred and sixty to go.

An hour later, we were thundering down the narrow main street of Langport, and a light changed against us. The engine roar ebbed slightly. Most of my body-moisture had seeped away, and, considering that it's supposed to constitute around ninety per cent of the average biped, it's hardly surprising that frailty of an advanced kind had taken its skinny hold. I wondered how William Faulkner, who had done this kind of thing for a living had ever found the strength to unlock his typewriter at the end of the night. With the slightly lower engine-din, Len found words.

"I wun't care," he muttered. "I don't even eat bleeding lettuce."

For the next seventy miles or so, through hot and silent Wincanton, Mere, Chicklade, Amesbury, we rolled, passing the odd yellow-lit outline in which iced Cokes and life-sustaining tea lay, out of reach. Len seemed a man whom normal metabolism had passed by; hunched slightly over his wheel, sucking an unlit fag, he pushed relentlessly on across the parched black desert of Wiltshire, un-curious of me or anything else. And eventually, at the point where the Grim Reaper was about to address me on a matter of the utmost urgency, just outside Andover, we stopped. The noise drained out of my ears, leaving only the occasional buzz and chime. After a few seconds, I could hear crickets, and the odd nightbird. I climbed down in a creak of dehydrated joints and followed Len across a gravel yard, and into a small stuccoed café. He ordered beans on toast and ate them without drinking anything, and then went through three cups of tea in three swallows. There were two other drivers at another table, with a *Daily Sketch* divided between them. Nobody in this special brotherhood said a word to anyone else. Until just before we left, when Len walked across and told them about the lettuces.

"Bleeding stroll-on!" said one.

"Diabolical!" said the other. "Bleeding stroll-on!"

Len walked out with me into the small hours. His face was shining victoriously.

"See?" he said.

And nothing else until we drove into Covent Garden at five am. Which is a curious experience: out of the silent, dawning emptiness of London, you suddenly and without warning fall upon a teeming, shouting, swearing, scuttling community, totally circumscribed within a handful of fruity acres, a place full of dungareed ants hurtling trolleys and crates about, up to their ankles in mashed vegetables, while buyers stroll with clip-boards from shop to shop, squeezing sprout and haggling in an oathy language all their own. Len, having left authorised lettuce-handlers to deal with his hated burden, led me to a pub which, provided you're a bona fide Garden worker, will dipense booze at the wierd and magic hour of six in the morning. We sat with Worthington E, as the sun rose over St. Paul's Church (which boasts not only the grave of Grinling Gibbons, but also the first pendulum clock in Europe), and Len, despite the promise of a beautiful day and the calming coolness of the beer, returned to the topic of green vegetables and the part they peren-nially played in his nocturnal life.

I'll tell you one thing: if Len ever appears in paperback, it'll be a black day for the lettuce industry.

MRS. Maureen Trunks of Costead Manor Road, Brentwood, who claimed that she had been raped by a Metropolitan policeman, admitted wasting police time today. *Southend Standard*

ILL MET BY MOONLIGHT

In which the Metropolitan Police are able to assist
ALAN COREN with his inquiries.

Doom'd for a certain term to walk the night—Hamlet I.v.

EXHIBITION ROAD, SW7, 4 am and dawn the colour of a
herring's belly seeping over the Albert Memorial. Ambassador-
ial London, this, and in a score of tall, white, faintly luminous
houses, diplomatic staffs sleep smugly in their immunity, dreaming
of Tripoli and Chad. The Regency streets breathe dull respectability,
silent; not a soul stirring.

Except a short man in bare feet and a red woollen dressing-gown
running down the road waving a ceremonial sword above his head.

"That's him!" shouted the police driver, slewing us into the kerb.
Who? Some crazed husband, chasing a lover from his wife's
drainpipe? An arab Consul bent on engraving some official oath
on the Israeli Ambassador's lawn? A retired general, waking from a
dream of Omdurman and sick for war?

The call that had squawked from the radio two minutes before
had dropped few hints: a disturbance, nothing more. And it was
that, all right. The doors flew open, and the coppers sprang into
South Kensington in the textbook position with the air of men who
have just found someone who may be able to help the police with
their inquiries. The swordsman, surrounded, stopped.

"My Aston Martin!" he cried.

It sounded like some discreet Victorian oath.

The two policemen, one tall and cynical, one plump and keen,
looked at him carefully.

"Tampering with it," gasped the man. He pointed the sword into
the air, towards the block of flats above his head. "My wife . . . "

A pale blob, looking down.

". . . heard something. So she telephoned."

Not, then, a villain, but a victim.

"What were you going to do with that?" said the taller copper.
The man looked at it.

"It's a sword," he said.

"Oh, is it?"

"I had a DB5 last year," said the victim, "and they stole that."

We all looked sympathetic. Life, said our eyes, is largely loss and sorrow.

"I got a DB6, now," he said. "And they're after that, too."

Clearly, a sense of persecution lay heavily upon him. Somewhere in London, he knew, a gang lived for his Aston Martins alone: followed him when he walked to showrooms; watched him pay; trailed him home; heard him switch off the lights; then nicked his transport.

"Has it gone, then?" asked the driver.

The man shook his head.

"They were there, though," he insisted. "My wife heard them."

So the policemen crept, and flash-lighted, and searched, but there was nothing out of place; they found a broken window, though, and woke the caretaker, in case of a break-in, and he said you don't expect me to mend the bleeding thing in the middle of the bleeding night, do you, I know all about that, it's been bust two weeks, but you know what bleeding glaziers are. What upset him more than anything, obviously, was the suggestion that anyone could dip their fingers into his block of flats without his knowing about it. Everyone thinks they know more than the police. Everyone's wrong.

It has been our fifth "shout" that night. We were operating out of Kensington Police Station, a huge and echoingly empty place that stands in Earls Court Road to watch over one of London's more complex and unstable acreages: on its Campden Hill boundary, it is a place of trend and affluence, where the summer nights ring to the fashionable shrieks of copywriters and Colour Supplement dollies, dining in tall thin over-priced houses and swopping one another with desperate dedication; a mile away, and the beat is an inter-racial warren of spielers and brothels, old, beat-up mansions full of transients and absconders and pimps and addicts and girls that go bump in the night. And it follows from this that the Kensington copper has to be much more than a man with the time of day and a swift half-nelson: he has to be sociologist, ethnologist, parish priest, headmaster, bruiser, welfare-worker, and frequently father and mother both. In the lunatic insistence by *soi-disant* intellectuals who scream for a police force staffed by university graduates (and who conveniently forget that the Chicago, New York, and Los Angeles Police Departments are the best-educated in the world—and also among the most brutal, inefficient and corrupt), little mention is made of exactly where young coppers might go to learn what they will need to know. A First from Balliol might well be of use to a constable called in by All Souls' to settle a row over the tertiary meaning of a paragraph in Wittgenstein's *Tractatus*; but the chances are that three years cloistered with his intellectual peers will stand a lad in pretty lousy stead when his first shout is to a stinking basement in Notting Hill—not to take a knife off a drunk or a shotgun off a jailbreaker, that's comparatively simple, an instructor can teach you how to do that, all you risk is your life; but to settle a bitter fight between two ageing queers who want to chuck one another on to the street, to soothe a woman whose husband has just hit her with a broken bottle, to do something for a child that nobody's bothered to feed for a week, to question a pregnant teenager, who's tried to open her wrists with a chisel, to pick up an addict in terminal deterioration, to stop a white landlord from braining a black tenant, or vice-versa. They send twenty-year-old coppers to do that, and if they staff of *New Society* would care to try it sometime, I'll pay their cab-fare and medical expenses. I spent six years at Oxford and Yale, and in case you think I'm boasting, let me just add that I could never handle the situations that a young copper finds himself in every night; and never would, despite the wonderful incentive of twenty quid a week, plus uniform allowance.

"She came in here two nights ago," said the Duty Sergeant, "a little old lady, very frightened, and she said that evil spirits were after her."

"Not much the police could do."

"Don't you believe it. I went along to her house, and I drew a cross on the pavement in front of it. In white chalk. And I told her they wouldn't dare touch her with that outside. And she was completely satisfied."

I laughed, and he smiled, and said:

"It's not funny at all, really. She was eighty years old, and she was petrified."

Nights at the station itself seem numbingly dull, mostly deskwork, a little tea, a few drunks and tarts to charge, and a procession of people with lost cats, lost keys, whined grievances, or foreigners looking for Wales. Activity centres on a small, rather dishevelled box-room full of switchboards and earpieces and policemen in braces, where messages are passed between stations, cars and beat-strollers; and, of course, on the cars themselves, who are most actively involved in rooting around the metropolis and nosing out such felony

"Well! I shopped and I shopped, but it was worth it. Like my new hat? Who's that?"

as dares to walk abroad. In this, routine patrol is as important as shout-answering: the atmosphere in a car is one of permanent suspicion, the eyes beneath the peaks ever on the *qui vive* for those tiny nuances which tell the expert retina that All Is Not As It Should Be. In Kensington, they're not the only patrolling wheels, either.

"Looking for toms," said the driver, as we low-geared irritatingly behind a beige Jaguar, two in the morning, an innocent-looking side-street.

"Toms?"

"Whores. They hang about round here, so the cars come looking for them. We've passed that bald bloke in the Jag three times."

"Hard up," said his mate.

"Or choosy."

We passed him again, and his bi-focals caught the lamplight. He looked guilty. Everyone catching a copper's eye looks guilty. There was a Mini in front of the Jag, and a Rover in front of that; they might have been looking for vacant parking-meters.

"They can't sound their horns, see?" said the driver. "Or we'd have 'em. I've seen 'em drive round for three hours, just peering out of the window. You'd think they'd stop fancying it, wouldn't you?"

"There we are, then," said his mate. "Hard up."

At which point the radio crackled and threw out a few cryptic, parroty cries, and we took off, leaving rubber, howled down Kensington Church Street, sprang across Ken High Street, snaked rapidly through half a dozen back alleys, and slammed to a stop in front of an all-night launderette. A second later, another police car swooped up behind us, and shot its contents into the night. The four officers sprinted into the laundry. The casual passing eye might have been forgiven for thinking that Ronald Biggs had just turned up to wash his vest.

Not so. There was no one in the place except two skinny teenage girls in anoraks, and a young pink copper. He approached his colleagues. He had the voice, remarkably, of a prep school games master.

"They won't go home," he said.

"Oh dear me!" said a colleague.

Which sarcasm was all very well, except that what looked like a brace of errant Brownies turned out to be two-thirds of a local *ménage à trois*, tossed out by the other third for failing to come across with what he was paying the rent for. They were also equipped with nails and teeth with which, the launderette being rather cosy, they were prepared to defend their new billet to the death. It took ten minutes to evict them.

"Someone," said the driver, engaging the clutch, "has been sharing a bed with that lot."

"Imagine," said his mate.

The drunken Irishman was somewhat easier. He cried when the policemen removed him from his ex-girl-friend's flat, eighteen years old, far from Erin, and the tears running down his beardless cheeks. And stupid-drunk.

"Will you be a good boy now and go home?" they said, nicely.

But he ran, and when they caught him, he kicked one of them, hard, and swore fit to strip the cellulose off the car. And, against their original will, they arrested him. The younger policemen rolled up his trouser, and nursed his shin. I asked him if the Irishman would get charged with assaulting a PO.

"No," said the PO involved. "He didn't know what he was doing, did he?"

Whereas a gentleman whom we shall call Adrian did. Adrian is the swinger mentioned in last week's final sentence (for those of you who hang on every syllable), and we first became aware of Adrian's presence on this planet when, cruising slowly along Kensington High Street, we saw a red light walking along the pavement, some fifty yeards away.

"Right," said the driver.

Adrian was six-feet-odd and bamboo thin, with hair like Veronica Lake's and a very nice beige cashmere suit, bell-bottomed, and a silk polo-necked sweater. To set this off, he was wearing a red hurricane lamp in his left hand; the deprived workmen's site stood accusingly, a few yeards away. Beside Adrian swayed a lissome, musky girl in a fur coat. They both laughed tinklingly. It didn't cut much ice. They were charged with taking away an etcetera, contrary to an and so on, and Adrian became somewhat over-wrought. He stamped his foot, and went into a little speil that the coppers, one felt, had possibly heard before, concerning the fact that Adrian was a taxpayer and why weren't they out apprehending thieves, for which service Adrian paid 11s. 9d. in the £?

"We are," said the driver. And that was that. We called for a van, and it came and collected Adrian and friend, and we all went back to Kensington nick, where, amid further petulances, the pair of them were charged. Personally, I thought it was coming it a bit strong for a childish prank, and said so.

"Ah," said the Duty Sergeant, "but he's not a child, is he? And this borough loses thousands of pounds' worth of stuff like this every year. Which also happens to be taxpayers' money. And there's another thing: he wouldn't have nicked it in daylight, would he?"

He glanced up at the station clock, significantly.

"People have got to learn that they can't get away with something," he said, "just because it's the middle of the night."

IN the meantime, life goes on, and a recent survey at Wayne State University, Detroit, found that "at any given moment in an American college, one fifth of the students are thinking about sex". And the other four-fifths? Probably doing something about it.

CHIMES AT MIDNIGHT

THE first line of poetry I ever knew was: *There were angels dining at the Ritz*. I didn't even know what poetry was at the time, but this was undeniably it. Three words encrusted with magic, despatched from another world to enslave the imagination and detonate the senses, trilled across the ether by those arch-druids Anne Ziegler and Webster Booth. I was nine at the time, four feet tall and crushed beneath the austere heel of the Attlee government: the winter of 1947, no coal, the bomb-sites deep in dirty snow, and London full of men in brown demob suits looking for work. And yet, gliding through this bone-cold gloom came these two impossible incandescences, she with teeth like a row of Rennies and professionally crinkled hair, he in white tie and tails and a face glimmering beneath four coats of varnish, ladling out romance to a sackclothed, disillusioned world like charity nobs at an East End soup kitchen. When they broke the news that a nightingale had sung in Berkeley Square, lumps rose in ten million listening throats to wipe out the unspeakable memories of snoek and whalemeat; it was a covenant offered after the great flood of war, a rainbow promising a return to gold and glamour.

It was my earliest glimpse of Night-people. No doubt, for a country child, the fascination of the night depends on such mysteries as the movement of voles and what owls get up to when the sun goes down. I have heard that flowers close. But for a town child, it means the locking of a million doors and the turning out of lights and a brief silence falling over the dull, darkened Day-people while the streets change character and prepare for a new population whose lineaments have been fed into his imagination by innumerable songs and films and books and similar high-gloss brochures for package-tours of Wonderland. Country infants may dream of men on white horses in enchanted woods, or talking badgers and gingerbread shops run by rats in aprons, of owning a barge and an edible cottage and milking their personal cow. I burned only for the night when I should dine with angels at the Ritz, those svelte and silken lay princesses with soft-scalloped necklines and bee-sting lips, and watch the dawn break over Crockfords in the company of long witty men in thin moustaches and collapsible toppers, all singing "Goodnight, Sweetheart" and "Me And My Shadow". I wanted to pop champagne corks, and overtip fawning cabbies, and buy fags from a girl in fishnet stockings, and order in impeccable French, and get Geraldo to play my partner's favourite tango, and come home with the milk. When, at the age of twelve, I got my first long trousers, possibility loomed and tantalised; instantly man, I sidled up on mirrors, winking each eye with the debonair subtlety of a midget Tyrone Power, my hands in the accredited *Teach Yourself*

Dancing fox-trot position, and wondered how far up Rita Hayworth my head would come.

Nightclubs! A word to shrivel the tongue, headier than the wickedest underlinings in my school Bible, fatter with promise than *Reveille*. They were all there, if you were tall enough, round about the middle of the Piccadilly Line, full of pianists called Sam who would play it again when I strode through the bead curtain, full of barmen who would leave the bottle when they heard that Lauren Bacall had left me, full of Peter Lorre, a man small enough for even me to break a chair over should the occasion demand it. "Limehouse Blues" would be weeping in the blue-smoke background, and I should have a double-breasted jacket and real bags under my eyes and a lighter you had to flick with your thumb.

We lived near traffic lights in 1950, on a main road into London. Past midnight, you could hear the cars change gear, and know that in the dashlight glow, hands bronzed by equatorial suns and sinewed by Oxford oars were lightly gripping steering-wheels in the scented company of something in a feather boa, resting her peach-bloomed cheek against his blue-black shoulder. The lights would change, and the clutches engage, and they would be off, roaring down the starlit road to a penthouse where the party never stopped, and slim young peers with DFCs threw deathless epigrams at doe-eyed starlets sipping glasses full of gin and chopped-up fruit. Most of the dancing took place on balconies, with which such environs were rife. The moon was always full.

Ah, Hollywood, F. Scott Fitzgerald, I. Novello, how much you have to answer for! Never before a generation like those you raised on beautiful pap: doomed to search their real world for that bogus landscape sloshed so indiscriminately on your canvases by brushes sopping with instant love, nostalgia, sorrow, joy, and vanishing, gilded youth. Hardest of all on the poor Night-people, cabbing from party to party, from bar to bar, from club to club, the carnations withering on their lapels, the make-up flaking on their noses, seeking joy like Dracula before the dawn comes up to leave them swaying on the pavements, trapped by the incoming tide of office cleaners and early Tubes.

Eventually, and inevitably, I became a Night-person, joined that thin, desperate line of traffic speeding into the West End against the fatter flow of those going sensibly to their exurban beds. And I remained a Night-person for some considerable time, shored up through innumerable disappointments by my belief that it had to be my fault that I never found anywhere or anybody to match the scintillating landmarks of my swollen imagination: I had driven past the turning, no doubt, come to the wrong place; or the right place on the wrong night; or the Jet Set had all just had an urgent call to Acapulco or Rio or someone's nuclear yacht; perhaps, I would murmur to my partner as a sniffing waiter dumped something inedible in front of us from his flaming sword, this club Arrived last month and was on the way Out; or, as a tone deaf trumpeter with a broken lip hacked his way through "Fascination" for the fifth time that evening, this was as yet only on the way In, and would Arrive next month. Maybe all these whey-faced nobodies were really Somebody after all, recognisable only to other Somebodies, and if I sat down with them and they accepted my password, then a key would turn, and a world swing open, and the decomposing skeleton of my old fantasies would suddenly be fleshed, and I'd get to dance with Ingrid Bergman, and for once I wouldn't get home, drizzle-sopping, at six am with a splitting headache from inferior booze and mud on my dinner jacket where I fell down the steps of Horse Guards Parade running for the only cab in London and my intestines shot to hell for a week afterwards and a wallet lighter by nineteen-pounds-four-and-something due to my being unable to read a bill written in yellow ink on cream paper and nothing to see by except candlelight and someone being sick on my shoe in the gents.

But nothing ever changed. I got older, of course, which merely meant that everyone demanded larger tips and I kept finding myself being woken up under Eros by younger and younger foreigners. So, gingerly, I climbed down from the carousel, paid off an overdraft which had left me with nothing but a few books of exclusive matches and occasional bouts of giddiness whenever the widow Clicquot insinuated herself into the conversation, and married. And last week, since five years had dribbled unnoticeably away, since fatherhood was imminent, since my comb was growing daily hairier, and since I wanted to flush the last clinging folly from the mind and at the same time call out to those still bound to the rack of the midnight chime and the neon Grail, I decided to undertake a last crash round of Nightplaces. Who knew but that it mightn't have changed at last, that *Time*'s award to Swinging London mightn't have been more than journalists' yak, that permissiveness and all its drear cortège might not have glossed the writing on the wall?

Fat chance. At Annabel's, most illustrious, most exclusive of the newer night-haunts, whose membership is as impregnable as Fort Knox and whose subterranean Edwardiana, heavily gorgeous, promises more than much, in this reputed Mecca of the beautiful and damned of seven continents, the small dark dance-floor was packed tight with tiny, walnut-faced businessmen (doubtless, of course, of wealth and influence) leaning their wrinkles on the embonpoint of tall wigged girls with pebble eyes. Sporadically, above the unswinging knot, the unmistakable head of a younger peer would bob like a marionette's, a mockery of bone-structure, and laugh at something simple. The couple at the table next to mine talked about shoes for most of the night, and across the aisle a half-forgotten TV face said nothing for three hours, then went, spilling cigarettes. Yawns were worn, real or affected who could guess? At the Revolution, discothèque nonpareil (I'm told), long lines of *boutiquiers jeunes* queued for a chance to wedge up against teenage columnists and such minor pop stars as could be persuaded by their PR men to spend ten seconds glancing through the door. The noise was an incessant gonging, the heat in the red darkness would have brought a stoker to his knees, had he been able to find a speck of ground; the joy was terrible. For old time's sake, we spent one night at the Savoy, centre of mythic elegance; the band played "Happy Birthday To You" for a party from Barnsley, who all did the hokey-cokey and shrieked, and a man came in with his hat on backwards and reduced his table to helplessness. At the Saddle Room, at The Garrison, a slightly dowdier crowd than those who packed Annabel's danced to the same music, made the same remarks, drank heavily and paid the same way, and all went home to Wembley and Gants Hill. Danny la Rue's, at least, was fun, good clean McGill transvestite stuff, but what was it, really? A pier show, transplanted to W1, blue jokes, red noses, inelegant and jolly, watched by middle-aged couples on their anniversaries who smiled through their tears when the band played "Always," and tucked in happily to their scoff. Later, each night, we gambled at the best half-dozen clubs and a few lower spielers, but gambling in London has no chic these days, professional as it is and for the most part shabbily or flashily dressed, played by thickset citizens whose noisy wives swop clichés at the bar, or rich young men who tend to sweat too much.

So we ushered in a few grey dawns, exhausted, bored, and re-assured: we had given the Beautiful People every chance, but they had stayed wherever it is that shadows hang their hats. Oddly, it was not until three nights after this committed binge that I actually *saw* as Beautiful a couple as dreams had ever sketched, behaving exactly as they should—tall and handsome and immaculate, strolling at four am along a Kensington street, hand in hand and humming. I was in a police car at the time, and we arrested them for theft.

But that's another story.

ALAN COREN

"But this is the way we did plan it."

COME ONNA MY PLACE

OFFHAND, I cannot recall a Western which didn't have a happy ending. From "Bite on this bullet, ma'am, doc'll be here real soon" to "Stand fast, men, here come the cavalry now . . ." the cliche dialogue is deliberately calculated to remove instantly any audience anxieties deliberately induced by the cinematic action.

The poison and the antidote are administered almost simultaneously. Even as the baddie smashes his pistol butt down on the oblivious hero's skull, you know deep down that Everything Is Going To Be All Right. For one thing, the star is unlikely to be killed off within ten minutes of the epic's commencement. For another, years of training in the four-and-sixpennys assures you that, finally, every man gets what he deserves.

Our training outside the cinema should have taught us that life is seldom so rewarding, yet no cinematic cliche could ever match the revived hope induced by "Would you like to come in for a cup of coffee?" There she stands in the porchway; her eyes cast demurely into the fairy grotto of her handbag and her fingers dredging nervously for her latch key. The evening's Good Time Charlie spending —and mental arithmetic in the taxi—has assured you that the rest of your financial months must be dedicated to a regime of austerity, your last bus has just gone screaming down the road, and it has just started to rain . . . Then she says: "Would you like to come in for a cup of coffee?" and suddenly Everything Is Going To Be All Right.

Offered in such a context, it would be fair to categorise a cup of *Nescafe* as an aphrodisiac—for what bubbling depths of anticipation are plumbed by its mention. How wide the chasm between a blue and white striped beaker of *Maxwell House* and the surging passions its image irresponsibly releases. In that simply worded offer of camouflaged hospitality, before the hot brown stuff has taken the skin off your drying lips, there is more erotic suggestion than in a full bottle of whisky. Too often the invitation is itself camp. Only the cynical experience of a handful of dashed hopes teaches a man that all he is going to get *is* a cup of coffee. It is why that other well known phrase or saying: "Come up and see my etchings" was invented.

I am not ashamed to say that I have asked girls up to my place on this flimsy pretext, not because I know anything about art, but because I know what I like. Currently the old faithful seems to have been supplanted by an invitation to "come up and hear my LPs or listen to my new transistor"—an alternative of lures which too readily establishes that all you are after finding out is whether she is looking for high fidelity or whether she is simply more interested in frequency—but I love doing the what comes naturally, and after nature, art. For one thing, a basic collection of etchings can come to something considerably cheaper than a full set of hi-fi, and only a fraction of the expense of a night on the town. It is only necessary to know how to use them to proper advantage.

The simple and relatively unimaginative method is to keep them in a portfolio which you can examine together in intimate juxtaposition as you sit with heads close together on the yielding springs of your patent "deep-in-the-centre" settee. Success here depends upon the girl's reaction quotient to erotic pictorial stimuli. Some like cards on the table early in the game. Others are inclined to deal a stinging discouragement before you can whisper so much as "Circa 1897 . . ."

These latter can be mollified in the early stages by a simulated search for the etchings when you first arrive home. A hunt through various desks and drawers in histrionic exasperation can finally lead to your throwing open a cupboard door behind which have been concealed a bottle of *Dom Perignon* and a couple of glasses ."A little something to be going on with whilst I find the damned things," you mention in tones of absentminded generosity. As she draws down a few glasses of the happy juice whilst you simulate searching sounds in an adjacent room, it will be a while before she realises that even if the etchings haven't been framed, she has.

Actually, the expense of framing your etchings need not be discouraging, because under such a system it is only necessary to buy a single picture to offset the cost of the frame itself. This should be hung carefully in position and illuminated by one of those long narrow tubes inside a metal reflector which is traditionally controlled by a long and dangling on/off string. The whole set-up should be positioned on the wall of an otherwise darkened room (the better to do full justice to the art work, of course) immediately above a club sofa and approached across an old and ragged rug. I have found that when confronted with the etching, and handicapped by her extreme short-sightedness (very short-sighted girls are the only ones I can ever get up to my place), and lady of necessity makes tracks across the room to submit the picture to a closer examination. Inevitably her shoe catches in the torn rug and she stumbles. The stumble develops into a head-down forward trot and is only terminated by a sharp contact between the wall and the top of her head. Nothing dangerous, you understand, but a blow of such surprise and suddeness as to render her slightly more stupid than when she agreed to set foot over the threshold in the first place. She than falls gently into position on the club couch so thoughtfully provided.

All anxious condolence, you are beside her in an instant, taking her in your fond arms and insiting that you kiss it better. The on/off switch cord is situated immediately below the etching and your hand finds it without even reaching out. Can you be blamed if your lips do not find the exact location of her bruises in a room that has been plunged in darkness? To be truthful, the tiny Charlotte Street *pied à terre* I dignify with the title "My West End luxury flat," in order to persuade people to visit it, is so diminutive in its proportions as to forbid such ploys as I have outlined. A pity, for like Sonny Liston's reference to the boxing ring when a reporter asked him how he would cope with a constantly retreating target, I could say: "Man, they can run—but there ain't no place they can hide." My place isn't big enough to swing a cat and, perforce, I have had to give the habit up. Consisting as it does of only a single bed-sitter room (usual offices adjoining) the architectural shortcomings are such that the first thing which greets your gaze on opening the front door is the bed. And faced with such an introduction, the average female's defence mechanism clicks resolutely into place behind the bland inscrutability of her baby-blue eyes. "I'll wait in the car. Bring the etchings down and show me . . ." she says icily, backing out like a shy dray horse.

I await the invention of the really disguised divan with impatience. Attempting seduction in a single roomed bedsitter is difficult enough without adding to your obstacles the female resistance indiced by a great, smirking, brass bedstead over there in the corner. A rich friend of mine who lives in Devonshire Street has a remarkable construction which is bookcases on one side and which pivots round to reveal two single beds attached to its back but I have seen these in a dozen cinematic murder-mysteries and every time you revolve the thing, a dead body comes round with the other side. Three's no company.

I have experimented in my time with one of those wall fixtures which fall down into the horizontal at the touch of a button, but neutralising their hazard is child's play to a really resolute female. I discovered that any time I made a move towards closer *rapprochement* the girl would beat me to the control button and the bed would clang down on top of my head, stuninng me for long enough for her to make her getaway. There *are* convertible couches, I know, but they don't allow for the sheets and pillows to remain in place, but hidden, whilst you are going through the motions of entirely altruistic hospitality in the early stages of the evening. And a man's intentions are transparently betrayed if his quarry returns suddenly from repairing her make-up in the bathroom to find him smoothing out a pair of Winceyette sheets and politely enquiring: "Do you like hospital corners?"

Maybe a Russian scientific breakthrough is the grisly answer to the whole problem. Soviet researchers have perfected a sleep simulator which plies the system with electronic impulses to disperse the fatigue toxins stored in the human frame during the day. They estimate that it should ultimately reduce the amount of necessary slumber to about one hour in twenty-four and will add to any user's life span the equivalent of about twenty years of waking life. The son of man may soon have no need to lay his head.

With the bed disappearing, its current copulation connotation will go too—and the generality of couches, sofas and settees in living quarters must remove them from the category of hazard which has psychologically so handicapped beds in the past. To *really* lonely men, the news that the sleep simulator ensures that its users are not subjected to dreams may come as a disappointment; but to my mind it is balanced by another recent scientific discovery —that the average man dreams far more about other men than about women; and usually about close male relatives, what is more.

For my money, the sleep simulator cannot be faulted on that score. With hundreds of millions of women in the world, I can do without dreaming about my uncle Fred.

JOHN TAYLOR

Where
Are the Cuddly Ladies
of Yesteryear?

I DON'T know much about calendars but I know what I like, roughly three hundred and sixty-five days, divided up between January and December, light on Friday the thirteenths, and heavy on those round and fully packed girlies clad only in fluffy ear muffs for winter months and red wellies for April's showers. It does not seem like much to ask but judging from the stock of 1970 calendar art I have perused thus far I am a dreaming fool. Something definitely has happened to the calendar girls this year. To speak of it as a falling-off is ridiculous understatement. It is more as if a famine has struck; and not only have the girls got skinny, they have also got nasty with it. Spindle shanked, lean jawed, narrow bosomed, the 1970 calendar girls stare out at you with cold contempt in their eyes and a hint of derisive laughter playing around their thin lips. Added to this, as if to rub something in, is the fashion among 1970 calendar girls to be covered with gritty sand. I cannot example it. I have no idea what the significance is. But there it is, on every 1970 calendar I have seen there has been at least one girl covered with gritty sand.

Where, one asks, are those round, milky thighed Vargas girls and full-bosomed, scarlet-lipped Petty girls who pouted and moued from the walls of the billiard parlours and petrol stations of my youth? Those old time calendar girls who inflamed the adolescent in the 'thirties, 'forties, 'fifties, and early 'sixties, have, like the D cup brassiere, the cami-knicker, and the black lace stocking top with matching suspender, disappeared without trace from 1970's calendars.

Girls there are aplenty on 1970 calendars. They are stripped down and lounging on exotic beaches from the South of France to the Bahamas, but all the girls lounging on all the calendars I have seen so far this year all look like they have been ordered to the sunshine for health reasons. Invariably they appear to be suffering from a lack of bulk in their diets, their breasts sag, their ribs show, and while not exactly running to dandruff they exhibit what we watchers of the telly commercials can recognise as dull and lifeless hair.

There has, of course, been a fashion for several years now for boyishly shaped girls, but until this year the fashion did not make any great inroads into calendar art. The calendar girl until now had been a last preserve of the old-fashioned dumb and cuddly girl in an era of steely hipped and hearted dollies. Somehow, however, without anyone getting to know about it, the sexual suffragettes have taken over the calendar girl business and so the sex kitten has disappeared, replaced by sand gritted, razor-boned girls in bikinis looking out at you as if to say, "Okay, jerk, ogle this if you dare."

That seems to be the spirit of the 1970 calendar girl. Gone is the coy hypocrisy of lacy foundation garments—with figures like these 1970 girls have you don't need to dig foundations. Gone, too, are the awful attempts at humour and those truly horrible and vulgar puns that lighted up many a dreary month with their moronic innocence. I have searched in vain for a March 1970 that would, for example, show a girl bending over picking up a glove with a gusty March zephyr billowing up her skirt, with the girl's mouth making a little O of surprise while the saucy caption quipped: PRETTY CHEEKY.

In the main the jokes on the vintage girlie calendars were of that intellectual calibre. But at least they did have jokes. There are no jokes on the new style 1970 calendars. No, it is all taken very seriously. There is no hint of old English bawdiness and backside pinching. You will notice, please, that the old time calendar girl *was* wearing gloves. Calendar girls in those days were always lady-like. And the girls were not only seasonal but also traditional. Harvest-time was, I remember from one calendar of not so many years ago, marked by an incredibly busty girl setting up a pile of Dame Nature's autumnal bounty (undoubtedly at her parish church) with the caption line reading: SOME PUMPKINS. Today's calendar girls all appear to be on beaches no matter what the month of the year.

As well as escaping the rigours of the British winter, the 1970 calendar girls have also turned their backs on pets. In the old days, all good calendar girls were very fond of pets, particularly little dogs. One of my all-time favourites had a curvy lady, wearing of course white gloves, walking her little Pekinese dog, the dog had evidently got to frisking about, its lead was all tangled around the lady's beautiful legs, hoisting her skirt to her waist. The caption was a tribute to native wit. PEEK-A-KNEES, it said. This calendar, I hasten to add, did not date from a prudish time when the glimpse of stocking was something shocking. What one actually looked at in the picture was not the girl's knees, your attention was focused just where it would be today. But the vulgarity was masked by the terrible pun and the frilly romance of a lady's unmentionables. Now, of course, such innocence has been shattered by people like Miss Mary Quant who has asserted loudly that girls today dress to the crutch. And, too, everyone is so hip on paperback Freud that they are afraid to admit to liking ladies' frilly undies.

Naturally, the cuddly well-padded ladies of the vintage calendars are in a direct line of fantastic descent from those pictures in children's books of woodland bunnies in waistcoats drinking tea by the blazing hearths of their tree trunk houses. And undoubtedly the Freudians can make good cases against both the woodland bunnies in waistcoats and the well-padded cuddly ladies looking surprised (the old time calendar girl was always getting surprised) as the wind reveals their frilly knickers. No doubt there is something psychologically unhealthy about a man whose fantasies run to such unreal creatures but I've got a wee bit of a suspicion (not bigger than a pair of fluffy ear muffs) that the fellow who fantasies over a sneering, skinny dame all covered with gritty sand is somehow going to beat me to the analyst's couch.

By STANLEY REYNOLDS

Lay that Pistil Down

By J. B. BOOTHROYD

"Facts of Life." Father of boy and girl would deeply appreciate a beautifully written essay on this subject.—The Times

YOU must have noticed that often when a lady and gentleman kiss on the pictures or TV it is not the same sort of kiss that you give your Mummy and Daddy, or even the same sort that Mummy and Daddy give each other. This is one of what we call the facts of life, just as girls and boys have different bicycles. They are different in other ways, too, though not as different as they used to be before jeans were invented. And, by the by, do not confuse jeans with genes, because these were invented much, much earlier, though you have only just begun to hear about them on the B.B.C.

I know you are very interested in birds, and love to see the blue tits hanging upside down from a half coconut, but I am sure you know that it is cruel to take their eggs—because if those eggs are left to ripen they will have other birds in them, and in time *they* will hang on half coconuts and *they* will have eggs with other birds in them. Yet there is a difference between the bird and the coconut, which does not have eggs but is a native of the Malay Arch-i-pelago, whence it has been carried by human agency to tropical and subtropical regions in all parts of the world. Perhaps you can most easily associate the word "coconut" with the word "shy", and if so I am very pleased as shyness was the next thing I was going to talk about.

Little boys and girls are very often "shy" with one another, though not, of course, if they are brothers and sisters. When it comes to the facts of life, brothers and sisters are not boys and girls in that sense at all, but often ride each other's bicycles and think nothing of it. I expect you have notice, too, that a boy throws a ball at a coconut shy quite differently from a girl, except when the girl is what is called a "tomboy". I expect that will remind you of a "tomcat", and it is true that a tomcat is very much more boy than girl, and cannot have kittens, any more than little boys can. Boys often ask their Mummies, "Can I have a kitten?" and do not understand why they are always told No. It is a fact of life.

One thing that must have puzzled you, since you were about six, was where you were seven years ago? You ask Mummy and Daddy where *they* were seven years ago and they tell you at once, Twicken-ham, or perhaps even Esher, but when you ask where *you* were they put you off with e-vas-ive answers. You must remember that even your parents do not know the exact answer to everything, and though there are such songs as "Only a Baby Small, Dropped from the Skies" these are not really giving the facts of life in a true form, as your friends at school may have told you. This does not mean that you should believe all that your friends at school tell you. It is much better to pay attention to a beautifully written essay like this and try to understand what is being said to you.

When a bird . . .

When a cat . . .

I realise that I should have said that coconuts are not the only natives of the Malay archipelago. Many of the natives there are Mummies and Daddies in the same way that your Mummy and Daddy are, exactly. The population was nearly six million in 1947, very unevenly dis-tri-but-ed, leaving large, virtually uninhabited areas of mountain and swamp jungles. When you are older I will lend you some books about the facts of life in that part of the world, by a writer named Somerset Maugham.

Rabbits are . . .

A bee is a fer-ti-lizer, but instead of being spread, like other kinds, it buzzes from flower to flower.

Perhaps the best thing is to think of your Daddy as a great big bee, with only one flower to go at (Mummy!). I expect he has talked to you about the facts of life from time to time, and seemed the biggest bee you ever listened too. If so, remember that that's just what *he* was feeling all the time.

"It takes up all his time but it keeps him out of mischief"

Too, Too Solid Flesh!

B. A. YOUNG on Shakespeare in modern undress

THE first details to leak out concerning the *Macbeth* film in which Ken Tynan and Hugh ("Playboy") Hefner are involved are not of the players' names but of the witches' nudity, and why should this surprise anybody?

It certainly won't surprise anybody who has had anything to do with witches. True, Holinshed, from whom Shakespeare got the story, calls the Weird Sisters "iii women in straunge and ferly apparel," and Thomas Heywood in his *Hierarchie of the Blessed Angels* thought they were

"*three Virgins wondrous faire*
As well in habit as in feature rare."

(Heywood also reminds us that Banquo's surname was Stuart, which makes a lot of things clearer.)

But in John Manningham's diary for 1602-1603—only a year or two before *Macbeth* came out—we read of a sabbat of "some six couple men and women dancing naked"; and the evidence against Jonet Wischert, the well-known Aberdeen witch, in 1593 included the charge that she was "naikit from the middill down." Even if Shakespeare hadn't read these documents, you can bet Mr. Tynan has. And after all, though it's true Shakespeare never said that his witches were nude, it's just as true he never said they weren't.

Apparently Lady Macbeth is going to be nude, or near-nude, in the sleep-walking scene too. Actually I've always believed that Lady Macbeth was a witch herself. *Macbeth's* a curiously short play, and my idea is that there is this scene missing from the beginning. In this, Lady Macbeth, having anointed herself with an ointment made from boiled-down children (an ingredient just as necessary as the eleosalinum, aconitum, pentaphyllon, solanum somniferum and bats' blood that your local chemist will mix you for a few shillings), calls up the witches in a private ceremony at the castle and briefs them about what they're to do on the blasted heath when the battle's lost and won.

This could also clarify the problem of Lady Macbeth's children, casually mentioned at the end of Act One but never heard of after. The passage in which the Weird Sisters insist on her including them in the ointment as part of the contract could be really grisly.

If the nude witches go down well in *Macbeth*, there are more witches waiting in the wings. The most obvious of them is Joan la Pucelle in *Henry VI;* she may seem heroic when she's winning, but she's not slow in raising a bunch of fiends when she's in trouble.

"A woman clad in armour," Lord Talbot calls her, but as I see her she will wear armour with nothing underneath it, a kinky effect that chould go down well with the *Playboy* members. Shakespeare is more helpful with Joan than with Lady Macbeth. When an English soldier interrupts her conference with the Dauphin and the French general staff, the stage direction says *They fly, leaving their clothes behind*. Obviously the conference was some kind of orgy. Joan's line "And now there rests no other shift than this" may mark the crucial point of a strip-tease routine.

However, it's no good only bringing on the nudes where Shakespeare gives the word. Ordinary practice in the permissive society should tell us where they ought to be. In *Pericles*, for instance, there's this scene where the virtuous Marina finds herself in a brothel. She's no great credit to the profession; the first we hear of her abilities is when a Gentleman coming out says, "Come, I am for no more bawdy houses; shall's go hear the vestals sing?" But after an introduction like that, what could be more aphrodisiac than to see Marina in the altogether? It would make the ensuing scene, from where Lysimachus says, rather ungraciously, "She would serve after a long voyage at sea" to her last-minute delivery to go and teach singing, weaving, sewing and dancing to the citizens of Mitylene, into a positive cliff-hanger.

Zeffirelli's film awoke us to the realisation that when Romeo and Juliet made love, they first took their clothes off. Shakespeare is a devil for keeping his passionate scenes offstage, but the film director can always nip off into the wings with a camera. Arthur Brooke's poem from which Shakespeare took the story is specific enough, Lord knows——

And now the virgins fort hath warlike Romeus got,
In which as yet no breache was made by force of cannon shot,
And now in ease he doth possess the hoped place.
How glad was he, speake you that may your lovers' parts embrace.

So if Juliet, why not Cressida, who comes as near love-making in public as anyone in the canon? Why not Cleopatra? Why not Hamlet's mother, whose love-making is described with such detailed distaste by her son? Why not Miranda, Desdemona, Ophelia? Why not Rosalind?

Well, there we come up against a snag. Poor Rosalind has to spend most of her time pretending to be a boy. No doubt an inventive producer could have a wonderful time thinking up ways in which she could almost, but never quite, present full frontal nudity to the unhappy Phebe and the gullible Orlando, but even in a movie it could hardly be easy. As for Viola, it sounds as if the game would be up when Orsino tells her "Thy small pipe is as the maiden's organ."

After the girls, the boys. Hamlet's first words in his letter to the King after the abortive trip to England are "You must know that I am set naked on your kingdom." "Naked!" repeats the King thoughtfully after finishing the letter.

Many a director might feel equally thoughtful.

When did you last sip Champagne from a lady's slipper?

ROUND about 10.30 am on the third Wednesday in every month the tea-lady comes into our boardroom, and puts in front of my colleagues the cup of iron filings boiled in tannic acid which they all seem to like. In front of me, however, she sets a pot of Lapsang Suchong China tea, and this, I fear, my colleagues regard as epicene, if not downright decadent, though they are too polite to say so. And that's about as near to an orgy as we ever get in our corner of SW1.

Studying, however, as I do, all these stories in the *News of the World* about sales reps whooping it up in Walthamstow, and the Bacchanalian revels that seem to go on after hours in Throgmorton Street, I'm beginning to wonder whether our board isn't missing something.

We have our usual Christmas party in the office, of course, and very enjoyable it is, too. I notice, however, that some companies are dropping this particular celebration. I suppose they feel that there's a risk of an unreflective little frippet from Accounts saying some-

Quentin Blake

thing to the managing director late in the evening which may un-balance the office for weeks to come.

One of our contractors, for instance, tells me that their office party last Christmas was disturbed by a young lady from the typing pool. She rushed into the general office observing, "I've been assaulted." Her friends crowded round to give her comfort. "Who could have done this dastardly thing?" they inquired. "Obviously one of the directors," she replied. "Who else would wear an Old Etonian tie, and make me do all the work?"

Business, of course, has been business down the ages, but some-how I think our forebears managed to mix business and pleasure with dreater panache than we do. Take the Romans. Petronius has a nice bit in *The Satyricon* about a dinner party given by a neighbour who wanted to acquire a few acres off him at a knock down price. History doesn't relate how the deal went, but it does record that the host kindly provided a little golden-haired slaveboy through whose curls the guests could run their fingers when they had got a bit greasy from the Umbrian chicken legs and ham bones. Now, that's really obliging. I doubt if you could get that sort of service in the Savoy even if you gave them weeks of notice.

Plautus had sensible views, too. In one of his plays he demon-strates that the best way to crack an egg is to place it between the navels of two young Nubian salvegirls standing face to face, and then instruct them to rotate simultaneously. But suppose you are taking out a couple of tough Dutch shipbuilders to lunch at the Ecu de France, you can't just send down to the Brook Street Bureau and ask if they've got a couple of Nubian egg-crackers on the books. They'd have you round at the Savile Row police station in a trice.

And what about the Rape of the Sabine Women? That sort of behaviour wouldn't go down at an English party even in this Per-missive Age. Imagine if you were asked to the Ladies Night at the local Rotary Club, and just as they were tucking into the Bombe Surprise you suddenly scooped up all the wives of the Committee, popped them over the bonnet of the Rover, and off away home you went to Potters Bar. Well, I mean, you wouldn't be asked again, would you?

I'm beginning to think that the whole of this Wine, Women and Song stuff is a bit exaggerated as far as British business is concerned. About American business I'm not so sure. What usually happens in fact is that you are taken out to the Tycoons' Club for luncheon to celebrate the deal. To a background of gin and musak, you're given far tee many Martoonis. You're then treated to a piece of steak the size of the West Rising of Yorkshire (and about as yielding) which you wash down with scalding hot, white, very sweet coffee, and after you've gone down in an elevator which leaves your stomach up on the top floor, you stagger out into Wall Street and send off a Telex to your chairman saying the deal has been clinched, to which he replies, sourly, "Why only three per cent?"

These are the facts. But in legend, ie, in *Playboy* magazine, things turn out differently. The boys take you out to dine in Greenwich Village, and shortly after the Pot Roast has been done with the Maitre D wheels in an enormous cake out of which erupts 38-26-38 of very undressed blonde who raises her glass in a bumper toast to the Discounted Cash Flow. This is an entertainment at which I have never actually assisted.

I must confess that I did once go to a Travel Sales Conference at the Coventry Street Corner House where a lady named Princess Ouida Ouigglebelli (or something like that) had been engaged to take off all her clothes slowly and quietly to music. The guests on either side of me expressed the opinion that she was a nice enough girl, though she was constructed on architectural principles too generous for their taste, and that next year they would prefer Morecambe and Wise. I, too, was beginning to wonder whether business and sex really mix.

There's nothing so helpful to the Good Old Days an a Bad Old Memory. My Uncle Charlie used to drop dark hints about celebrating a successful coup by taking some charming little Thing out to supper in a private room at Rules, and drinking champagne out of her slipper. Even if he did, I believe the operation must have been a great deal more complicated than it sounds. And knowing my Uncle Charlie, I bet he made a right mess of it, too. The nearest I've ever been to it myself was during the war when I went to a Hogmanay Party with the London Scottish, where they were reduced to drinking oatmeal stout out of a NAAFI girl's gumboot. The experiment was not a success.

The Russians, of course, have to be different. In their funny Victorian way they still foster the idea of the tired Western business-man relaxing to the sound of throbbing balalaikas whilst the current Mata Hari adjusts the bugging device behind the armoire.

Some while ago I went to Lenningrad with a deputation from the British Tourist Authority. On the first night after our arrival the Russian Travel boys threw a party in our honour. It was a fine party (they wanted a good deal from us) and by midnight we were awash in vodka. Knowing that I had to make a speech next day I slipped away to my room, undressed, and went into the bathroom

in search of Alka Seltzer. Slightly to my surprise I found an elderly Chinaman sitting in my bath washing his toes. "Hi," I said loudly (in English, of course). To which he replied, "Hi," equally loudly in Chinese, which, in these circumstances, sounds roughly the same. I put on my dressing gown, and in some confusion ran out into the corridor, and into the welcome arms of my colleagues Lord Geddes and Sir Charles Forte. They led me back to my room explaining comfortingly that I was not drunk but had merely forgotten that in the Astoria Hotel, Leningrad, each bathroom served two bedrooms, and that unless you also locked the other door from the inside you were bound to find someone like an elderly Chinaman in your bath. Relieved, I retired to bed, and slept the sleep of the just.

But at breakfast time next morning our interpreter, Tanya, bore down upon us with lowering brow. We asked anxiously if ought was amiss. Indeed there was. As a matter of fact there had been a diplomatic détente; a démarche, even. It appeared that the Deputy Chairman of the Soil Erosion Committee of the People's Republic of Outer Mongolia had been insulted in his bath by an Alcoholic Nude.

My friends tutted and clucked, but loyally did not give me away. I'm sorry to say that I sat silent in smug content. There could be few international Travel Conferences, I felt, that had ever been addressed by an Alcoholic Nude, and a member of the House of Lords at that.

By LORD MANCROFT

Bring Back Virginity!

By KEITH WATERHOUSE

WHAT, exactly, are the aims and purpose of Virgins for Industry?

The aims and purpose of Virgins for Industry are, foremost, to restore British virginity to its former prestigious position in the markets of the world; secondly, to impress upon young men and women the economic and social advantages of retaining their virginity before it is too late; thirdly to rid Government, Industry and the Trade Union Movement of dangerous non-virgin elements whose avowed objective is to establish Great Britain as the Sodom and Gomorrah of Western Europe; and fourthly to campaign unceasingly for the removal of the iniquitous Tax on Virginity.

Is Virgins for Industry, then, a political organisation?

Virgins for Industry is completely unpolitical. We believe, however, that the present trend towards permissiveness is directly traceable to the folly of socialist politicians who publicly admit to being active non-virgins. We also believe that millions of man-hours are being lost each year as the result of lust and fornication on the factory floor, as well as behind filing cabinets. It is our contention that only a Virgin Government can lead Great Britain back to strength, chastity and economic sanity.

Virgins for Industry was recently accused by a Socialist Member of Parliament of being interested only in increased production and profits at the cost of other people's pleasure. Is there any truth in this scurrilous libel?

The socialist politician who made this vicious and cowardly attack under the cover of Parliamentary privilege is, it is openly admitted, the father of two children. Thus he publicly flaunts his confessions that he has been in bed with a woman on at least two occasions. Where he to present himself at the House of Commons with a mattress strapped on his back, it could not be a clearer indictment of his direct interest in the permissive lobby.

But let us examine these groundless allegations. What is the so-called "pleasure" which it is said we seek to deny the British people? Let us make no bones about it, it is the "pleasure" of sex—which, as many doctors have testified, leads *directly* to rape, incest, abortion, prostitution, venereal diseases, adultery, illegitimacy, nervous exhaustion and like perils.

And who really wants this "pleasure"? Not, you may be assured, the Virgins of Britain. No virgin lathe operator ever approaches the foreman for half a day off so that he may defend himself in a sordid paternity suit. No virgin secretary fails to turn up at her desk because she is suffering from morning sickness. We do not see virgin company directors ashen-faced with worry, and unable to deal with important export orders, because some woman has just rung up to say that she must see them at once, and it's very urgent.

No, the British virgin is happy to forego such "pleasures."

Other critics, with the best of motives, claim that Virgins for Industry is impracticable. They say that if we were all practising virgins, Britain would be uninhabitable within seventy years.

Certainly there would be a marked decline in the demand for subsidised housing, free education and other perquisites of the Welfare State which (since the Exchequer does not look kindly on the single man) are largely paid for by the iniquitous Tax on Virginity.

But it is wrong to say that Virgins for Industry is reaching for the moon. We are realists, and we recognise that there must always be an unhappy minority who will indulge in sexual intercourse, just as there will always be drug-addicts, alcoholics, perverts and criminals.

However, just as we would not expect to be governed by drug-addicts, alcoholics, perverts and criminals, neither do we wish to be governed by those who indulge in the sexual act.

You have convinced me that criticism of Virgins for Industry is either ill-informed or malicious. Now, speaking constructively, could you outline the economic advantages of virginity which you mentioned earlier?

Even allowing for the iniquitous Tax on Virginity, the practising virgin earning, say, £2,000 a year, is many times better off than his fornicating opposite number. Here is one case from among hundreds on our files.

As a *direct result* of losing his virginity at the age of twenty-three, John B., a chartered accountant living in Middlesex, is now the father of three girls under the age of twelve. Having kept careful records of his expenditure he has been able to calculate that the cost of this brood in the way of clothes, food, shelter, education, birthday and Christmas presents, toys, holidays, horse-riding lessons, Brownie uniforms, soft drinks, sweets, ice-cream, pocket money, subscriptions to *Jackie* and the remainder, has so far amounted to the fantastic sum of £10,700.

By remaining a Virgin a young man of equivalent income would be able to *save* £10,700 within twelve years.

You might have added that such a sum when invested would actually appreciate over this period. But money is not everything. What are the social advantages of virginity?

An independent survey has shown that the Virgin has *twenty-five times* more leisure than a non-virgin. Leisure in which to read improving books. Leisure to take up a rewarding and profitable hobby such as coin-collecting. Leisure to peruse the correspondence course that may rocket him to the top of his profession. He is also, from the employment point of view, a more efficient working unit, far less likely than the non-virgin to arrive at desk or work-bench with circles around his eyes, waste precious hours mooning about in the typing pool, or write pornographic letters on the firm's stationery Remember, too, that it is the virgin with *twenty-five times* more leisure at his disposal who is best able to serve his country in Government at all its levels.

Twenty-five times more leisure! Surely this is a staggering figure which will come as a revelation to all thinking men and women?

It is indeed a staggering figure, and one that perhaps deserves to be explained in a little more detail. Our argument, which is based not on theory but on fact, is that the average virgin is, hour for hour, twenty-five times more productive than the average non-virgin, irrespective of the quality, use or desirability of that which is being produced.

Time-and-motion studies show that for every fifteen minutes spent in copulation by a non-virgin, *five hours* is consumed in pre-paratory activities such as bathing, dressing, applying after-shave lotion and other unguents, drinking cocktails, dining by candlelight, dancing, groping in taxi-cabs and professing a mutual interest in certain gramophone records. Even then the end-product—such as it is—is not guaranteed.

In a comparable period, a virgin who has decided to spend his evening sorting through his collection of day-of-issue stamps will not have wasted a single minute. Nor, according to independent costings, will he have incurred a restaurant bill for £8 9s. 6d. plus fifteen per cent tip.

It is clear that sex is wasteful, time-consuming, expensive and that there is no place for it in modern Britain. How do you propose to drive this message home?

By disseminating literature such as this in schools, youth clubs, offices and factories. By setting fire to hotel beds. By spreading rumours that the Pill causes women to grow moustaches. By patrolling Hampstead Heath shouting "Disgusting filth!" at courting couples. By discouraging office parties. By taking a full-page announcement in *The Times* newspaper denouncing HM Government as lechers and fornicators.

Naturally, all this costs money, and we exist entirely on voluntary subscriptions. We rely on *your* support.

I would like to join Virgins for Industry. How do I set about becoming a virgin?

Naked as Profits Intended

A nude Macbeth, a nude ballet, and at last Equity has stepped in on behalf of members reluctant to appear in nothing but their talent. E. S. TURNER dipped eagerly into their postbag.

The Secretary,
Equity.

Dear Sir, My Client has been offered the part of Anna Karenina in a forthcoming film production, with the stipulation that certain scenes are to be played in the nude. I shall be obliged if you will send me a copy of your Special Rates card covering such performances. Yours faithfully, Jasper Crick, Theatrical Agent.

Jasper Crick, Esq.

Dear Sir, We have no Special Rates card. The agreement on Exposure Increment, to which you probably refer, is a long and complex document which can be consulted only in these offices. In general, such increment is calculated on a basis of salary and varies with the performer's sex, physique, degree and duration of exposure, strength of lighting, nature of the medium and other factors. As an example, a male film performer earning not more than £200 a week would be entitled, in respect of continuous or intermittent frontal exposure in full-strength lighting, to increments as follows: First 15 seconds (or fractions thereof) £5 per second (or fraction thereof); next 30 seconds, £2 per second; thereafter, 2s. 6d. per half-hour. The rates for women are, in general, two-thirds of the male rate, with special bust allowances which help to bring them up to the male level.

I may add that there is a loading of four hundred per cent for close-ups and scenes in slow motion and a loading of one hundred per cent for all nude performances enacted under water or on ice. I trust this information will be of some assistance. Yours faithfully, Giles Gradgrind, Secretary, Nude Performances Division, Equity.

Giles Gradgrind, Esq.
Equity.

Dear Sir, I have now made a careful study of the agreement on Exposure Increment in your offices. It appears to my Client and myself that the rates are wholly unrealistic in respect of an actress who is called upon not only to appear nude but to recite passages of Tolstoy as well. As my Client puts it, she might as well be posing with a pitcher on her head at the Windmill. May I have your comments, please? Yours faithfully, Jasper Crick.

Jasper Crick, Esq.

Dear Sir, The question of additional payment for a nude Tolstoyan actress is being referred to our General Policy Committee, who will be be reporting in a few weeks' time.

Meanwhile, I feel bound to point out to your Client that female trapeze artists who appear unclothed are entitled to no additional payment. Yours faithfully. Giles Gradgrind.

Giles Gradgrind, Esq.

Dear Sir, I learn with regret that you are unable to furnish a quick ruling in this matter. Your suggestion that playing in the nude is a feat comparable to circus acrobatics is one which my Client and I find deeply hurtful. Surely the great trade union movement has some regard for the claims of culture?

Would it be too much to urge that you consult Mr. Vic Feather in this matter? Yours faithfully, Jasper Crick.

Jasper Crick, Esq.

Dear Sir, I am reluctant to widen this correspondence into a philosophical debate. Our function as a trade union is to obtain for our members the highest possible remuneration for the deployment of what they conceive to be their assets, whether physical or cultural, or both. In recent months our task has been rendered difficult by the rush of inexperienced performers anxious to appear nude, irrespective of their talents and physique, at salaries which they would have rejected if called upon to wear clothes. We are the victims of market and other forces beyond our control. Nevertheless, we shall make every effort to maintain our existing rates of Exposure Increment.

I regret that it is not possible for me to anticipate or accelerate the decision of our General Policy Committee. Yours faithfully, Giles Gradgrind.

Giles Gradgrind, Esq.
Equity.

Dear Sir, I appreciate the points you raise, but I cannot believe that there is an overwhelming rush of actresses anxious to play Anna Karenina in the nude.

While your Committee is deliberating, perhaps you would advise me on whether it is reasonable for my Client to assign to the producers of the film unrestricted global television rights in perpetuity for .05 per cent of the network fee. My Client points out that if her children, her grandchildren and even her great-grandchildren are to see her in this role at the domestic hearth she is entitled to a far higher percentage to offset the injury to her modesty. Yours faithfully, Jasper Crick.

Jasper Crick, Esq.

Dear Sir, I am sorry you have introduced the red herring of modesty, which has never been taken into account in the assessment of Exposure Increment. If our members had any modesty, they would not be our members. What they are prepared to do in public has occasionally surprised us, but our role is simply to ensure that others do not unfairly reap the rewards of their audacity.

I am referring the question of the proposed television fee to our General Policy Committee, along with the other matter. Yours faithfully, Giles Gradgrind.

Giles Gradgrind, Esq.
Equity.

Dear Sir, My Client informs me that the offer of the part of Anna Karenina has now been withdrawn and that the director is considering playing the part himself. As a result my Client is forced to accept a greatly inferior part in "Once More Nude Around The Clock."

I am forwarding copies of this correspondence to Mr. Vic Feather, the Editor of *The Times* and Mrs. Mary Whitehouse. Yours faithfully, Jasper Crick.

Psst! You want a woman?"

O Pioneers!

By JANE CLAPPERTON

ONE of the things that bemuses me about life in the United States (the other is how they've managed to get along all these years without egg-cups) is the curiously schizoid attitude of manufacturers to their very own dream girl, the American Housewife. There she goes, prancing through the advertisement pages: an alarmingly vital sprite who can whip up a bushel of nauseous bite-size bitlets in less time than it takes to open the packet and who clearly never had a day's illness in her life. And yet a quick, strabismic peep at the aids to modern living with which she is encouraged to cram her split-level home makes one wonder whether all this bouncing health is just a hollow mockery. It's been common knowledge for years that the poor girl can't bend; hence the electric scrubbers, electric polishers and, for all I know, electric tongs for picking up Sunday newspapers, empty Coke bottles, babies and other articles too bulky to be taken care of by the vacuum cleaner. More recently her condition has deteriorated to the point where she hasn't the strength to open a tin, and has to fall back on the Auto-Magic Kitchen-Mate which is not, as you might think, her husband, but an electric tin-opener which rips the armour off the baked beans, along with any fingers and thumbs you are anxious to dispose of, in a matter of seconds. And now, as God is my witness, the woman can't even clean her own teeth—though indeed why should she when for a mere seventeen dollars and ninety-eight cents, plus tax, she can kit herself out with an electric toothbrush (simply approach the mechanism to those great rotting molars and the wonders of science do the rest).

That's one side of the picture, and if it keeps you awake at night don't blame me. But here comes the catch. This frail, lacklustre being whose muscles have all the tensile strength of damp spaghetti is expected to be able to put a wardrobe together with a mere flick of the wrist. The line taken by furniture manufacturers, aided and abetted by delivery men who hate to carry wardrobes upstairs—as a matter of fact they hate to carry *anything*, preferring if they can get away with it to stack their burdens against the front door and run like mad—is that having presented you with the component parts, impenetrably shrouded in forty-two layers of corrugated board, they have done their share and the rest of it is up to you.

My first and most traumatic brush with this aspect of the American Way of Life came the day I moved into an unfurnished flat and discovered, slap in the middle of the living-room floor, a windowless prefab for large gnomes. A long inelegant tussle with sticky tape eventually revealed that this structure contained my new bed—in bits. Anyone who has ever put a bed together single-handed and without any tools will know that this is the sort of thing that marks you for life. An octopus could have done it in half the time, but equipped only with the courage of despair and the miserable two hands I was born with the contest was unequal.

It's not much of a game, really. You start by laying the pieces out on the floor, staring at them in a forlorn attempt to rationalise their unpromising appearance and fighting down the dark suspicion that all this junk has nothing whatever to do with beds and is simply what was left over after a gang of drunken amateurs had finished assembling a combine harvester. Attached to one of the girders is a little linen bag which is not meant to open; in the end you set about it with your teeth, and eight screws and a wing-nut fall out and roll under the radiator. Also in the bag is a bit of paper that says: "Assemble frame, taking care that side rails are at side and head and foot rails at head and foot. Tighten wing-nut, *having first adjusted adjustable clamp.* Insert castors in sockets provided (see diag.)." Diag., incidentally, is a nice little drawing of a castor; a bit too representational by current standards, but for somebody who'd never seen one before it would obviously have its uses. But *clamp* . . . *What* clamp? Why wasn't it in the little linen bag with the rest of the stuff? Or perhaps it was? Then it's still under the radiator. Down we go.

This beastly scene has been re-enacted with minor variations shortly after the arrival of every single piece of furniture I own—chairs, tables, book-cases, the lot. The fan took a particularly heavy toll (Philadelphia summers may be described, if you like euphemism, as sultry, and if you can't afford an air-conditioner you compromise with a gigantic window-fan which nudges the hot air around in an officious manner, thus converting a turkish bath into a turkish bath with a draught). What set the fan apart from the rest of the occupational therapy was that nestling among the cardboard ramparts was a glossy, artistic booklet of instructions instead of the usual three enigmatic lines on a scrap of ricepaper. The instructions, though kindly meant, tended to confuse; for reasons which Freud would know all about I mislaid them within half an hour so I can't quote at length, but one sentence that has stuck in my mind, where

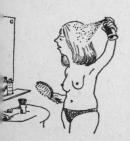

Hans Haëin

it is doing me little good, went like this: "It is essential that flange with protruding lip should face away from inside of room."

The whole thing is further bedevilled by the conviction, deeply and irrationally rooted in the feminine psyche, that it's a waste of money to buy expensive tools. The pride of the flimsy collection tangled up in my kitchen drawer is a fiendish invention which offers four tools, none of them satisfactory, for the price of one. It is designed on the Russian Doll principle (a hammer containing a chisel containing a screwdriver containing Old Macdonald and his farm, and so on) and every time you start knocking in a nail the weapon disintegrates and the loose covers are cut to ribbons by flying ironmongery. Using the screwdriver leads to a more subtle form if dissolution; the base of the device slowly but inexorably unscrews itself and the contents quietly leak out one by one and lodge quivering in your instep. The furniture manufacturers, whose spies are everywhere, are clearly aware of this, and the fact that they continue to package their gimcrack products so that they can only be assembled by two strong men with a chain saw and a brace-and-bit has been ascribed by many thoughtful citizens to sheer sadism, if not to Communist infiltration.

Myself, I think they're overcomplicating. As I see it, these tycoons are in it together; the people who make the dishwashers, for instance, are assured of a steady sale because they know perfectly damn well that after erecting an all-steel kitchen cabinet with the aid of adhesive tape, safety pins and a plastic letter-opener no woman is going to be in a fit state to start slaving over a hot sink.

All over America, in buses, on trains, on hoardings, you will see posters depicting a nervous-looking lady gnawing her knuckles, over the following caption: "1 out of 10 of your fellow Americans is emotionally disturbed. Your Understanding Can Help Her To Find Herself." Note the pronouns, that's all I ask, just note them. So: who assembles whole gigantic suites with just a lick of flour-and-water paste? And who is emotionally disturbed? Right. Any more questions? Because if not, here is where one dear old cabinet-maker retires to a darkened room with a jug of Californian Burgundy and gets absolutely stoned.

Con Amore

By R. G. G. PRICE

MR. P. G. WODEHOUSE has explained that whenever the moguls of Broadway feel a musical is getting snarled up in plot they order "Bring on the girls," and this, of course, is a formula used also in landscape painting, crime fiction and films about cattle-rustlers. Sex has recently spread to the literature of war and even of exploration. Historical novelists get away with quite frightful things and I have even met some sultry reading in novels about internecine warfare in the world of finance.

Literature, however, is a vast field and never completely tilled. There may be pulse-stirring stuff in space fiction and autobiography and farce and even hints in topographical verse but there will still be corners that have yet to be hotted up. I add some suggestive extracts.

From *A New Middle School Algebra*

Tom, Dick and Harry date Mary, Ann and Betty. If Mary lets Tom go twice as far as Ann lets Harry . . .

From *A Guide to the Ceremonies of the University of Oxford*

Entrancing in their furry hoods, the Bachelors from the Women's Colleges move forward on their high heels to receive the Degree of Master and assume the flowing hemline, the fascinating pierced sleeves and the wine-red hood of Masters of Arts. The sharp outline of the rectangular mortarboard seems to emphasize the melting softness of the eyes beneath. Addressing each in Latin the Vice-Chancellor . . .

From *How to Clean Up British Boxing*

. . . under Rule XXXVI. One cause of fouls is undoubtedly over-anxiety to win owing to the presence in ringside seats of girl-friends. Intent on hitting his opponent for six, the welter-weight suddenly catches sight of a vision in enticing head-scarf, with tight sweater and liquid lips, as she leans forward glowing and breathing hard, reminding him of past delights and delights to come if he can earn them, radiant and bewitching and nubile to her smooth, red fingertips. The use of metal in the gloves . . .

From *Studies in Early Rumanian Philology*

. . . glottal stop. In a paper read at a Congress in Oslo, Dr. Hilda Wunf argued that the Minden-Mulfgang theory over-estimated the time-lag in prepositional development. Tall and fine and blonde, she stood at the lectern like some rare Valkyrie and not a scholar present but his heart swelled and throbbed at the sight of her strong, firm teeth and her arms, so capable of bending the stoutest bow or cleaving a helm with one stroke of an axe. Her thighs, swelling beneath her black tweed skirt, and her primeval feet matched well with the harsh blue light that sparked from her hard, clear eye . . .

From *A Thames Valley Recipe Book*

. . . until thoroughly stewed. Being calory-free, Slough Cold Pie will not put an ounce on to the slim, fluent form of the most gluttonous yet figure-conscious young woman. As she rubs her pliant shoulders against the back of the dining-room chair in an esctacy of greed, as her pimpernel lips part in a radiant welcome to the dish, as she whispers "Oh yes, yes," when offered a second helping, she need have no fear of padding out those shallow pelvic curves. When served with a sprig of parsley the recipe is known as Stoke Poges Cold Pie . . .

From *A Primer of Conjuring*

. . . satisfy the audience that the lady is firmly held in the frame before you pick up the saw. Then linger. Let the audience look at those soft, shapely legs in their sheer silk as they vanish provocatively into the delusive protection of the abbreviated skirt. Gaze down on her as she lies extended at your mercy, palpitating, smiling invitingly, feminine, grappled by bands of steel . . .

From *The Macedonian Question 1943–57*

. . . Mixed Arbitration Commission. No one can fail to see the strong Hellenic influence in the young girls of the region as at evening they tuck up their skimpy dresses and, giggling with shy lasciviousness, paddle barefoot in the stream, crying out somewhat broad jests at any youths who are caught spying on them. These nymphs, with their dark eyes that shoot fire and laughter and their graceful necks and their proud, well-developed busts, are a thousand years, a thousand miles away from the sultry, statueyque beauties of the great Slavonic plains. At the census of 1933 . . .

From *Revised Winter Timetable, Mid-Wessex Bus Service*

aa Sats only. Continues to Girls' Remand Home, giving passengers just long enough.

"Other jumpers from Peter Cazalet's stable worth nothing this week are King, Hal's Hope and Fier Chimiste."

Sunday Times

They're ringing their solicitors.

SPROSON (Tatton)—Thank you, Jane, for the birth of our daughter (Julie Ann). I love you. Thanks also to the staff of RAF Cosford who helped to make this possible.   *Wolverhampton Express & Star*

"Richard! I thought we'd turned our backs on suburbia."

Mr. Wonderful

By BILL HARDCASTLE

I WAS given a bottle of *Brut* last Christmas but it hasn't done a damn thing for me. I was coming to the conclusion that my case was beyond the reach of even the most exotic after-shave. I was preparing to quit the starting-gate and go out to grass like some spavined selling-plater. Until one day I was mooning round a station bookstall and spotted a copy of that most worthy journal *Woman's Own.*

"Who are the world's most fascinating men?" the magazine's cover asked. I slapped down my bob and hurried to the station buffet for an elevenpenny cup of tea and an individual fruit pie. Over these, and a leisurely drag, I studied my purchase.

"When he bent to kiss my hand it was almost too much. Far from shattering my illusions, the real man was proving to be more overpowering than I'd ever imagined." Thus Miss Eleanor Harvey, normally one of *Woman's Own's* most self-disciplined authoresses. And who made Harvey lose her cool? None other than Rossano Brazzi.

I immediately saw a glimmer of hope. Maybe Rossano's pectorals haven't got the adipose layer that mine possess. His hair has to recede another couple of inches before it reaches the Hardcastle snow-line. But Rossano's been around this planet just about as long as I have. Our mileage must be roughly the same. Then I saw the "most fascianting" choice of another *Woman's Own* writer. Hers turned out to be Paul Getty, for Heaven's sake.

Hardcastle, I said to myself, you're back in the race and running. Maybe all I need is a *change* of after-shave.

But I paused and considered. What I (and presumably Rossano Brazzi and Paul Getty) have learned is that half-measures are never enough. A woman's magazine had given me a blinding revelation; it had snatched me back from the brink of despair. Brushing the last crumbs of the individual fruit pie from my lips I returned to the station bookstall to purchase the prescription that would complete my transformation—the *men's* magazines.

I was a stranger to this territory, but I had heard that *Playboy*, despite its title, was not a trade magazine for out of work male chorus dancers. I also knew that it sold billions of copies each month and enabled Mr. Hugh Hefner to have personalised rear-engined jets like the rest of us have two-stroke lawn mowers. So at considerable cost (I went without baked beans on toast for tea that day) I bought it, and the magazine fell open at the picture of a girl with no clothes on in the middle of a rather damp-looking forest.

She appeared to be cunningly constructed of one of the more modern kinds of inflatable plastic. But anyway this sort of thing did not seem to be of practical assistance to me in my immediate problem. So I flipped the pages again and came upon a house advertisement which read, "What sort of a man reads *Playboy?*" The answer apparently is "The guy with an eye for something special . . . in the décor of his bachelor pad or newly formed household."

Hefner, old chap, you may be making a bomb. Frankly I envy you your executive jets, even though I wonder what happens to your plastic stewardesses under pressurisation. But I warn you that you're missing the top end of the market—the people who have long departed their bachelor pads and whose households are as oldly formed as Stonehenge. I refer to Rossano Brazzi, Paul Getty and myself.

It was clear I'd got off on the wrong foot (or breast, I suppose you might say). To be fair *Playboy* is an alien product, and I had gathered that strenuous efforts have been made in recent years to build up—like computers, carbon fibres and British port-style wines—a strong domestic industry in this field. So back to the bookstall for further major expenditure (it meant doing without cheese and onion crisps with my brown ale later that same evening).

I have since completed my survey of the British male-magazine press. It seems to break down into three distinct categories. The first is for people who can't afford to go to Copenhagen and have to make do with what will pass muster by Scotland Yard's pornography squad, Mrs. Mary Whitehouse, the Home Office and W. H. Smith and Sons. In these publications the nudes are less plastic, the correspondence columns more neurotic, and the advertisements more explicit. For readers of this type of work, frustration and a dirty macintosh are essential.

The second category still features girls with no clothes on, but also stresses hairy-chested articles and fiction about motor car racing and grappling with grizzly bears. They are rather like *Reveille*, with knobs on, and I was touched by the free gift that came with a new man's magazine ("NEW—for today's man!") that came out during the period of my survey. It reminded me of the free German's spy's magnifying glass, and similar goodies, that used to be folded into the pages of the *Wizard*, *Rover* or *Hotspur* during my boyhood. In this case the gift was suitably masculine and adult—a money clip—but mine seems to have lost its virtue, and keeps falling off my money.

But I digress. The third category turned out to be what I was really looking for. *Men in Vogue* (and it was clear from *Woman's Own* that Rossano, Paul and I *are* in vogue) is a magazine of severely practical advice.

"In the high income bracket, apart from all their gourmandising, very few men in the middle age group take any exercise. Self-driven or chauffeur driven, they move to and from their desks. Hey you, in your think tank, trapped in mounds of flesh, there's assistance if you want it!"

Thus, Miss Jessica Jessel, *Men in Vogue's* expert on how to avoid the effect of advancing years ("Instant baby face can be yours for as little as two quid!").

"It's okay to drop your aitches," Miss Jessel avers, "but if anything visible droops or sags, you're better off dead."

Jessica, baby, you pull no punches. But are you right? You're certainly flying in the face of the judgement of *Woman's Own*. Paul Getty's face, to name but one, sags like a dejected bloodhound. But let us move on into the broader pastures of *Men in Vogue*.

Astonishingly enough this magazine has somehow managed to do exactly the same as its female equivalent and discover a group of male models in an advanced stage of emaciation. Certainly not the type to appeal to Miss Eleanor Harvey and the rest of the gang down at *Woman's Own*. They also get themselves up in some pretty odd duds. "Green linen thigh boot with grey snakeskin foot, held up by matching snakeskin waist belt." Not me, I thought.

As I wandered through these pages from yellow butterfly hat to bush suit in green velvet to trousers in cherry lambs' wool I began to wonder. Just to make sure I returned to *Woman's Own* and Miss Eleanor Harvey.

"The evening was warm, the moon was full. Suddenly I heard his voice calling a greeting. That voice—there is no mistaking it."

Exactly. Who needs *Men in Vogue* when a good pair of tonsils can do the job for you? Let me just add a point made by *Woman's Own* in its editorial.

"Why not drop us a line telling us who *your* dream man is, and the reason for your choice?"

Why not, indeed, though far be it from me to make any suggestions.

"Priest who wed Nun appeals to Vatican."   *Daily Sketch*
Bet you he doesn't.

Tell Me, Daddy, About the Bees and the Fleas

By RALPH SCHOENSTEIN:

"THIS," said a California newspaper, "is war."

What triggered such belligerence from the Anaheim *Bulletin*? Was it the theft of a ship that belonged to the Seventh Fleet? No, it was a seventh grade probe of a subversive act called intercourse.

While millions of American parents have been seeing such films as *I, A Woman* and *I Am Curious* (*Yellow*), millions of others are opposing the reaching of the curious callow, teaching that has turned the three r's into four by adding reproduction. In nervous cities across the nation, people are rattling sabres over sex education. Should we teach our grade schoolchildren how to make other children or should we just let them drift along with their innocent ids, each one a tiny Columbus on a tittilating voyage into puberty?

The very battle itself shows the distance we have come since the medieval days of my youth, when I learned about sex not in a grammar school but in the University of the Gutter. The foes of sex education insist it belongs neither in school nor gutter but only in the home, a point that would be valid if most partents had the skill to turn their children's eyes from the TV to the ovary. Although my own parents gave it a touching try, their abbreviated guidance was really the ideal birth control: they prepared me for little more than hygienic kissing.

The sexual briefing that I got from my father was memorable for the way that it avoided textbook jargon and came directly to the point: he took me into the library one day when I was twelve and solemnly told me that the time had come for me to know that I was never to use a men's room in the Broadway subway. Since this dissertation left a certain gap in the story of procreation, my mother tried to fill in by also taking me to the library, this time the public one, where she spent more than an hour trying to find a book that explained how I'd been brewed; but in those dark days, the secret was never published for tiny eyes.

My teachers did no better than my parents in telling me about the birds and the bees. Not only was there never a word about the passions of my own species, but even the birds and the bees were handled platonically. Once when I returned to school after having been sick for several days, I heard a rumour that one of the teachers had told a suggestive story about a rooster; but from that day on, in spite of the strain of my innocent ears for some juicy stuff on crows or canaries, I heard nary a bawdy word.

It remained for a pal named Mickey Higgins to take me into an alley one day during the Battle of Midway and reveal the facts of life in all their ageless beauty.

"It's somethin' your mother 'n' father do to each other," said Mickey, carefully choosing his words. "Your mother 'n' father—they're definitely the ones involved. Y'see . . . well, y'see . . ." And here he smiled with embarrassment and disbelief. "Well, this is gonna *kill* ya 'cause believe me it's really *stupid* . . ."

The story didn't kill me, but it left me with a wound, for the earthy scholarship of that little curbstone Kinsey moulded my view of amour. Perhaps it was Mickey's Rabelaisian presentation or perhaps his story *was* inherently silly: I only know that no matter how sweetly the violins are playing, I can never approach love without also approaching laughter. At least I have the comfort of knowing that Richard Burton shares my affliction, for his wife has said that he also laughs in bed. Was there a day in Wales when a Mickey ruined him, too?

Although Mickey's romantic tale fell somewhat short of *Ivanhoe*, it was good that he told me how the population explodes because I went on to have two little pops of my own. By loosely following his instructions, I managed to sire two daughters, one of whom has just requested the flaming facts from *me*, the facts that every father hates to declassify. One day last week, Eve-Lynn, my eight-year-old, came to me and said, "Daddy, what's *mating*?"

There it was: the new American trigger word; and for a moment

I felt like joining the militants called POSE: Parents Opposing Sex Education. I was silent for several seconds after Eve-Lynn's question, but not because I didn't know the answer, for mating was something that I almost understood. I was silent because I didn't know if some racy little two-reeler from the Board of Education—perhaps something called *I, A Mommy*—was already playing in her classroom. And so I made a quick decision: I would explain only *external* fertilization and let all other thrills come from the teacher.

"Honey," I said, "mating is when two bees or fleas or fish decide to make *more* bees and fleas and fish."

It was hardly a marriage manual, but it was prettier than Mickey's tale. Carefully remaining on a low zoological level, I went on to deliver a veterinary *Kama Sutra*, shrewdly avoiding pauses for questions; and by the time that I was done, Eve-Lynn knew exactly how to keep herself from ever being compromised by a lobster.

I couldn't have gone any further and still protected the American way of life, for I've recently learned from leading conservatives that sex education was invented by Karl Marx to wreck the family unit, corrupt the young, and destroy the domino theory. Moreover, it has now been established that for the past two decades, the Communists have been following a programme of conquest by pornography, distributing French postcards whenever political subversion has failed, while Americans in the silent majority have looked to prayer and impotence for a patriotic counter-attack.

"The long-range plan to bring sex education into the American public schools for children from kindergarten to the twelfth grade is part of a giant Communist conspiracy," says the Reverend Billy Hargis, for whom POSE also means Preacher Opposing Socialist Erotica.

And so I gave Eve-Lynn just enough information to satisfy her curiosity while still keeping her loyal. All the naughtier details will have to come from the Vietcong.

Unfortunately, however, I now have a problem with my older daughter, Jill, who may well be headed down the road to socialised hormones. Yesterday Jill's class saw a movie that told how cows are born. When I asked her about it, she said she'd explain the whole business to me when I take all the THINK AMERICA stickers off her books.

A Day in my Life

By PATRICK CAMPBELL

SIX o'clock in the morning, every morning, finds me wide
awake if still in bed, coiled like a spring to pounce upon the
literary tasks of the day.

This comparatively early awakening may be force of habit. I,
however, prefer to regard it as Mother Nature's warning to her
son that the few functional hours of the day have already begun
to slip away and that it's time he was up and doing.

Some writers—and a pallid looking lot they are—tell me that
their most fertile time is after midnight, while all the world is
still and they can be alone with their thoughts. Plenty of black
coffee, they say, some classical music playing softly in the background, and they can advance their novel by as many as two pages
a night.

"A gruelling work programme such as this," I suggest to them,
"must render it impossible for you to get up until lunch-time the
following day. What, then, do you do all afternoon and evening?"

"We think," they say, "about what we are going to write during
the coming night."

They are brave men, and I tell them so. "But what happens," I
then inquire, "if you've begun to write at midnight and find at,
say, one-thirty a.m. that you've failed to make a mark on the page?
To whom can you turn at that underpopulated hour for little chats
on the telephone? Is there a shop or a public house open? Will
the window cleaner arrive? Is there one chance in a million of people
dropping in for drinks?"

Before they can reply to this stern questioning I tell them of my
own method, one which is far less exposed to the terrors of a state
of isolation in which there is nothing else to do except to write.

It begins with the coiling of the spring, in bed, at six am. I said
earlier that this process was a preliminary to pouncing upon the
literary tasks of the day but, in fact, much of the energy created by
it is expended upon necessary tasks outside the literary field. Like
shaving.

I solved the problem of shaving, before writing, years ago by
shaving with an electric razor while reading in bed.

Shaving takes, perhaps, five to seven minutes, so that I still
have the best part of two hours to employ before the newspapers
arrive at eight o'clock.

In view of the fact that the contents of the newspapers may change
the whole of my thinking, it is clearly uneconomical to begin to
think until after they have arrived. So I continue to read.

"But surely," people ask me, "surely during this time thoughts
must be formulating themselves, ideas must be running through
your mind? Surely you couldn't help it?"

"Not only can I help it," I tell them, "I can actually stop it—

by reading. Such publications as *Motor Sport* and *Esquire* are most beneficial in this field."

I've always had an uneasy feeling about thinking before the actual moment of composition. It can create a block which no amount of battering can break down—as in the case of the venerable reporter who covered the funeral of Queen Victoria for the *Morning Post*.

This old gentleman was the star of the reporters' room. He was turned loose only upon occasions of major national importance, and for this one the most elaborate preparations were made.

A room was set aside for his especial use. Reams of gleaming white paper were provided and all manner of pencils and pens. There was also a bottle of whisky, a large jug of water and two siphons of soda.

The old gentleman sped back from the funeral in the fastest hansom cab that could be found and as he shot into his office his lips were seen to be moving.

The younger reporters observed to one another, in awe, "He's already begun to compose."

The door banged and silence fell for what turned out to be nearly an hour.

By the end of the next hour a measure of anxiety was beginning to spread itself throughout the office. Time was getting short. The machines were ready to roll.

In fear and trepidation the Editor took it upon himself to tap very softly on the old gentleman's door. There was only silence from within.

The Editor, holding his breath, opened the door, and saw a dreadful sight.

The star reporter was lying face down across his desk. The bottle of whisky was empty and hundreds of sheets of gleaming white paper were spread about the floor.

The Editor picked one up. Written upon it was the sentence or, rather, the beginning of a sentence: "Not since the death of Jesus Christ . . ." And upon all the other hundreds of sheets of paper were exactly the same words.

The star reporter had thought too hard, and begun too high. It's to avoid this kind of thing that I like to keep the mind as far away as possible from the approaching conflict—up to the moment, that is, when the papers come through the letterbox.

Now, for the first time since waking, the intelligence is permitted to manoeuvre around the possibility of formulating a theme, by studying the events of yesterday.

This hope is based upon the newspaperman's expectation that newspapers make news or, to put it another way, that he will find something to write about today in something that another newspaper wrote about the day before.

I recall, as we're all here, the first editorial conference I ever attended, after some fifteen years of working for newspapers.

I entered the conference absolutely unencumbered by thoughts, ideas or even faint possibilities and was immediately shocked to see that the other lads all had notebooks and stacks of clippings, suggesting that every one of them, given the opportunity, could fill the newspaper on his own, without aid from anyone else.

I was a lot calmer ten minutes later, because it turned out that all their ideas were based upon the certainty that there must be a good follow-up to something that had already appeared in *The Times*, the *Mirror* or the *Sketch*. Furthermore, all of them had selected exactly the same stories to augment or improve. I found the sense of claustrophobia almost overwhelming, but the Editor described it as "A damn good productive kick-around."

So, at eight o'clock every morning, having been intellectually alert for a full two hours, I read a couple of newspapers in their entirety, leaving out only the situations vacant for computer programming assistant clerks in the Nigerian civil service. I can't bear to read these because £1,700 a year, rising by yearly increments of £45 to a maximum of £2,600, never seems to be nearly enough for knowing how to programme a computer.

By nine o'clock I have completed my study of the two newspapers and absorbed two boiled eggs and toast. I'm still in bed but I've been awake so long that I could have been in Glasgow, by now, if I'd had a mind for it.

I have achieved one practical benefit from my newspaper reading. An analysis of the sea of parboiled repetitive tosh in both of them convinces me that it is not possible for me, or anyone else, today, or tomorrow or at any time in the future, to add a single new drop of anything to it.

This discovery gets me out of bed at a run. Time is fleeting and, unlike the midnight oil mob, my working day tends to shut itself down, for good, shortly before lunch.

By ten am. I am seated at my typewriter. Before thought can impede action I write down, very quickly, "Well," he said, "what about Harold Wilson now?"

This is purely a defensive measure, aimed at preventing what we senior technicians call "white page glare." The longer a sheet of typing paper is left alone the more paralysing does this glare become, until in the end one actually has to leave the house to get away from it.

Strike quickly is my motto, and make a mark while you still can.

The typewriter, if it's any good at all, will look after the rest.

"DURING the last four days, plain-clothes policemen were sent to watch the dancers and many of them disregarded our earlier instructions not to strip and dance naked on the stage," said its spokesman.
Straits Times

Well, you *said* plain clothes.

IDEAL SUMMER GIRL

By KEITH WATERHOUSE

IT'S not given to all of us to be H. E. Bates, so there is no point in starting anything about the yellow strings of laburnum flower that we are unable to finish.

Beyond doubt it was summer. Certain unidentified birds sang in a variety of trees. The flowers, whether laburnum or otherwise, flourished.

The scene was a patch of arable land which may or may not have been a meadow.

To paraphrase Peter de Vries she was stark naked except for a PVC raincoat, dress, net stockings, under-garments, shoes, rain-hat, gloves, umbrella and a bucket-bag containing Kleenex tissues. She wandered along the hedge-row gathering the white hedge-flowers, or hedge-blossom, from the—well, hedge-trees. If she had concentrated more on the sheets of buttercups that dazzled under a high blue sky we would have been on botanically safer ground, but I approached her just the same.

I asked her name and she said it: "Rose." What else, in weather like this?

I explained that on this ideal cuckoo day I was looking for a girl on whom I would eventually be able to look back through the mists of time and remember as the lost ideal of that high distant summer. She asked me what high distant summer and I replied this one: the present one. The bluebells were going out all over Europe and they would not bloom again, if blooming was what they had been doing, in our lifetime. I wanted to remember the last English rose of that last high carefree June before the world grew dark.

She asked me why the world would have grown dark and I said there were any number of reasons why it would have grown dark. A world holocaust, for example, or a slump, or the nationalisation of steel. The point was, if she would just listen and stop interrupting, to be able to look back on a carefree bloody June with a carefree golden girl. We would make daisy-chains, wander by the river tickling trout and other fish. There would be sticklebacks, kingfishers, hawthorn, willow-herb, reeds of various kinds, cowslips. We might not be able to classify this flora and fauna but this I could promise her: sheets of buttercups dazzling under a high blue sky. Any silly fool could recognise buttercups. We would lie down in them and our hands would touch in the red evening twilight.

She raised a point about the colour scheme. Was the sky high blue or red evening?

I said that it would have been high blue to begin with but it would have become red evening later. If we stayed around long enough it would become golden night, and we would lie on our sheets listening to the whip-poor-will.

She said that she had not understood much of what I was talking about but she thought she had caught the general drift. For her own part she was a Danish au pair girl called Jorgenson. Her employer, a Mr. Rogers who was in the motor accessories business, called her Rose because he could not pronounce her first name.

She lived in the Big House across the meadow. (Actually, when we face facts, it was not so much a meadow as the site for six bungalows. The full dark song of the blackbird, or it might have been a thrush or an escaped parrot, was lost in the low throbbing of a cement-mixing machine.)

It was an ideal magpie day and we walked together over the sheets of buttercups and the hot tarpaulins towards the Big House. When I say Big House, I suppose more accurately it was a Span maisonette. But the garden was heavy with blue hibiscus—blue hibiscus? Blue something, anyway. Not daffodils. Irises, possibly— and the air was still, and it was an ideal chaffinch day.

"You will come to my room?" she said, but I had not planned on that at all. I asked her, what about the sheets of buttercups?

"It will be damp," she said, and indeed the high blue sky had turned an ominous grey as if the shadow of a world holocaust or slump was already falling across that last golden June. I imagined her room with its open window overlooking the thick currant bushes; it would be heavy with the scent of—well, currants, I suppose. There would be blue hibiscus or irises in cool stone jars, and tree ferns pressed in the pages of *What's On in London*. There would be good rough cider from the wood, or Scotch and ginger ale for those who preferred it.

So I agreed that we would go to her room.

"But not today," she said. "We have only just met."

I pointed out that this was the whole charm of the deal: you meet this total stranger in a meadow on this golden day before the world has grown dark; the pair of you make beasts of yourselves on sheets of buttercups under a high blue, or ominous grey, sky; and then you stroll off independently, never to meet again. The thing was practically folklore.

She said: "Today I must go to the launderette, and then bring the children from the ice-skating rink. We will meet again. I would like to see *Dr. Zhivago*."

We arranged to meet when the hawthorn would be in bud and the lush grass covered in cuckoo spit (we would take a groundsheet) and the martin would be singing its plaintive/jolly song.

This left it all a bit vague. I went back to the meadow a couple of times between June and October. There was a bird singing, but it sounded more like a seagull to me. The flowers were gone. The bungalows were built, never saw her again but I remembered, such as it was, that ideal buttercup day.

That's No Kandy-Koloured, Tangerine-Flake, Streamline Baby, That's My Wife

SATURDAY morning, late lie-in and a luscious pillow's-eye view as my allotted portion of wedded bliss shucked overhead her St. Mike's mini-nightie and, unadorned as Oliver Reed, only different, confronted the dressing-table mirror.

"Would you mind," I asked, "if I painted you?"

"On canvas?"

"No. All over."

"All over what?"

"All over you."

"All over me? Have you gone kinky?"

"No. Female body-painting is the latest rage. The *dernier cri* of *avant garde* fashion. Queen Mary Quant prophesies that in the 'seventies, 'we shall move towards more exposure and body cosmetics.' "

"I'm more in favour of a new fur coat myself."

"But you've got to move with the swinging times. At our age . . ."

"At whose age?"

"Well . . . at my age then, you can't afford to vegetate. All I'm doing is trying to keep a bit of magic in our marriage and . . ."

"All right, Oberon," she said, rubbing her face with perfumed skin polish that would have beggared Midas. "Let's see you get up and flap your fairy wings."

"Body painting is all the go in America already. In Seattle, over-wrought businessmen can now relax in their lunch hours at studios and paint pictures on naked girls for six pounds five for the first twenty minutes and two pounds for each additional quarter of an hour."

"That works out at over twelve quid an hour. Hundred pounds a day. Better even than sitting on a million. Are you offering me that?"

"Well . . . no. Because we're married, aren't we? Body painting on your own dearly beloved must be one of a man's basic conjugal rights. But you needn't be bothered about any expense. I'll buy my own materials."

"You're too good. How much are they?"

"A full set of the new Colour Me Body Paints costs fifty-seven and six. Twelve brilliant shades of pelt varnish guaranteed harmless to the epidermis and removable with soap and water. So you don't have to worry about getting it off."

"I'm not, because you're not getting it on."

"I'll do it all with a special Doddy non-tickling brush. I won't start any finger-painting hanky-panky, either, you can rely on that."

"And so can you. If you want to paint anything there's the wall in the downstairs loo been waiting for its second coat for seven months now."

"I don't know why you're so unreasonable about it. It's not really all that new. Goldfinger gilded Shirley Eaton all over, hand-painted dollies wiggle on *Laugh-In*, and if, in your Ancient Briton incarnation I'd been King Caractacus and you'd been Queen Boadicea, you'd have been only too pleased to have me sloshing the woad on your royal back for state occasions."

"If I'd been Boadicea," she said, buckling on her chest harness, "I'd have cut you off at the knees with my chariot knives before you got within brush-range. And now, get up out of that bed and see to the boiler."

"You could be sorry one day for not encouraging me in my artistic ambitions. Locked up inside this Tarzan body there could be an epidermal Picasso trying to get out. Picasso Ryan, King of the Body Painters, President of the Royal Academy of Flesh Decorators, who never lays a brush on a bird's buttocks for under two thousand guineas."

"Which reminds me you haven't given me any house keeping yet for this month."

"Though now a millionaire and doyen of the dolly-dabbers, Picasso Ryan had the rotten hard time of it at the outset of his career because his selfish wife refused to allow him to practise his art on her anatomy. Thus forcing the young genius, desperate for canvases, to stand in the rain on street corners calling plaintively to passing young ladies, 'Anybody want free sunflowers painted round their nipples, pierced hearts over their navels, or roses round the door?' Which brought him further setbacks when the uncultured fuzz kept knocking him off, and stark frustration was his lot until he hit upon the cunning ploy of painting up his missus while she was asleep at nights and unawares . . ."

"If you do that," she riposted, halfway through the first round of the daily all-in battle with her girdle, "I'll write four-letter words on your forehead with cochineal."

"Lord Ryan gained his first international recognition when he won the Scunthorpe Courier 'Paint Your Lady' Competition with that amiable Flossie from the dairy depicting 'Poetry in Motion' and stencilled all over with eleven verses of 'Come Into The Garden Maud' and a like number of replicas of the LPTB Underground map. His fee rose to the four-figure bracket during his Action Body-Painting Period when nude wenches, a round dozen at a time, ran willy-nilly about his tarpaulin studio while he sprayed them with luminous distemper from aerosols and hurled handfuls of wet chiaroscuro at them from his Jackson Pollock catapult."

"You'll be sorry," she said, having counted out the girdle. "If that boiler's out and you have to relight it."

"At the next Biennale, the Master swept all before him with the first of his Epic Mobiles. Using his favourite twenty-two-stone model, Mighty Elvira, he delineated on the vast oceans of her bosom, 'The Battle of Trafalgar.' The billowing Atlantic seascape covered her torso and, as Nelson and our British hearts of oak sailed into flag-bedecked battle down the left-hand swell, Villeneuve ranged his gaudy French men-of-war in line of battle up on the right. And when Elvira did her little hula-hula, the stormy winds did blow and the raging seas did roar to such realistic effect that they had to take Robin Knox-Johnston outside and give him sea-sick pills."

"I was wondering where to go on holiday this year. A cruise might be a good idea."

"In his unforgettable Electric Period, Picasso R. heightened the glory of his palette by festooning his subjects with fairy lights, neon necklaces, and exquisite strings of artificial glow-worms for illumination where Mr. Mellors left off. He made a third fortune, of course, with his Corporeal Collage in which he pasted hand-signed blow-ups of jam labels, baked bean stickers and fag packets all over any female barmy enough to strop off and stand still long enough . . ."

"If you stay still in that bed much longer, that boiler'll be taking over from the 'fridge," she said, pulling on the all-covering slip and closing the show. "And, anyway, I really can't see any sense in painting yourself up with all the colours of the rainbow. Sounds a bit vulgar, to me."

And forthwith proceeded to decorate her face with peach foundation, green eye-shadow, buff powder, black mascara, coral lipstick and golden scent, the complete impasto being applied with fingernails incarnadine enough to Lady Macbeth. I left the bed and went along to my daugher's room to see if she'd volunteer to be painted up psychedelic, but she said that she'd already had younger offers and didn't like to risk being run in for artistic incest. So I snitched her eyebrow pencil and went downstairs to sit beside the dead boiler and play noughts and crosses on my paunch.

By PATRICK RYAN

LOVE
is a multi-departmental thing

Take your secretary home to meet the wife, says a
psychiatrist, and avoid tense situations.
MILES KINGTON suggests a different approach.

IT was a beautiful morning. It was a sizzling, swashbuckling
morning. It was the sort of morning that makes people want to
take their clothes off and run down Regent Street towards the sea.
The policeman in Piccadilly Circus could hardly believe his eyes.

I took the morning mail into my boss.

"I see mid-summer madness is in the air again, sir," I remarked.

"Yes indeed, Miss Lefebvre," he sparkled. "In fact, a time to
throw off restraint and listen to the call of the bloodstream. How
would you like me to reserve a bench in St. James's Park at lunch-
time, just for two?"

"Oh yes please, Mr. Preston," I breathed. "And after that a
week-end in Brighton, with the curtains flapping timelessly in the
breeze and the never-ending sound of the cicadas outside our
window!"

Mr. Preston drew on his thick spectacles and stared strictly in
my rough direction.

"Miss Lefebvre, you sadden me. I need hardly tell you that for
the second Friday running you have failed the Company's weekly
personal standards test. From where I sit your moral fibre looks
sub-standard. This is not good."

"No, sir."

"But I have faith in you. I know that somehow next Friday
you will prove yourself to be strong, and good, and resolute."

"Oh sir!" I cried. "But I am so frail and weak and the Company
is so firm and manly. Shall I ever be worthy?"

"Of course you will, Miss Lefebvre, but it is a long and hard path.
The Company is praying for you. It is also paying for you, so we shall
do some letters."

The day grew hotter and hotter. Word came along the grapevine
that several Australian citizens had been arrested in Trafalgar
Square for surfing in the fountains. A police car arrived in the
street below to prise the traffic policeman out of his patch of melted
tar. From where I sat I could hear their strong, upright voices
floating up to me and suddenly I found myself standing on the poop
deck of a two-masted brigantine, watching the lithe sailors flashing
silvery through the waves. There was a man at my side and even
before I turned to look at him I knew it was Mr. Preston.

"In two days we shall be in Martinique, Miss Lefebvre," he said,
"and when we arrive I shall put my strong brown arm around you
and show you the plantation I have bought for us."

"I am sorry, Mr. Preston, that you should have strengthened and browned your arm to no avail. I must ask you to turn the boat around and take me back immediately to Lower Regent Street."

His handsome face grew dark and he bit his moustache.

"As you wish, Miss Lefebvre. But you are the first woman who has ever said nay to Jack Preston. I would deem it a favour if you could keep this matter a secret."

I gave him my word and all through lunch in the canteen I breathed no hint of my narrow escape. The workings of a large corporation are not made easier by the temptations which spring from hot weather and when I thought how near I had come to hurting the shareholders' feelings, a blush came to my face.

I took the afternoon mail in.

"This is indeed a time to be thankful for our calm Nordic temperaments, Mr. Preston," I remarked.

"Darling!" he said. "All through lunch I couldn't stop thinking of you . . . three times I addressed the chairman as sweetie pie. I have booked our room at Brighton. Do you want a pink, blue or plain hot water bottle?"

"Oh Jack! I don't care what colour it is, as long as it's warm, resilient, durable and reminds me of you!"

"Then you'll be on Platform Three at Victoria at 5.37?"

"There's no other platform I could possibly bear to be on."

"Miss Lefebvre, you are no doubt aware of the Company's monthly ethical spot check-up. I only mention it now, because you have just failed abysmally. I cannot understand your lapse, especially when only this morning you promised me to be chaste for the Company."

"Oh sir! Believe me, when you are not here, I am off-hand to you to the point of rudeness. It is only your presence that affects me."

"You must learn to control it, Miss Lefebvre. An ecstatic firm is not a happy firm, you know."

"No, sir."

The afternoon became golden and somnolent. The traffic in Piccadilly Circus had come to a standstill in the absence of the policeman, who was later found in a Trafalgar Square fountain waiting for colonials to go surfing. The owner of the café opposite brought chairs and tables out on the pavement, where they immediately disappeared into the pockets of passing French tourists. From multiple transistor wirelesses came the lilting rhythms of a drawn county cricket match. But I hardly paid attention, obsessed as I was with proving that I was second to none in my devotion to duty.

My chance came sooner than I expected. I was taking an afternoon stroll in the convent garden. The birds were singing in every bush and from the nunnery buildings came the soft murmur of a thousand vows of silence. Suddenly, a face appeared from behind a bush. It was a white hawthorn and Squire Jack Preston.

"Sister Lefebvre!" he said urgently. "I have come to get thee from the nunnery. I have a pony and trap waiting without."

Furiously, I produced my pad and pencil and wrote NO!

"Then at least come behind my hawthorn bush with me."

"I am a Sister of God!" I wrote. "Would you ask God to sell you His sister?"

His face darkened and he toyed with what was left of his moustache.

"You are right, Sister. I have sinned and see the error of my ways. I would deem it a favour if you were not to pass a memo on my lack of success to any third party."

As the sound of his horse's hooves faded in the distance, I rejoiced that I had proved strong. Then I put away my things, covered up my typewriter for the week-end and hurried into the rush hour crowd.

Half an hour later I made my way on to Platform Three at Victoria, and there stood Mr. Preston.

"My own!" he said. "So you really came!"

"I really did," I said.

"I have the tickets here in my pocket. I have reserved a compartment facing west to catch the setting sun and anything else of interest in that quarter. I have asked the attendant to put two gins and tonic on ice. Now all I need is your assurance and signature that you really truly wish to come with me."

"Oh yes, Jack. Yes, yes, yes."

"Miss Lefebvre, I'm afraid I must tell you that the Company has today decided to institute a new staff relations adequacy test. It is perhaps unfortunate that it should occur on a day in which you have already twice shown yourself unworthy of the firm, but it cannot be helped. I will be frank with you. You are fired."

"Oh sir!"

"Yes, Miss Lefebvre?"

"I would just like to say that even if I am far from the Company, I will go on being faithful to it."

"I think I speak for all of us if I say that the Company will go on loving you in its own way, Miss Lefebvre. So no hard feelings?"

"No, sir."

"Good girl."

He glanced at his watch.

"But look at the time! We'd better hurry if we're going to catch that train, my darling."

"Can we go to an orgy at the Bennets after choir practice?"

Disenchanted Evening

NICHOLAS TOMALIN looks for Swinging London

"I'VE got a temperature of one hundred and three," said the Bishop, staring morosely out of the taxi window at the swirling snow. "I'm not in the mood for gambling. Can't we call this off?"

I knew at that moment the evening would be a dud. My tape-recorder bumped disconsolately round my knees.

"It's been a hard day," said the Bishop. "All my sense of moral indignation has dried up with this flu. And I imagine you'll be wanting me to thunder." The firm lines of his famous face were drawn, his normally piercing eyes sat dully in their sockets, the resonant *timbre* of perhaps the most recognisable voice in modern Christendom was reduced to a tender whisper.

"I tell you what. I'll just do my bit here in the taxi-cab. Take it down on your tape recorder thing, and link it in with what the other chaps say later. When you've cooked up a proper argument, show me the draft. I really must go home to my wife, she's doing me a light supper with hot Bovril."

I thought of Quintessence of Evil and Dolly Girl, sitting expectantly in The Frugging Filly, waiting for The Confrontation to begin. The photographer would be there also. (Did he know them? Would he have the wit to introduce them to each other?)

"Swinging London!!" said the Bishop, grasping my arm just above the elbow. "Have you turned on your machine? Swinging London!! How exciting it sounds! How gay! How full of promise! How fab! And yet, and yet ... we all know, don't we, that underneath there's something missing? Something cheap? I don't want to seem priggish—about that word 'fab,' I first saw it from a train at London Bridge the other day. Someone had chalked the words 'circumcision is fab' on an alley wall. Extraordinary. Don't print that—Heaven knows I hate the kind of clergymen who always act the dismal jimmy. But when there is so much opportunity for real purposeful joy—you have told the driver to go to Paddington Station I hope—in this world, why spoil it with febrile stimulation?"

The whole evening had been so meticulously planned. Everyone else had moralised about the new sinful London. I was to be the first journalist to take a Bishop, in the flesh, round it. In company with the most infamous rake willing to join the expedition for all-expenses-paid plus forty quid gambling money, and a dewy teenager chosen after two weeks' auditions. Innocence, and two types of experience, witnessing before my eyes and my tape-recorder the whole scene going. A brilliant, beautiful editorial idea. But who could have predicted it would be the coldest, most unswinging night of the year, and the voice of Christian conscience would be struck down with Asian flu?

"It was, I believe, George Eliot who so succinctly demonstrated in her fine novels how gambling diminishes the human spirit, vulgarises the sense of excitement—lord, my throat is so rough tonight—blunts proper ambition and titivates frivolous and improper lusts. Now, two bob on the Derby, or the odd sixpence in an office sweepstake: there's absolutely nothing wrong in that. But when it ceases to be fun, yes *fun*, I'm not afraid to use that old-fashioned word—I'm warming to this subject—then gambling, and jiving, and all the rest become a real evil. A substitute for reality, for God if you like. I'm no gambler myself. In fact, this visit to erumperump—you put in where the others are going, my boy—is my first real experience of this kind of thing. But as I look round—these places aren't too dark to look around in, are they?—I'm amazed, yes amazed. I may be a terrible old square—no, cut that out please—I am, I hope, as 'switched-on' as the next man.. I brush up against lots of young people in my work, you know. Attractive young girls like you my dear—put in her name, will you? —and ordinary young chaps like yourself——"

"Quintessence of Evil is thirty eight, sir, and wouldn't like to be called ordinary."

"Very well—and dashing chaps like yourself, and they *don't need this*. Life itself is exciting enough. To visit erumperump is a revelation. Look deep into the eyes of the people here. For once, just for once, abandon your preconceived notions and with real sincerity look at their eyes. Empty. Desperate . . ."

We had arrived at The Frugging Filly.

"Actually sir, we've arrived," I said.

"This isn't Paddington?"

"I'm afraid I cheated."

"Very well, I'll come in for one bitter lemon. But just one. It's very unfair catching me like this. And just when I was beginning to enjoy myself."

As we entered The Frugging Filly I saw it was just as I had imagined. Quintessence of Evil sat with his hands on his knees, staring straight ahead of him. I had wanted him to be truculent drunk, he was clearly benevolent drunk. Dolly Girl was peering in an agony of nervous embarrassment into her vodka and tonic. Three tables away the photographer fiddled with a large pile of leather-clad equipment.

The Bishop, his purple robes billowing beneath his top-coat, his golden cross lolloping to and fro on his chest like an overripe bosom, clashed sensationally with the scarlet and vomit decor as he walked in.

Quintessence waved at us wanly. "I'm quite high, old man. Been hard at it in Muriel's all afternoon. I love the whole world, even you."

"Good evening," said the Bishop. "I'm afraid I haven't read any of your novels."

"Pleased to meet you," said Dolly Girl.

The Confrontation looked well, I had to admit. The Bishop was slowly recovering, Dolly Girl looked coy instead of nervous, and Quintessence, with his round, red sweating face, his oiled upper-class locks drooping caddishly over his forehead, his fat gold cufflinks and shiny suede shoes appeared—if not exactly a *trendy* devil's advocate—quite corrupt enough in period style to perk up the Bishop's reflexes.

Quintessence was a boyhood hero of mine. He had indecently assaulted a parlour maid at the age of fourteen, been expelled from three public schools, a direct-grant grammar school, university and four regiments for a series of dashing gentlemanly misdemeanours, and was now making a decent living by recording it all in a series of romantic novels. He had seven times been declared bankrupt.

As I brought the first round of drinks, he turned aggressively towards the Bishop, mustering his intellectual resources. I turned on the recorder.

"I believe, sir, you were at Lancing with my father," said the Quintessence of Evil.

"Yes," said the Bishop. "I believe I was."

The Dolly Girl's uncle had also been at Lancing; so, for that matter, had the photographer. I changed the tape after twenty minutes talk about Lancing.

The Quintessence had to go to the lavatory. He dragged me with him, his fingers soggily round my arm precisely at the point already bruised by the Bishop's hawk-like grip. "How can I rough-up a nice old bastard like that? He went to Lancing with my father."

"But what a well-mannered young man," said the Bishop while Quintessence swayed to-and-fro in the Men's Room. "I can see it's all a pose. You can't seriously expect me to condemn a person of sensitivity like that. I will, however, have dinner with him if you like. My wife will understand."

I can't remember much about dinner except that the photographer knocked over two imitation silver candlesticks (with real, burning candles), that we drank sour claret and the Bishop had his own jug of iced bitter lemon, that The Confrontation nearly came to life when Quintessence asked the gipsy violinist to play "Nearer My God To Thee," and that we were squired by The Frugging Filly's PRO who dominated the conversation with highlights of his youthful career in ice hockey with the Toronto Maple Leafs. Two more tapes passed through the recorder.

"Have you heard?" said the PRO (who would have done so

much better than Quintessence), "The discotheque world is ablaze with the news. Harold Wilson is a trigamist. They've unearthed his second wife in Warrington and they're going to distribute her signed statement to the world's press on the morning steel nationalisation comes up. Dynamite. Zowie! We had a chap in from Conservative Central Office telling us all about it the other night."

"I don't see how a man's personal failings necessarily affect his potential talents as an administrator, or indeed as a Socialist," said the Bishop, whose brother was later made a Life Peer by the trigamist.

"I've always wanted to know about Socialism," said the Dolly Girl. "Would you tell me what it means to the modern world?"

"Could I borrow your hat, old man?" said Quintessence to the PRO. He bent forward, as if to examine the label, and was sick into it. "I did that once before with Graham Greene," he told us.

Moodily I changed another Socialism-laden tape.

We had to skip most of the swinging itinerary as we were behind schedule. Proprietors, band-leaders, dress-designers, with-it groovy personalities in Ronnie Scott's Club, the Colony Room, The Pheasantry, a typical Kings Road Pub, waited switched-on in vain. We taxied straight to the gambling club.

"I feel like Marina passing through the brothel," said the Bishop, as we rang the doorbell.

"Brother, you look like her," said Quintessence.

The trouble about the gambling club as a symptom of sinful modern life—I subsequently sacked the researcher—was that it was empty. We were the only customers. Fifteen elegant Louis XVI rooms, all of them echoing and empty except for a band playing to itself in one room. We spent two hours surrounded by footmen in electric blue livery, half-a-dozen pimply croupiers who didn't speak English, and the manager nervously offering us drinks on the house.

The Bishop took me aside. "You'll have to modify some of that stuff I gave you in the taxi unless things liven up a bit. I suggest you substitute along these lines: As I look around me, do you know what I feel? I feel how sad it is. Yes, how truly *sad*. I have been in my time to some of the poorest, most squalid areas of this country of ours. Even there I have found a spirit, a vivacity, which is lacking in these pathetic domes of so-called pleasure. What are people after who come here? Emptiness, emptiness. Shadows chasing shadows."

"Exactly why do you say it's sad?" said Quintessence, who had also overheard. "The only real pleasure I get these days is feeling lusty when I'm more than a hundred quid down."

"I beg your pardon?"

"There is no vulgarity greater than the vulgarity of self-conscious puritanism. Virtue is only an absence of spirit."

The Bishop flexed his fingers. "Second-rate depravity mustn't be confused with spirit," he said. He turned to Dolly Girl, who was losing heavily at roulette. "Second-rate depravity mustn't be confused with spirit. Don't you agree, my dear?"

"Absolutely. Francis, you're a boring old sot. Shut up and stop being rude."

"Come, my dear. I think we should listen to that band," said the Bishop. Quintessence went off gloomily to lose sixty of my pounds playing the manager and his wife at *chemmie*.

We found the Bishop and Dolly Girl an hour later. She was teaching him the rudimentary technique of The Madison. His purple robes swirled fetchingly against her pillarbox red felt dress.

I had a headache, and an all-too-clear vision of the nightmare days ahead, coping with a succession of bored, or shocked, shorthand typists transcribing totally useless words off a defunct tape-recorder.

"One thing is clear," I announced. "If I ever manage to turn this evening into a viable article I shall have to so transform you all that any resemblance to actual people, living or dead, will be purely coincidental."

"What a ghastly, boring, frightful, lousy, ugly, vulgar, hopeless place," said Quintessence.

"I don't know," said the Bishop. "I think it's rather jolly."

"Francis, you're a square," said the Dolly Girl. "Leave us alone."

"Welcome to the colony. That's odd—we always thought that you were Mr. Brewster and that you were Mrs. Brewster!"

Some Enchanted Evening

MARGARET DRABBLE on the strategy of modern love

IT was the kind of party at which nobody got introduced. The room was dark, lit only by candles in bottles, and although a certain amount of feeble shuffling was going on in the centre of the floor, most of the guests were grouped around yelling in a more or less cheery fashion to people whom they were lucky enough to know already. There was a lot of noise, both musical and conversational, and the general tone seemed to Humphrey to be rather high, a kind of cross between the intellectual and the artistic. He could hear from time to time words like "defence mechanism" and "Harold Pinter" being bandied about above the deafening body of sound. He supposed, upon reflection, that one might have expected this kind of thing from his host, a young man whom he had met in a pub the week before, who had been most pressing in his invitation, but who had hardly seemed to recognise Humphrey at all when he had duly arrived, some time ago. Now, after half an hour of total neglect, he was beginning to feel rather annoyed. He was in many ways a conventional young man, and had not the nerve to go and accost a group of strangers, who anyway seemed to be getting on quite nicely without him, simply in order to add his own unoriginal views on Harold Pinter. On the other hand, he did not really want to go.

The situation was made even more annoying by the fact that everyone looked so interesting. That was why they were all getting on with each other so splendidly, of course. The only people who were not shouting or shuffling were extremely boring-looking people like himself, who were propped up sadly in dark corners. And the girls, one could not deny it, were most impressive. He liked artistic and intellectual-looking girls himself; he could never see what other people had against all these fiercely painted eyes, these long over-exposed legs, these dramatic dresses. They all looked a little larger and brighter than life, and talked with a more than natural intensity, and laughed with a more than natural mirth. He found them most exhilarating. He gazed with frank admiration at one exotic creature with long pale hair and a long maroon velvet dress: her legs were not over-exposed but on the contrary totally enclosed, though she made up for this modesty elswehere, displaying to the world a vast extent of pallid back, where angry pointed shoulder-blades rose and fell as she gesticulated and discoursed. All he saw of her was her active back: her face and front were bestowed upon others.

Even she, though, had nothing on a girl he could see at the other side of the room, far away and perched on top of a book-case, whence she was holding court, and whence she smiled serenely above the heads of others and above the sea of smoke. Her slight elevation gave her a look of detached beauty, and her face had a cool superiority, as of one who inhabits a finer air. She too was surrounded, naturally, by hordes of friends and admirers, who were plying her with chat and cigarettes, and constantly refilling her glass. And she too, like the pale girl, had long hair, though hers, as far as he could distinguish, was not pale, but of a dark and fiery red. He decided that he would cross the room and distinguish a little more closely.

This decision was sooner made than executed. It was remarkably hard to cross the room: instead of parting to let him pass, people seemed to cluster closer together at his approach, so that he had to force them asunder with his bare hands. They did not seem to object to this rough usage, but continued to ignore him altogether, and managed to talk uniterruptedly as though he simply were not there, as though he were not standing on the foot of one and sticking his elbow into another's chest at all. He steered his course by taking the face of the red-haired girl as his beacon, shining dimly for him above the raging social waters, and finally, a little battered, he reached her vicinity. When he got there, he found that his luck was in: by squeezing himself into a small gap between the book-case and a table, he could get very close to her indeed, though he was of course directly behind her, with no view of her face at all, and with his head on a level with her waist. Still, he was near, and that was something; so near that he could have stroked with ease her long descending hair. Not that there would have been any future in such a gesture. In an atmosphere like that she would not even have noticed. In fact, now he had got there, it struck him that there was not much future in anything, that this was really as far as he was likely to get. He had given up hope that somebody would come along with those oft-scorned but now desired words, "Hello, Humphrey old chap, let me introduce you to a few people." This lot were clearly far too *avant-garde* for a bourgeois convention like introduction. He wondered how they had all got to know each other in the first place. What was one supposed to do? Surely one couldn't go up to someone and say, "Hello, I'm Humphrey, who are you?" It seemed, apart from anything else, a positive invitation to rudeness.

The red-haired girl seemed to be called Justina. The name suited her, he thought: there was something finely dramatic and vital about it, and yet at the same time something superior. As well as remarkable hair and a remarkable face, she was the lucky (and conscious) possessor of a remarkable voice, which she was not at all afraid of using. From where he was standing, directly behind her, he could hear every word she uttered, so deep and clear and vibrant were her tones. She seemed to be fond of brave abstract assertions like

"Well, in my opinion, the abstract is a total bore, anyway. I like things that *happen*, I don't like *talk*, I think that action is the only true test, myself."

He was so entranced that he was content to listen to this kind of thing for a few minutes, but then he began to get a little restless, for, like Justina, he preferred action to talk, especially when the talk in question wasn't directed to him. He began to think of imaginary witty replies, things that he might have said had he not been such a non-participant. He even thought at one point that he might say one of them, loudly, just to see if Justina and her admirers would turn round, but by the time he had summoned up the courage the remark was no longer appropriate, and he had to start thinking up a new one. Then he wondered what would happen if he really took action, and pushed her off the book-case. That would make them notice his existence, at least. She might even like it. Or perhaps he might just grab her from behind and shout gaily "Hello, let me introduce myself, I'm Humphrey." And then again, he thought, perhaps not.

Sadly, for the twentieth time that evening, he reached for a consolatory cigarette and put it in his mouth, the miserable last of a miserable pack. And he didn't seem likely to get offered any more, either. When I've finished this, he said to himself, I'll go home. Then, reaching for a match, he found he had lost his box: for some reason the eternal introduction of "Have you got a light" never even crossed his mind, occupied as it was on far more desperate levels, and he reached to the table behind him for one of those candles in bottles that served as illumination and decoration to the whole dreary scene. He lit his cigarette and stood there, candle and bottle in hand, staring gloomily into the small wavering flame. Thoughts of dramatic calls for attention continued to flow before him: what about that chap he had once known who had put a cigarette out on the back of his hand because some girl said he was a physical coward? He had been drunk at the time, of course, and it had left a horrible scar, but the girl had been most impressed: indeed she had screamed loudly and burst into tears. Humphrey reflected glumly that he could have put out all twenty of his cigarettes all over his person and nobody would have batted an eye-lid. One had to be introduced first, before one could embark on that kind of thing. One had to have an audience.

When it happened, it happened so suddenly that he never quite knew whether it was inspiration or accident. As he did it, he did not quite know what he expected to happen: clearly he could not have hoped that she would go up in a sheet of flame, nor even that she should sustain any injury, however mild, for he was a kind and unmalicious person. She did not go up in flame, anyway: hair is not a particularly flammable substance, not even long flowing fiery-red hanks of it, and he did not apply the candle with much violence. But it did singe and scorch, with a most alarming and dangerous smell, strong enough to cause a great commotion.

"Good Lord, Justina," said one of her admirers, "you're on fire!" and he only just had time to put the candle down before she twisted round to clutch at the singed ends, shrieking with dismay and delight, and lost her balance and fell into his arms.

"You did it," she said, challengingly, from a breath-taking proximity. "You did it, you set me alight."

And he, reading in her face nothing but pleasure at having created so large a disturbance, held on to her tight and said:

"Let me introduce myself, my name is Humphrey."

"What did you do it *for*?" she cried, in a positive blaze of admiration, the kind of excitement kindled by duels or the *Rape of the Sabine Women* or indeed any violent and decisive action taken in the cause of passion.

"Oh well," he said, with nonchalant pride, as though such inspirations came to him every day of the week, "I just wanted to attract your attention, that's all."

"Right, clothes off everyone; this is a dress-rehearsal."

FOGARTY'S WEDDING

By ALEXANDER FRATER

FOGARTY sat on a bollard by the Grand Canal, cracking humbugs between his teeth and gazing at the pearly palaces and gunmetal skies with apprehension. Venice was mirrored darkly in his patent leather boots—the gilded, sun-dappled plaza of St. Marks, the passing bumboats and moored steamers—and, for the fourth time since brunch, he mumbled, "This is the biggest day of my life."

"Oh, stop saying that," I said. "You don't have to convince me."

"I was talking to a barman last night who said that Venice is a great place for weddings. They've had some pretty wild ones here, apparently. Have you ever heard of a Peruvian timber tycoon known, I think, as the Stinkwood King?"

"No," I said.

"He loved animals," said Fogarty, "and flew a selection from his private zoo across to add a bit of colour to the reception. The barman said that several escaped. Apparently two gorillas pinched a gondola and set off for Yugoslavia, rowing strongly, and a female warthog burst into Florians and tried to give suck to the espresso machine."

"What arrant bloody nonsense," I said.

Fogarty frowned. He looked at me with a worried gleam in his strange, wine-coloured eyes and said, "The hotel porter told me this morning he could smell fog. That's all I need. Here I am, marrying a Venetian lady on a goddam duck sanctuary in the middle of the lagoon, and somebody smells fog. Can't we change the venue? There are plenty of spare churches right here in town."

"Her family has always been married on that island," I said. "Anyway, all the guests will be out there waiting."

Fogarty sighed, and we waited for the two gondolas to come. They hove into view eventually, the first empty, the second carrying a heavy-breasted girl in white lace, clasping a massive bunch of snapdragons, and an elderly lady with blue hair. Fogarty swallowed. "Got the ring?" he said.

I nodded. The leading gondola drifted into the landing and Fogarty and I ran down the steps and jumped in. "Well, hi," called Fogarty to his bride, reaching out across the water for her hand.

"You no touch her, Fogarty," snapped the girl's mother. "Not till after the priest finished his business."

"Yes, signora," said Fogarty, sitting down in the cushions. He seemed suddenly happy. As we moved off over the lagoon, he beamed across at the girl, making little popping noises with his lips and stretching sensuously till his limbs cracked. They had met some months before when Fogarty was on vacation; he was swimming at the Lido one morning when she had damn near truncated him with her speeding pink water skis. Her name was Immaculata, but she was known as Lulu, and she brought roses and pomegranates to his hospital bedside and accepted his proposal of marriage by letter a few weeks after he returned home. Fogarty and I had flown out for the ceremony the previous evening. We lit cigarettes and lay back, enjoying the salt air and the slapping of the water against the hull. Then, some time later, the gondolier muttered and shook his head. "What did he say?" said Fogarty.

"I think he says fog is coming," I said.

He wasn't joking. Fogarty groaned and watched as it swept down on us like smoke, thick, pearly clouds of it rolling in from the Adriatic, smelling of oysters and old wrecks. Soon Venice was ephemeral and half-seen, a pink, marbled moon city hazy through streaming cirrus, and then it was gone. "Bloody hell," said Fogarty, looking around for Lulu's craft, some way behind, but it had vanished; our gondolier shipped his oar, wrapped himself in a blanket and sat on the deck, smoking. Fogarty tried to organise community singing. "It will keep our spirits up," he said. "They did it in the war, of course, when they took to the boats. I understand the Admiralty even issued song sheets along with the salt pork and biscuits. 'Eskimo Nell,' and stuff like that. 'Eskimo Nell' was a great favourite of Winston's, you know. He sang it at the Yalta Conference. Stalin took his hat off. He thought it was a hymn." He turned to the gondolier. "Allora cantiamo, sport. Arrive derci Roma, or something. Okay?"

"You go sug eggs," muttered the gondolier.

Fogarty, with his missionary talent for seeing the best in people, said, "He speaks quite good English," and glanced at his watch. "I wonder where they've got to? Lulu!" he called. "Lulu!" but there was no reply. "I don't much like this," he said. "Right now she's probably drifting helplessly towards the African coast, following the Babylonian tin route with her mum." He suddenly leant forward and looked at me hard. "She'll like England, won't she?" he said. "The dynamism of the cities and the lush green countryside? Besides, we have many shared interests, like our love of winter sports and sparkling wines. Oh, this marriage is going to be a notable success. Isn't it?"

"The gods have always smiled on you, Fogarty," I said.

He nodded and lay back in the cushions, staying that way until abruptly he sat up and pointed. A high, rust-streaked shape was looming towards us, towering like the side of a cliff and painted with the words, barely perceived, "MV *Spirit of Thames Ditton*." "Hey, she's British!" exclaimed Fogarty. He stared up at it, then said, "Shall we go aboard? It's at anchor. Perhaps, they'd give us coffee, or something. I could do with a cup of something hot."

"Good idea," I said. "We can at least ask," and I motioned to the gondolier to make fast to the gangway and wait. We climbed the swaying stairs and, when we reached the deck, stood there, calling softly. A woman's voice said, "Who's that?" and a tall, angular figure in boots and a worsted poncho appeared through the mist. "Are you the men with the fruit?" she said.

"No, ma'am," said Fogarty. "Our gondola is fogbound and we were wondering whether you could possibly let us have a hot drink." She considered us a moment, then nodded. "Very well," she said. "You'd better come to the galley," and we followed her along empty decks, past humming ventilators belching warm, egg-and-beans scented breath, and arrived at the vessel's kitchen, a small, dimly lit room hung with butchers' calenders and a picture, torn from a magazine, of a grinning Negress, naked but for pads and a Surrey cap, whacking a ball through the covers at some tribal cricket match.

"Tea or coffee?" said the lady.

"Coffee, please," we said. She nodded and placed a kettle on the stove. She had cropped blonde hair and a bony, introspective face. "Are you a passenger? I asked.

"No," she said. "I am the master's wife. I always travel with my husband. He's asleep now. We attended a Mariners' Costume Ball ashore last night and got back rather late." She sighed. "He went as King Kong and I as the Statue of Liberty, and it wasn't a very pleasant evening. During the Excuse Me I was forced to smack a little Cunard purser across the chops with my torch. He came as Lassie the Wonder Dog and, under the influence of alcohol, he rather rudely widdled on my plinth. The atmosphere was somewhat chill."

"I'll bet it was," murmured Fogarty, with a glazed look.

She nodded. "I could do with some sleep myself, as a matter of fact. It's been a hell of a trip, this one. We had to transport thirty-five church organs across from New Orleans. The pipes were battened down on deck and all the way over the wind blew steadily, making this awful moaning music night and day. Then we hit a hurricane. Dear God," she murmured. "It sounded like Bach stewed to the eyeballs, if you will pardon the expression, and using the keyboard as a trampoline. What wild, insane melodies we heard! It got so bad that a French killer sub crash-dived as we came by. Wooop wooop wooop, wailed its hooter, and it disappeared in an acre of boiling foam. Off the coast a Navy sloop came racing up to investigate the racket. When we reached Gibraltar they sent us a monkey and a tin cup by Admiralty messenger." She sighed and placed the coffee mugs before us. "Now tell me," she said, "what were you doing out on the lagoon?"

"We were going to my wedding," said Fogarty.

"Your *wedding*?" She stared at him. "Well, bless my soul. That takes me back a while." She laughed. "Here, I'll give you some advice. Know what my mother said to me before *my* wedding? She said: 'Play your partner like a stringed instrument.' Isn't that droll? I tried of course, with George, but it was like strumming an old suspension bridge. Know what I mean?"

"Some people are stringed instruments, and some are not," said Fogarty.

"Exactly." She nodded.

"I myself am woodwind, I think," said Fogarty. "Sort of reedy and haunted. I am a muted sort of person."

"Oh, George is muted too," she said. "No question of that. In fact, if he wasn't so bloody muted he could be commanding a big refrigerated cargo job right now, instead of this scow, speeding prime beef from the Argentine."

We sat drinking our coffee. Then there was a knock at the door and a Tonk stoker stood there with Lulu, who looked wraith-like and chilled, with beads of mist in her hair. She ran in and seized Fogarty's arm. "We drifted past this Ship," she said, accusingly, "and saw your gondola. What are you doing?"

"Having coffee, love," he said, passing his cup.

"The fog's thicker than ever," she sighed. "It could last for days."

The captain's wife, who had been considering them morosely, suddenly stood up. "She's right, you know," she said. "But I have an idea. If you two are really determined to go ahead with this, why not let George do it? Ships' masters can marry people. He once spliced a Spanish torch singer and her child groom a couple of hundred miles off Nome. Hang on, and I'll call him up." She unwound a speaking tube from the wall and blew into it.

"Captain here," said a nasal voice.

"Climb out of your pit," said the lady, crisply. "We have a proposition to put to you."

"Muriel?" said the captain. "Muriel, it's time for my egg nog. And will you please lower your voice to a sorta muffled bellow and tell me what's happened to my goddam chest expanders? They've gone. Have you got them?"

"Aw," she said, with disgust, and replaced the speaking tube. "He doesn't make much sense at this hour of the day," she said, earnestly. "I'll just pop up and see him. Meanwhile, why don't you just sit here and discuss the matter yourselves. Back in a moment." She went out the door. We waited till her footsteps had receded then Fogarty, very pale, grabbed his bride and we crept out too. Silently we loped down the deserted decks towards our rocking gondolas, poised and waiting to carry us on across the lagoon.

"It spoils everything—the pictures,
TV, and now the cricket."

Mothers of AMERICA

Recent events having proved that any red-blooded American kid can get to be President, it didn't seem a bad time to take a look at how the other 199,999,999 got brought up. Here RALPH SCHOENSTEIN casts a Mother's Day eye over the ladies who do the upbringing.

IT is said that when a Chinese mother is due to have her baby, she excuses herself to the field hands, trots indoors, offhandedly delivers, and then returns to the rice, just another automatic Asiatic who was able to multiply on the fly. But if an American mother ever attempted such a coffee break delivery, it would only be for the purpose of setting a new world's record, for the chance to tell all the other mothers in town, "I took fifteen seconds off the fastest known time of the Cantonese communes."

Dr. Francis Bauer, a noted psychiatrist, has said, "Since the usual symbols of status—money and goods—are so accessible, mothers have turned to the only things left to manipulate, their children." And so the moment that an American child is born, it is entered in a kind of infant Olympics, in a desperate competition against the progeny of mommy's friends. The issue is simply issue: which woman has most grandly reproduced. Although she has performed an act that is not beyond the skill of a backward chimpanzee, the American mother takes supreme satisfaction in the fruit of her womb, no matter how big a lemon it may be.

The first cause for boasting is the baby's looks. I have passed many insincere hours in New York maternity wards, where I have yet to hear a mother say, "You know, he really looks like a nondescript prune, but at least I think he's honest." Never insult an American mother by telling her that her baby looks like a baby, for she knows in her swollen chest (an Everest of milk and pride) that this particular child is a living piece of the Sistine Ceiling, a feeling that would be true if the Ceiling bore diapered Eisenhowers. Some of the dreariest moments of my life have been spent hovering over cradles, solemnly intoning my catalogue of superlatives, but still unable to summon the rhapsody being requested for the pink chicken beneath me.

"Did you ever see anything so *gorgeous!*" the mother will hint. "And you can easily see that he's going to be a great man."

"I'm sure of it," I reply. "He already looks like Beethoven."

Once the American mother has made it clear that she has produced a six-pound Mona Lisa, she moves on to establish the child's earthshaking superiority in all other departments. The next achievement is to triumph in toilet training, a triumph that brings enormous prestige to the mother of the first rump to control its pump. In a kind of urethral one-upmanship, each child is grimly driven to become the captain of his kidneys, for nothing so warms a mother's heart than to be able to take a drier-than-thou tone towards the mother of the soggy little chap next door.

The new world's record for toilet training has been claimed by Mrs. Henrietta Windish of Akron, Ohio, who succeeded in putting her son on automatic at the age of nine months. This record, however, has not yet been verified by the Official Elimination Committee, which is now checking if Mrs. Windish cheated by making the boy sleep uphill.

Once an American child is both uniquely gorgeous and splendidly dry, it can then go on to conquer its peers with mental and social feats. There are, of course, the routinely fierce contests to see which children can be the first to kiss, to walk, and to talk; but since kissing and walking are also the achievements of baboons, most mothers concentrate on talking. In America, it is all right to have nothing to say just as long as you start saying it sooner than your peers. In fact, the reason for the impressive number of mature American bores is that they were forced to hit conversational peaks much too soon. They were driven by their mothers to achieve oral parity with the glibbest babies on the block.

The talking contests are hard to sustain once all the contestants have reached three or four and even the dumbest have learned to play back an adorable blend of TV commercials and domestic obscenities. Then the mother has to score points by inspiring the development of less common skills.

"Grace, you'll never guess what a *brilliant* thing little Myron did," says a mother to one of her frilly foes. "He stuck his finger in a fan and then pulled it *right out!*"

"*All* of it?" says Grace.

"Yes, *all* of it! Isn't that *amazing? You* know how fast those fans go around."

"Jane, that's really *something*. I mean, my Harvey can walk between raindrops, but to have the kind of timing that you need for a *fan* . . . I wonder what Myron's IQ is."

"About five points below Nietzsche's, but he has *much* better manners."

"Well, Harvey's is only a hundred and eighty-three, but he's already got two little hairs on his cheek. He may be the first five-year-old to reach puberty."

"Oh, Grace, you must be so proud. I mean, if you can't have the highest IQ, a gland case is still a wonderful thing."

By the time that the American child has reached the age of three, he is known as a sub pre-teener. He is also known as a big baby, but only in those unenlightened circles which refuse to realise that his childhood is over. At the age of three, the average American child, whether or not his bladder has been tamed, is set to enter both scholarship and society, the next campaigns in mommy's war games.

Studies start in nursery school, but not just any one that will keep him off the streets; for the kitchen commando called mother fights to put him in the very best of schools, in one that will lead to a prestige kindergarten, where only well scrubbed thumbs are sucked. This kindergarten, in turn, will be the gateway to a golden grammar school, whose sole function is to launch the child into a college that can place him in a medical school. In short, therefore, that over-sized foetus chewing his blanket in the admissions office is about to begin his introduction to surgery.

The best nursery schools have long waiting lists, for the mothers so love their children that they can't wait to throw them out of the house and into academic orbit. The competition, therefore, to enter these schools has been known to drive tots to suck toes as well as thumbs. Those three-year-olds who've been wasting their time with non-accredited play are made to stop their dissolute ways and take the cram courses necessary for storming the hallowed halls of lower education.

"George, we've got to start tutoring Debbie," says the mother to the father. "Her interview for Nugget Nursery is only a year away."

"You're right," he says. "There are one or two subjects we could work on. For example, I think I'll teach her to stop setting fires. The whole problem may be that Bunsen burner she got for her birthday. I mean, I know that we're insured, but . . ."

"Well, I'm still glad we got it. So we've lost a couple of rooms; but meanwhile we've given Debbie the fundamentals of chemistry; and since all the *other* kids already know math, it's a way for her to impress the interviewing committee. Yes, she's strong in chemistry, all right."

"But she's weak on elephants: she keeps calling them whales."

"Well, they may give her credit for imagination."

"She also keeps forgetting her name."

"Well, *that's* the kind of thing you can look *up*; it has nothing to

ROY DAVIS.

do with wisdom. By the way, we could use more recommendations. Is there still a chance to get one from the Cardinal?"

"I'm afraid not. My friend at the archdiocese was transferred to Kenya. But I just met a guy who knows the Secretary of Agriculture, and that's as good as the Cardinal, especially if Debbie's going to major in sandbox."

Once the sub pre-teener is established in an institution of maximum maternal prestige, he can then make mommy's life a total triumph by letting her give him the sophistication that has turned many American children into pocket-sized adults.

If the mother's weapon in the struggle for status is a little girl, she can buy her a "beginner bra," whose official size is 28AAA. This particular piece of anticipatory lingerie is not as pointless as it sounds, for it can also be used as a tourniquet. If the mother wants to make the child a definitive siren, she can also buy her one of the children's wigs whose ads announce, "Now your daughter can be as glamorous as you." All over America, small boys are huddling at gum machines and whispering, "Does she or doesn't she?" a question that once referred only to sleeping with a night light.

My nine-year-old niece not only has been sporting both a beginner bra and lipstick, but since she was six she has also been attending catered birthday parties, where the tails aren't pinned on a donkey but worn by the maître d'. Other elegant frolics are held in private homes, where little sirens in nylons and hairdos beckon to runty Romeos, where blind man's bluff has given way to a sport that's considerably funnier, for two ten-year-olds necking is like two turtles having a debate. And hovering over it all is that fluttery field marshal, Mother, wondering how many points she'd get for the first bastard on the block.

"This one has the hallmark of a real sizzler—grubby cover, crumpled pages, and an absolute mass of date-stamps!"

The Secret Life of Mrs. Mitty

Just You Wait, 'Enery 'Iggins

By KATHARINE WHITEHORN

TREAD softly, because you tread on my dreams—and a pretty squdgy mass you have underfoot at that. Emerging starry-eyed and embarrassed from a review of all the tales I have been talking myself to sleep with since I was a child, I hardly know whether to be more horrified at the saccharine quality of most of it or at the raw Sicilian vindictiveness of the rest. I only hope, therefore, that everyone will accept my proposition: that a woman's dream life, as much as Walter Mitty's, is always about the exact opposite of what she is up to in reality.

But what she dreams about is what she cannot get. What I couldn't get at the very earliest age was a houseboat. I would spend bedtime after bedtime planning it out in every detail—the lights and the lockers and the tablecloths and the picnic baskets; I even designed tasteful green and white bathing dresses to be worn upon it by those of my family who were sufficiently in my favour at the time to be allowed on board. I need hardly say that I had never actually *seen* a houseboat, and suffered, then as now, from instant seasickness; but the idea of a floating home was strong within me. Occasionally it was supplanted by a parallel plan of owning a caravan, but religion dealt that one blow from which it hardly recovered. One day in Sunday school we were asked to draw the caravan in which one or other of the children of Israel (or possibly Judah) had crossed the desert. I remember experiencing that tingling feeling you get at any age when the conversation comes round to your subject; and I set to work to draw my dream caravan, only making the windows narrower at the top than at the bottom as a concession to Hebraic culture. And then the woman came round and said No, what they wanted was a line of camels. *Camels!* I went back to my houseboat for good. The boat had its more mobile moments, when it was inhabited by the nautical children from Arthur Ransome's *Swallows and Amazons*, and I suppose that at some point the tides of puberty must have washed it from its moorings altogether. For the next time I remember constructing a boat it had become a yacht, and on it was a Man. Not just any man, but a twentieth-century pirate; and not just any pirate but a literate one who shaved and quoted Byron and knew about birds.

The story owes a good deal to Daphne du Maurier's *Frenchman's Creek*, and as one good plot begets another, I still think it will make a rattling good soft-centred novel if ever I fall on hard times (journalists, like the Victorian poor, being forced to rely in moments of financial crisis on soup). However, it had its own variations. It started with a schoolgirl who had snatched a day off on her way home at the end of term to row herself moodily about the Thames Estuary in a hired boat, sucking her hat elastic and brooding about the injustices of boarding school. She is capsized and rescued by the pirate who, owing to being on the run from the police, is unable to stop and put her ashore.

Through the weeks that follow she listens to him recite poetry, explain philosophy, and order about the toothless ancient (who is the yacht's only crew) in tones that are benign but manly. She is entranced, but he insists that she go back, as soon as he can find some port where it is safe to dump her. However, he takes her out for a final evening of whoopee in some French seaport town—and a brawl develops. Versions of this vary: in some she cowers tremulously against the wall, in others she hits his assailant over the head with a chair. But in both versions she disregards his order to proceed to the British Consul, covers his retreat to the yacht, and races after him. She scrambles on board; he speaks to her from the darkness, moved by her display of loyalty . . . as the ancient steers the boat for the open sea, she walks down the darkened ladder into his arms. Versions of that vary quite a bit, too.

The idyll follows; and idylls make poor stuff for dreams. So we flash fairly quickly to the time when he is insisting that he cannot distort the life-pattern of one so young, and she returns to her parents, a stuffy, upper-class lot utterly unlike, I may say, my own set. For four years she trudges through the sub-deb life of her kind; comes her twenty-first dance and she elects to have it in an uncle's house on the cliffs of Cornwall; as a mark of eccentric despair, she insists on wearing black velvet for the occasion. All is dust and ashes to her, and in the middle of the ziz-boom she slinks off to a little music room overlooking the sea, and listlessly taps out "We'll go no more a-roving" with one finger on the grand piano. Suddenly the glass door to the sea slams open; the wind blows in and there, framed by the darkness, is the pirate, looking more like Laurence Olivier than ever. He carries her off, this time finally and legally; and once aboard the lugger she is fine.

This was not, of course, the only lump of marshmallow; there was one about a woman leaving her husband and coming back, no vows broken; and another about a girl and a tall, shy coloured man, and another about a Ruritanian Princess who falls in love with a huntsman—though this one, to my disgust, went hard-centred on me and ended, after the Revolution, with them facing each other greyly across the devastated earth with absolutely nothing to say to each other. But the focus of them all was the same: the moment of discovery. From Jane Austen to *Woman*, it is the moment of reversal when ill fortunes change to good, that is the essential of escape fiction; and a good half of the plot mechanics of this sort of thing consist simply in setting up a situation, that shall not be too obviously preposterous, in which both parties can manage to be fully committed to each other without either realising the state the other is in (this is why inequalities of race or social standing are useful). In real life, of course, this absolutely never happens, girls always knowing ages before a man proposes so much as a dinner date, let alone the altar; but it is easy to see why it is so vital to dream life. You spin these fantasies when you are yourself less loved than you would like; to make the heroine ignorant of the burning passion which is about to flare up and ignite her is to tell one's subconcious that there may be a Romeo, even now, lurking in the shrubbery of one's own life.

I puzzled a bit over the piracy element, but I think that too is explicable in terms of wanting what you cannot have. Girls read adventurous books just as boys do, they too absorb *Autobiography of a Super-Tramp* or *Travels with a Donkey*; but they themselves are unfitted for the picturesquely picaresque: for the one feminine disadvantage which no amount of female suffrage can remove is that women can get raped. So it is travels with a revolver in the Cevennes, if at all; drifting, for those of us who insist on doing it, has to be done in slow motion, with jobs here and jobs there and no nonsense about riding the rails in between; and even hitch-hiking, which we all do and brag about it afterwards, is no fun at the time. French driving is frightening anyway; one is always scared of French lasciviousness; and the double worry about what the lechery will do to the driving makes travel in such circumstances a horror. The only conceivable vagrant life is one you can share with a tough protector; and since the men you actually meet always want to do *their* tramping either alone or in a ruggedly masculine atmosphere, the shared adventure remains a daydream. Wives of adventurers, too, find this out.

It has to be admitted that marriage is a great barrier to exciting daydreams, even for those who do not talk in their sleep. There is little point in dreaming about a man who is lying only a foot away, and if he happens to be what you want, there is equally little point in dreaming about anyone else. Even the artificially constructed dreams of "What would I do if I had a million pounds?" or "What would I do if I had only a year to live?" lose whatever vitality they ever had when the chances are that one does not want to do anything very different from what one is doing already. So one is pretty well reduced to dreaming about work, writing imaginary letters, and slicing up one's enemies.

My favourite work dream consists of constructing the ideal magazine, on which all my old friends from the *Spectator* would work, but with shining improvements: Brian Inglis would write about bugs as well as bogies, Monica Furlong would go back to reporting with affectionate amusement on the antics of the Church of England, Bernard Levin would relight his Taper, and I, personally, would have the joy of cutting down all articles on foreign subjects from three columns to one and a half. Sometimes this ideal magazine links up with my other secret indulgence, and becomes the instrument through which I expose the hypocrisy and evil intentions of my enemies; but mostly my revenge on them has a more personal flavour: I am refusing a dime for a cup of coffee to a man who once sacked me, or being in a position to see that someone who once sued me for libel never gets a respectable job again. Sometimes the ideal revenge I plan simply consists in pairing them off, and I revel in visions of Lady Hulton unexpectedly married to Sir Henry Brooke.

When, as so often happens, one's enemy is also one's employer, one spends a lot of time composing a letter of resignation designed to bring home to him not only the rottenness of his organisation but also the extent of the talent he is now losing; and when, as is the case at the moment, one actually likes one's employers, a substitute has to be found. My favourite right now is the letter I am writing to resign from the circle of Fashion Editors, explaining exactly why I never want to look at another dress show in any circumstances ever again so long as I live.

These letters, I suppose, are the direct descendants of the ones one used to write in one's head when single, the interminable letter to explain, accuse, demolish, forgive or assimilate the hurts and strains of the *affaire de coeur* just ending. These one sometimes did actually write and post, though the consequences were always disastrous; either they had to be returned unread because the chap had by then married someone else, or they had the effect of starting the whole thing up again, and upon my Sam I don't know which was worse. It is odd, now I come to think about it, that the enemies arranged for a carve-up of the imagination never seem to include old boy friends. Either it is all too long ago and far away, I suppose, or one is, in retrospect, so appalled at what would have happened if they *hadn't* behaved like snakes that one forgives them.

Letters can often take the place of straight wish-fulfilment: you dare not dream of being engaged, but you phrase and rephrase the letter breaking the glad news to your mother ("Tell her," said my husband unfeelingly when it actually happened, "that I'm un-employed, penniless, and have the chest of a boy of fourteen and the lungs of a man of ninety"). For dreaming directly about what you actually hope may happen is something, I think, that few women have the courage to do. They are far too superstitious: too accurate a visualisation would work as a bad magic and make sure you never got the thing in the end. It is far too dangerous to think about the college entrance, the first job, the wedding ring, the filled cradle—one can only look at them out of the corner of one's eye, working out the clothes one would need, or where one should live, or how the finances of it might work out.

Which is simply another proof that the secret life and the real one must never meet. The secret life is a strange garden on the far side of the mirror, peopled by gods and demons; and hopes that are planted there will catch unreality like a sickness and fade and die. It works the other way round too, of course: sometimes one does not want one's secret life upset by reality. I nearly met one of my enemies at a party the other day and had to leave abruptly: I might actually have said something civil to the man, and *then* what about that dream of spitting in his eye?

"And I don't want to be lumbered with anything that is going to be a dead loss at a wife swapping party."

It's Love that Makes the Rain Come Down

By ANN LESLIE

"WHAT men or gods are these?" cried Keats to his Grecian urn: "What maidens loth? What mad pursuit? What struggles to escape?"

What struggles to escape, indeed. The maidens are obviously far from loth, and aren't escaping at all, merely beating a temporary tactical retreat.

After all, if they're not there for a spot of jolly rustic rape, what *are* they there for—skipping winsomely about like that in the undergrowth, draped in bits of ill-fitting scarf, bared bosoms bouncing about like beanbags? Clearly such saucy misses were always hanging about in Arcady waiting for some godling to ride by, or even a herd of corpulent satyrs to come thundering out through the olive grove with twigs in their hair and bunches of grapes dangling about their privates.

No, the maidens' anxious glances obviously are not directed at their pursuing lovers, but at the terrain: any minute now, if they don't pick up speed, they'll be flung down in some nettle-patch or bit of dank bog and used as a sex-object-cum-lilo—and too bad they

171

didn't quite make it to that cosy patch of ant-free moss ahead where they'd planned to sink prettily to earth in strategic surrender.

It's about time really that the liberated nymphs of the seventies turned rapist in order to avenge woman's centuries of ordeal by alfresco sex. Womanhood must now wheel around and leap off in hot pursuit of yelping lovers as they scamper desperately over cowpat and thistle, felling them with neat karate chops and seeing how much *they* fancy being ravished in a gorse bush for a change.

Of course, you could reach some kind of compromise by suggesting the use of a groundsheet—although such a measure tends to be viewed with lofty contempt as being yet another, typically feminine attempt to destroy the essential spontaneity of outdoor eroticism. Moreover, it's a direct attack on his virility: how dare you *even* suggest that being impaled on a bramble bush could materially diminish your ecstasy once he's treated you to the full splendours of his sexual technique?

Back home in Barons Court, your feller may well have been mugging up on the secrets of the 143 positions received under plain brown cover, but let him come within sniffing distance of meadow or copse and you can forget all about that: as far as Man is concerned, Woman's sexual position in the great bug-filled, horsefly-haunted outdoors is always, quite literally, inferior. A chap feels so much safer that way . . .

I once had a boyfriend whose principal erotic ambition was to make love naked in the snow. I was to peel down like a grape glacée, but he'd be all togged up as usual, snug as a bug in his Lillywhites' oiled socks, ski-boots, string vest, fairisle woollies, long coms, y-fronts, stretch pants, furry mitts, anorak, pompon hat and goggles.

Okay, I said sourly I'd do it, but only if he took off his clothes as well. He found the suggestion profoundly lewd: "*Me?* Take off my *clothes!* Who do you think I *am?* And besides", he added in pained reproof: "You *know* I get chilblains."

I retorted rudely that *my* joints would play up something horrid once he'd deepfrozen me into the Eigergletscher, and how about *that* lover-boy? and he retorted sulkily that I wasn't very romantic was I, no imagination, in fact downright *frigid* he'd say. And I yapped back that I certainly *would* be frigid if I went in for many such Sex-on-Ice Spectaculars, and he said very funny, ha, ha, and eventually went off, masculine modesty still intact, and found himself a massive Finn who simply adored roguishly romping about in snowdrifts while being beaten on her big pink botty with a birch-twig . . .

If snow is nasty, beaches are nastier. There's nothing less passion-provoking than lying prone in the freezing spume, with seaweed making rubbery squawks and pops beneath you and little sudsy waves playfully filling your eardrums with gritty foam and rendering you deaf as a post for hours. You emerge rubbed raw, beaten flat and encrusted with sand like some jumbo-sized wienerschnitzel ready bread-crumbed for the pan.

In fact sand is highly inimical to enjoyable sex. One girlfriend of mine, having reached the age of twenty-five, got bored hanging around Saving Herself for Mr. Right, and decided to go on holiday to pick herself the sexiest Mr. Wrong she could find.

She lit upon a Spanish squid fisherman called Miguel—who surged about in the gigolo's regulation crotch-strangling jeans, raking every female under ninety with his fierce, steaming glances—and decided she'd have to surrender her All to him on the beach, since that's where he seemed to spend his life when he wasn't actually out at sea, or under it, or surging profitably in and out of wealthy widows' bedrooms.

The experience was horrendous and she swears she's been right off sand, and virtually off sex, ever since.

Boats aren't much better than beaches. Small boats have skittish ways and tend to tip you both into the harbour oil-slicks, more often than not in full view of shrieking boat-loads of unspeakable school-boys with braces on their teeth. Large boats are generally better—although it does rather depend how many devotees of love-making under the stars are crammed on to any one boat at any one time.

I was once on a working cruise round the Adriatic islands with a bunch of randy travel-agents of both sexes who, swiftly awash with slivovic and freed from the pruderies of home life in Crouch End and Potter's Bar, paired off—and then spent the whole of the first night reluctantly playing Sardines en masse on deck.

All night long, the yacht rang with muted thumps and twangs and clonks as frustrated lovers softly ricocheted off steel ropes and anchor chains and fire-buckets, desperately hunting for a patch of unoccupied deck, occasionally uttering stifled grunts and hisses like "Ouch!" and "Oops!" and *"Muriel!"* and "Sorry old chap!" and "What the hell . . .?" and "*****!"

From below one could dimly hear them blundering about like a herd of blinded elk, and none of us on board got a wink of sleep that night, and judging by the uniformly filthy tempers of the star-crossed adulterers next morning, they'd not been able to get a wink of anything else either . . .

Incidentally, have you noticed how people still wax absurdly lyrical on the subject of outdoor sex in our rural past? One can still stumble across sentimental parlour-Rousseaus who'll bore you rigid with explanations about how all those lads and lasses having it off in haystacks were, in some primeval way, acting out folk memories of fertility rites among the ancient corn gods.

Actually I think they were always having it off in haystacks because it was more convenient than having it off at home—what with the place being full of cattle and pigs and hens having fits and the wimminfolk a-guttin' rabbits and the menfolk a-packin' dung and Grandma stickin' pins in wax dolls and some spavined cousin a-layin' of the hired girl behind the butter churn as usual.

Spirituality scarcely reared its pretentious head one suspects, in truly bucolic sex: you got yourself a good woman if she had all her own teeth, proved to be good breeding stock by dropping a lusty son every nine months—and then stoutly shaking her skirts and going straight back to work again, bashing beets and strangling chickens.

Idealisations of rustic lust were still being produced until relatively recently, largely by middle-aged literateurs whose slim volumes on rural Venuses tended to be financed by Papa's liver-pill fortune or great-aunt's Brazilian holdings, and whose knowledge of nature was pretty well limited to what they saw out of train windows on day trips to Box Hill.

Oddly enough one *can* be made to feel dimly guilty about not liking sex out there under the skies, in the great embracing bosom of nature.

For after all, is one not Woman—whose great groundswell of spirit apparently answers to the ebb and flow of the seasons, whose blood is said to rise with the sap, wild calling to wild in the core of her being, whose soul they say lies deeply-rooted among the burgeoning mysteries of bogmyrtle and bladderwort? Whose breasts are like the hills, whose eyes like stars, whose hair like tangled moonbeams; who's as capricious as the summer's day, and yet full of deep intuitive wisdom; the fleshly expression of the universal lifeforce from whose fecund loins springs the eternal Man-child . . . and all the rest of that Earth Mother codswallop.

And do you mean to tell me that this mighty mysterious spirit isn't keen on a bit of slap and tickle among the bog iris *merely* on account of it's cold and it's wet and the sea fog's rising?

Yes, I do.

*"Something with a **plot**?"*

The Birth of a Father

By ALEXANDER FRATER

SAM GRINDL sat on a teak bench commemorating Khartoum; along the back a frieze of laurelled heads and muzzle-loaders were carved in relief and grimly he noted that someone's cheek bone, General Gordon's, he suspected, was pressing hard in his spine. He moved and a Nubian chin caught him in the kidneys. He was meditating lying full length when a nurse sped by. "Hey!" he said, scrambling to his feet. "How's my wife? Mrs. Sam Grindl?"

"No one of that name here," said the nurse. She wheeled into an ante-room and filled her pockets with syringes.

"But I brought her in not four hours ago," he said. "To have a baby. At five this morning she grabbed my elbow and shouted: 'Sammy, the waters have broke; I'm gonna lay my egg!' so I threw her in the Mini and planed up here with horn blowing and blinkers flashing . . ."

The nurse stuck a spatula in her belt and smiled. "There are no Grindls in our book," she said. "Go see for yourself. You obviously took her someplace else and returned here to rest . . ." Somewhere in the building a siren hooted; "Crises!" she boomed. "Trainee nurses, over the top and follow me!" and, with a grinding of starched skirts, she vanished into the subfusc gloom. The smell of antiseptic was strong and Sam Grindl returned moodily to the refuge of the Khartoum bench. Across the way hung a chipped but gilded mirror; his face he noted, was thin as a bird's and unlovely, occupying almost accidentally the south side of his noduled head. It was curiously haphazard, the face, as though some time back it had been hung on a wall while the features had been fired at it from an air gun and then somehow taken root. His spine curved and drooped sideways, like a thin stem bearing the weight of a heavy bloom; tiredly he tossed aside *The Leek Planters' Weekly*, from which the social page had been torn, and considered his place on the planet. He wanted much. He wanted a silver-grey Silver Ghost and a bijou penthouse with elms in the roof garden; he wanted a sea-going yacht with an Epstein figurehead and a collection of Modiglianis in the saloon, a Ming vase, from which to drink his morning coffee, a little black slave with an MA from Harvard for Mrs. Sam Grindl, an Arabian thoroughbred to crop the grass in front of his semi-detached. He wanted his teeth filled with sapphires and a brilliant blue smile . . . But circumstances stood in his way. And men; they jostled him perpetually in their dealings, and for thirty years he had been riding his heals in a life-long skid; but one day he would grind to a halt and pursue his star, jealously, lovingly, to its very apogee. He would cast aside the jostlers and bask in the warmth of his birthright. He *knew*; the gypsy who had eyed his palm before puberty had had impeccable references.

A sister appeared. "Come quickly," she said. "Your wife wants her back rubbed; soon the infant will come."

He sprang up and, swathed in lint and clean cotton, stormed into the ward. Proud of his strong hands and calloused thumbs he started manipulating the back before him; it was, he noticed, firmer than before with a mauve birthmark shaped like a lima bean beneath the shoulder blade which was alien to him. "I must get to know you better," he muttered.

"Harder," she said, into the pillow.

"Harder, Mr. Huggitt," said the sister at his elbow.

"I'm not Mr. Huggitt," he said.

"Of course you are," said the sister. "This is Mrs. Huggitt, the lady whose back you're rubbing."

He tapped Mrs. Huggitt on her third clavicle. "Look at me," he commanded. She did so and uttered a thin scream.

"You see?" he said triumphantly. "She rejects me. Now where the hell is Mrs Sam Grindl?"

"She's next door," said the sister, "feeding her little boy from a polythene bottle."

"Little boy?" he murmured. "You mean . . ."

"An hour ago," she snapped. "You should be ashamed of yourself; go to her at once." She stepped into the corridor. "Come here, Mr. Huggitt," she boomed, "wherever you're hiding yourself. You can't put off things like this."

Sam Grindl shrugged and went to his wife. "Hey," she said. "What's eating you this lovely day?"

He gave, as he had given faithfully right through the humid years of their married life, no sign of having heard. He lowered himself into a creaky cane chair, noting bitterly that it didn't creak for him, and examined his son. It looked anthropoid and shrunken. He could see no resemblance and the only aspect of the child that pleased him was the name Grindl, ticketed in bright red crayon on wrist and ankle. He rose, kissed his wife and retreated to the chair.

"Everything go all right?" he asked.

"Marvellous," she said. "They gave me this gas and I had these marvellous dreams, all about pagans dancing the hoochi coochi on the beach at Honolulu."

He nodded. "Baby all right?"

"A little gem of a male," she said. "All extremities present and correct. Come and look."

He lit a cheroot. "If you shove that rubber teat down much further," he observed, "you'll throttle the little cow."

She peered at him with a worried smile. "Sammy," she said. "How can you talk that way about your wee boy?"

He didn't answer directly, regarding directness as the mark of the poofter. "If his mouth's fulla rubber," he daid, "how can he breathe?"

"Through his nose, Sammy."

He digested this in silence. "I didn't tell you," he said. "Yesterday at the office, Fred got the new coffee machine put beside *his* desk. Not mine as they promised; isn't that lousy? He took Mr. Wurrer to lunch and then sent his wife orchids."

"They all jostle you, Sam."

"Yeah."

"Look at your little son, Sam. Isn't he a lovely boy? Only an hour old and already he can drink. I tell you, he's gonna be fiercely intelligent; I think he might be Prime Minister, or perhaps some kinda tycoon. I got a hunch he might go into Spare Parts like you."

"I'll beat them all yet. You see."

"Sure you will, Sam; I'm prouda you. Me and the boy here, we're really damn proud of you."

Sam stared at the child. "You think he knows who I am?"

"I don't know, Sam. Perhaps not."

"Some day I'll powder his little bum."

"That mighten be enough, Sam. I have the feeling you resent him in a way; am I right?"

"Yeah."

"Why?"

"Mrs. Grindl, I have a hunch he wants to compete."

"Who with?" she asked.

"Me, for Chrissake."

"You? Little Barney compete with you? Why, he's just fresh from the womb."

"Fresh or not, I don't want him leaving me in his wake. You know how jealous I can be, Mrs. Grindl. My pride couldn't stand it."

"Well, really," she said. "It's the most extraordinary thing I ever heard. Pass me that flagon of gripe water. This is your son, Sammy, your partner. One day him and you'll work together, standing shoulder to shoulder against the rest of the world; society will soon recognise the Grindl men, you mark my words. And when we're old, Little Barney will provide for us."

He beamed. "You really think we could do it together? One for all and all for one? He won't try and get the better of me?"

"Certainly not. He's a gracious, loving boy."

He kissed Mrs. Grindl farewell and chucked his son beneath the chin. The child eyed him coldly and vomited. Sam kept the rosy image in his heart as far as the vestibule, but when he stepped into the softly falling rain it had faded and he stood alone, girding his loins for war.

Sideways With The People

MOST disturbing statistic of the week was that the average size of the English bosom has risen (if that's the word, and we sincerely hope it is, when you think about the alternatives) from 34 in. to 36 in. over the past eight years, an annual growth rate (according to the Sun Intelligence Unit) of 0.8 per cent. All very well, until you match it to the information that the average height of English women has gone up by only half an inch, from 5 ft. 4 in. to 5 ft. 4½ in., or 0.1 per cent per annum. Should this trend continue, the Englishwoman of 2071 will be 5 ft. 11 in, with a six-foot bust. Still, even this drear wind is not entirely ill: following the depredations wrought on the industry by Women's Lib, bra manufacturers must today be facing those broad sunny uplands with a little more confidence.

SOME LETTERS TIED WITH BLUE

PATRICK RYAN
has unearthed a remarkable correspondence
between Elizabeth Barrett Browning and
Sir Robert Peel

50 Wimpole St.
17th August 1844

Dearest Bobbity,

How proud am I of our secret love when I read of the welcome the country gives your Bill for Working Children. Your humanity in fixing the minimum age of employment at eight years, and your charity in limiting a child's working week to sixty-six hours have brought many plaudits from readers of my poem "The Cry of the Children." How strangely move our destinies that you, a guest of queens and seneschal of empire, should come to cherish a poor, wandering singer, singing through the dark and leaning neath a cypress tree. I trust that the ill-manners of my naughty Flush at your last visit have not caused you any lasting ill. I wept that he who loves me blindly should so assail the one I hold most dear. Do haste to tell me you are well.

Your very own
Ba

---

10 Downing St.
20th August 1844

My very dear Ba-lamb,

Pray do not discompose yourself, my love, about the playful nip which dear Flushie, impelled indubitably by purest motive and diligent only for his mistress's defence, put upon my person as I stooped to retrieve your reticule. The visual damage to my nether garments which necessitated my immediate withdrawal from your presence was no doubt alarming to a delicate, feminine eye, but it greatly exaggerated the superficiality of the physical injury beneath. My resulting obligation to remain standing upright before the Front Bench throughout the Parliamentary day, does perhaps confuse the Speaker a little and lead him to believe that I wish to address the House on every subject, all the time. But this uncertainty serves happily to reduced the time available for the fulminations of the vulgar, young Disraeli. Soon, I trust, I shall once more be able to sit down on your dear sofa.

Your devoted
Bobbity

50 Wimpole St.
15th September 1844

Oh! Bobbity Bobbity!

Gods of Hellas! Take me from the ashes of my grief! I seek but Acheron's portal and greet with eager hand Persephone. Breath freezes on my lips as moans my agony. From a desert of despair, I reach, beloved, for your strong hand to succour me. That which did haunt me now has come to pass and I am left with naught for company but tears. Come to me, Bobbity, come to me!

De profundis
Ba

Windsor Castle
18th September 1844

My beloved Ba,

I have but this night received your letter of the 15th, having been commanded without forewarning to attend Her Majesty at Windsor to discuss the coming visit of King Louis Philippe of France. I hope to be released from Royal duty tomorrow evening when I will hasten to your side and bear the burden of your woe.

Your own true
Bobbity

P.S. Accustomed as I am, my love, to the Calliopean splendour of your prose, I cannot quite make out what has happened to you.

---

50 Wimpole St.
20th September 1844

Dearest Bobbity,

I've lost my dog! Dear Flushie was stolen on the street. I could not sleep. I could not eat. Did I but close my eyes there echoed through my brain his dear voice crying in captivity. But happily he is back with me now. So you need not hurry home from your treasured Queen. My brave brother, Henry, hunted down the dog-stealer who demanded six guineas in ransom. Is there no law that can protect us from such rascals?

Your happy, happy
Ba

---

10 Downing St.
23rd September 1844

Dearest happy Ba,

I was most relieved to learn that your dear Flush is restored to you again and that a smiling face will greet me on the happy day when next I mount your stair. As to the law, my love, I must advise you that, under existing legislation, a dog is not recognised as legal property and, therefore, its owner can obtain no redress against a dog-stealer. I promise you I will give some Parliamentary attention to the matter as soon as we have quietened Mr. Cobden and Corn Law contentions.

Till soon, my Ba, and bliss,
Bobbity

50 Wimpole St.
3rd October 1845

My dearest, wounded Bobbity,

How lovely it was to see you on Wednesday and feel your strong arms lap once more about me. And what a pity that silly Flush should mistake the ardour of your embrace for an ill-disposed wrestling-lock. Arnica, Miss Mitford always says, is a sovereign remedy for dog-nips, and I hope that it will rapidly restore your dear, abused thigh. I have lately heard that Mr. William Wordsworth has suffered some financial disappointment and wonder if my dear, kind-hearted Prime Minister could give him some small assistance from the Patronage Fund?

Your very anxious
Ba

---

10 Downing St.
5th October 1845

My dearest Ba-lamb,

Pray agitate your mind no more about my trifling hurt, which so soon responded to the wisdom of Miss Mitford that I no longer need to preside perpendicularly at Cabinet meetings. I have authorised a suitable grant to Mr. Wordsworth from the Patronage Fund. You will recall, my love, that, at the behest of your tender heart, I have previously made grants to Mr. Southey, Mrs. Hemans and Mr. Alfred Tennyson. Such concentration of official charity on poets might lead a cunning mind to detect our attachment. And so I trust that your new bardic acquaintance, Mr. Robert Browning, will not later require such benefaction. We cannot be too careful with Benjamin Disraeli ever-anxious for means to encompass my downfall.

Your own true
Bobbity

---

50 Wimpole St.
14th October 1845

Bobbity! Oh! Bobbity!

Ah, Fate! Ah, Me! Ah, Agony! Icy death creeps up my heart and the grave would be but warm quietus to my misery. I am Electra incarnate and Life makes ready my sepulchral urn! Let me look once more, dear Bobbity, on your sweet face ere I go heart-weary from this traitor earth.

Miserere, miserere, miserere,
Elizabeth

Southampton
16th October 1845

My darling Ba,

I take it from the tone of your last letter that you have lost your dog again? Pray possess yourself in patience, my child, and take comfort in this grievous time that these villains ply their trade to make money rather than to accumulate dogs. Therefore, in due course of time, they will bring forth your dear Flush for ransom. I can write no more just now of all the love and sympathy that overflows my heart, since I am about to board the ferry for the Isle of Wight, whence Her Majesty has urgently summoned me to advise on the purchase of some property at Osborne.

> *Loving you always,*
> Bobbity

> 50 Wimpile St.
> *18th October 1845*

My dear Bobbity,

Possess myself in patience, indeed! Is such pious adjuration all I may expect in my hour of purgatory from he who pledges me his secret heart? They snatched poor Flushie from our very doorstep while Arabel was looking out her latchkey. Can you not do something, Robert, to catch these miscreants? Is a Prime Minister quite powerless? Can you not call out the police for me? If you can't, then who can? You invented them, didn't you? Do they call them Peelers for nothing?

> *Your weeping, weeping*
> Ba

> Osborne, IOW.
> *19th October 1845*

My sweet, tearful Ba,

The Queen insists I stay another day about some new additions to the estate, and how can I gainsay Her? How can I reveal that I would rather fly post-haste to London to kiss away your tears and scour every street in the metropolitan area until I find your long-lost Flush? Believe, my love, that I will come to the foot of your chaise-longue at the earliest practicable juncture.

> *Your sadly separated*
> Bobbity

> 50 Wimpole St.
> *20th October 1845*

Dear Bobbity,

The Queen! The Queen! Always and ever, Her Majesty the Queen! I'll warrant if she lost one of her stomping, fat dachshunds, you'd soon have every police force in the kingdom out looking for it. And like as not, call out the specials, too. You seem to be forever dancing attendance on the Queen these days and I vow you love her better than

> *Your neglected, forgotten*
> Elizabeth

My dearest Elizabeth,

Conscious though I am, my love, that you are no doubt over-wrought by your present trying circumstance, I cannot forbear to say how grieved I am that you can find it in your heart to conceive that the frequency of my visits to Our Gracious Queen are impelled by any emotion less proper than simple devotion to my Prime Ministerial duties. I have not, and never would, my dear, consider for a single moment that the rumoured regularity with which Mr. Robert Browning now visits you in my absence, indicates any purpose less spiritual than literary dissertation. I shall be with you tomorrow evening without fail.

Your offended but constant
Robert

---

50 Wimpole St.
26th October 1845

Dear Robert,

How fortunate it was that my brother, Septimus, at payment of six-and-a-half guineas, recovered Flush for me before you arrived on the 22nd. And how unfortunate that my poor, frightened pet should have misinterpreted your intent as you stooped to fill his water-bowl, and have taken the impression that you were bent on drinking its contents yourself. I do hope that the small impact of his dainty jaws will not have inflicted any lasting inconvenience. I wondered, after you had gone—and Mr. Browning today echoes my thought—whether Flush connected you in some way with the man who stole him and therefore attacked you as the best means of his own defence? Perhaps, there is some superficial resemblance, do you think? Do please let me know how you are.

Yours affectionately
Elizabeth

---

10 Downing St.
28th October 1845

My Dear Elizabeth,

I hasten to assure you that I am in as good health as can be expected after this last savage attack by your spaniel. My wife, Julia, unfortunately, is beginning to wonder why I take breakfast so frequently from the mantelpiece, and has been heard to query the household's consumption of armica. Mr Disraeli has been asking malevolently in the Smoking Room if a man can contract chronic dog-bites. I cannot but resent most deeply your suggestion that I bear any resemblance to a petty criminal and would assure you that there is not the smallest likeness between myself and that odious dog-thief, Taylor.

Yours Affectionately
Robert

Dear Robert,

Taylor? How, might I ask, do you come to know the name of the villain who stole my dog? You could not have got it from me because, until today when I asked Septimus after receiving your letter, I did not know it myself. My mind cannot help but mark the coincidence that poor Flush seems to be stolen each time he bites you. Is his theft and incarceration by way of being your revenge? Is that why you have ever been loth to call out your Peelers? Could it—but Mr. Browning assures me that the idea is too monstrous—could it be that you are in league against my Flushie with this beastly Taylor?

Yours sincerely
Elizabeth Barrett

---

10 Downing St.
30th October 1845

Dear Elizabeth,

This is utterly preposterous. I happen to have noted, in the course of my official duties when Home Secretary, that Mr. Taylor is the King of the Fancy and, as such, the controller of London's dog-stealers. I profoundly resent the implication—fed into your innocent mind, no doubt, by the subtle Mr. Browning—that I, the Prime Minister of Great Britain, would stoop so low as to connive such retaliation upon your lap-dog. Though God surely knows that from the savage way the spoilt little brute attacks me whenever my back is turned, I have every justification for doing do.

Yours sincerely
Robert Peel

---

50 Wimpole St.
1st November 1845

Dear Sir Robert Peel,

Spoilt, little brute, indeed! I would have you know, sir, that Flush has bitten many finer and more sensitive men than you can ever hope to be. He has bitten, to my personal knowledge, Mr. William Wordsworth, Mr. Benjamin Haydon, Mr. Thomas Carlyle, Mr. Alfred Tennyson, Mr. Robert Browning and other geniuses of the cultural world, none of whom, sir, has seen fit to blackguard him in the manner that comes so naturally to you.

Yours faithfully
Elizabeth Barrett

---

10 Downing St.
4th November 1845

Dear Miss Barrett,

La commedia é finita.

Yours faithfully
Robert Peel

50 Wimpole St.
1st September 1846

Oh, Bobbity, my own true Bobbity!

Woe! Woe is me and dolorous my day. The bitter cup is pressed once more upon my lips. I am Cassandra come again to Mycenae. Black poppies deck my brow and weave into my funeral wreath. Make soft your heart, for old time's happiness, and lend your power to help me from my pit of last despair . . .

In anguish
Elizabeth

Drayton Manor
Tamworth, Staffs.
6th September 1846

Madam,

I am directed to say that Sir Robert Peel infers from yours of the 1st inst, that your dog has again been stolen, but regrets that, since he is no longer Prime Minister, he cannot be of any assistance to you in the matter.

I remain, madam, your obedient servant,
Horatio Cleghorn
Private Secretary to Sir Robert Peel.

Hotel de la Ville
Paris
22nd September 1846

Sir,

Mrs. Elizabeth Barrett Browning requests that Mr. Cleghorn inform Sir Robert Peel that she has recovered her dog once again from *his Mr. Taylor* and that she, and her husband, wish Mr. Disraeli every power to his jawbone.

Yours faithfully
Elizabeth Barrett Browning (Mrs.)

TO "Worried Mind" of Kingston: this cannot possibly affect your ability to father children; your eyesight is perfectly safe as well, so stop fretting. *Jamaica Sunday Gleaner*

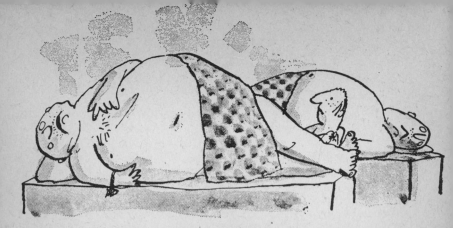

A NIGHT IN THE TURKISH BATH

"A pleasure so exquisite as almost to amount to pain"—Leigh Hunt

THOSE of you whose memories are still cluttered with the worthless effluvia of a traditional English education will instantly recognise the gobbet below my title as coming from a letter written by Hunt to Alexander Ireland, dated June 2, 1848. The rest of the text escapes me, along with trigonometry, the doings of the Corn Law League, and most of the exports of Java, but it's almost certain that the aforementioned correspondent spent June 1, 1848, broiling his frail Victorian parts in a Turkish bath. No other length of shimmering tropery could quite as accurately call up the dreadful joy of squatting naked on a marble slab and watching your body drip slowly into the gutter provided by a thoughtful management.

The Savoy Turkish Baths, Jermyn Street, meeting place of London's overweight nudes, is a spot that Hunt would instantly recognise (as you would be able to tell from the shudder racking his dehydrated frame): Turkish baths have not appreciably altered since the Turks themselves nicked the abominable principle from the Romans, a race given to shuffling between the tepidarium, the caldarium, and the laconicum, those three chambers of progressively intensive heat that go to make the bath the purgatory it is. The Romans also went in for a frigidarium, which in Jermyn Street has been replaced by an icy pond that is undoubtedly more terrible than anything that even Caligula would have suggested to his plumbers.

GOING DOWN

Nevertheless, it is here that every night the clogged pores of the metropolis foregather; it is an inauspicious doorway, hemmed in by shirt shops, in a discreet Piccadilly lane, and one wonders how many late-night strollers pausing to gaze at ties and boots are aware that beneath their feet several tons of fat are quietly steaming, like so many suet puddings, waiting for dawn. Because the baths themselves are deep underground, which, considering their temperature and endless supply of agonies, is no unsuitable location; and though, on

185

the evidence of one visit, overt sin seems absent, there is about the place an atmosphere of lasciviousness being purged. Men who have over-eaten, over-drunk, over-spent their bodies and their wallets, congregate here as at some great evangelical camp-meeting; stripped of their clothes and worldly possessions, they are punished and cleansed and given food and rest, and sent back into the dirty world. It is a kind of physical confessional.

COMING CLEAN

Which is the largest part of its pleasure. There's no point in telling a Turkish bather that it's not doing him any material good whatever, that the weight he loses will insinuate itself back by morning, that the heat and the freezing showers and the massage won't tack extra years on to a span prescribed deep inside him by fallible organs and other stuff beyond the reach of steam and masseurs' thumbs. It makes him *feel* good, he says, and he doesn't mean just physically; the bath carries with it the spiritual and psychological satisfactions of a good belch, a well-squeezed blackhead, a suddenly unblocked nostril, and that purifying evacuation that is the concession a recalcitrant bowel will make to those who will only have the patience to wait. In a sense, one is arguing from the opposite pole— examine the language of the Authorised Version, and you will find that when Godliness wants to hammer home a point, it falls back on the language of cleanliness to make it.

Not that the Turkish bath is exactly up there with Winchester Cathedral when you're ticking off the top ten shrines; its prevailing mood is non-denominational, with a strong Islamic tang. They take your shoes away at the entrance. This gives a somewhat socky tone to the air of the ground floor, and it is wise to strip off fairly nimbly, slip into the gingham tea-towel provided, and pad down into the pit below, your earthly identity retained only in the strap on your wrist to which is attached the key to your locker and, for some obscure reason, a little bell. (In the annihilating steam room, visibility is cut down to about four inches; and being in there with the rest of the inhabitants moving slowly about tinkling, one has the impression of groping through some hot Highland fog, surrounded by disorientated cattle).

The first room, which hasn't even got an -arium to its name, runs out at around a hundred degrees, which, apart from an odd sweet smell of flesh, is tolerable. It is filled with nudes reviving, lobster pink. The next, the ludicrously understated tepidarium, is sub-divided

"*She's being stoned for adultery.*" "*BITCH!*"

into sections of 165° and 200° intensities, and I spent most of my cooking-time in the cooler of these, with brief exploratory forays into the hotter. I glanced into the calidarium, which was chugging along nicely at 250°, and the very glance baked on my eyeballs: there was one man sitting there, who winked at me. I was not immediately certain whether what was on his mind was sodality or sodomy, but left quickly, giving him the benefit of the doubt on the grounds of the temperature being such that enterprises of great pith and moment with this regard their currents turn awry, and lose the name of action. A general word here about the unfair reputation generally foisted on to Turkish baths would seem in order: the ratio between perversion and respectability among the clientele is certainly no higher than it is elsewhere. The casual eye, fed on paperback psychology, may draw conclusions from the groups of middle-aged cab-drivers flicking one another with wet towels to make the buttocks blush, but they'd be the wrong conclusions; the object is merely to restore to life those cells numbed by a lifetime of leatherette seating. At least, that's what I'm told.

After about an hour of punishing dry heat, it gradually bore in upon me that my body and mind were actually enjoying this apparent hell enormously. As I mentioned earlier, the sensation is almost entirely compounded of virtue deriving from self-castigation, with a little masculine vanity thrown in by one's realisation that one is actually surviving. In all, not unlike (I'm guessing, mind) the feeling a nun gets at the end of a successful working day. Thus encouraged, I gave myself into the hands of a broad, Chaucerian masseur, who worked in silence with stiff brushes, some private oleaginous goo of his own invention, and fingers the size of bananas. Whole areas of subcutaneous adiposity broke loose beneath his hands and moved, like an amoeba's offspring, to new locations, where they settled, tired but happy. This sculpting done, I was swaddled in towelling like a Tunisian virgin, and bedded down in a dormitory full of similarly bandaged shapes; the overall effect recalling some field-hospital at Sevastopol, shortly after Florence and her amputating minions had done their worst.

I called weakly for tea; but never saw it brought. Within seconds, a deep, sensual fatigue seeped through every beaten molecule, dragging me down not into sleep, but unconsciousness. At 9.30 they woke me, and in a touching little ceremony involving the exchange of coinage, gave me back my shoes. I walked down the narrow corridor, feeling cleaner than I had ever felt before, and out into Piccadilly, just in time to catch the first thick fall of morning traffic grime.

By ALAN COREN

's the big idea, stupid! You nearly hit her!"

Are Latins Lousy Lovers?

By CATHERINE DRINKWATER

SOMEONE once asked Sophia Loren what was the best thing about being rich. "Not having to travel by Roman autobus in summer," she answered. Well, she must have had trouble in winter too. But certainly in summer every Italian male who wants a quick re-check on his virility seems to head for the nearest autobus. At 7 am they breathe last night's salami down one's neck like some asthmatic horse. By mid-day it's butterfly kisses up and down any female arm still young enough to strap-hang—with a lightning belt under that same arm into the first vacant seat. After dark I often expected to find that the pattern off my dress had been imprinted on some total stranger's suit.

But why the autobus? Well after one has known the hunters as husbands, fathers, brothers and sons, one suspects that it's because after ten minutes consternation among the girls they can swagger off feeling like the advert picture on something like Old Sea Salt deodorant; dangerously male, rakish and a very swine with the women. A picture for which surprisingly many are as well equipped as an expert dog-paddler posing on the high diving board—all right, so Mario didn't turn out at all like that last summer—well maybe someone had pushed him off the deep end already.

There's another reason why the open season for autobus hunting starts in April. Italian women may sport cleavages down which one could drive a coach and pair with ease, but few Italian men are misled by appearances. An Italian Signorina, when stalked by bold-eyed males, comes over all haughty. Swishing along like a cow's tail she manages to look deeply insulted while giving the come-on. But few Italian men make the mistake of coming-on too far. Anything precipitate could bring down the family shotguns— even to the last second cousin if it happens to be Sicily, Sardinia or the Boot. Oh yes, the Signorina will become the Signora eventually, but in the meantime those foreign birds will do very nicely as practice prey.

The ardent young male knows from his older brother that a coach party will be here today and in Milan tomorrow. He reckons every young Miss will be a swinger, though from conversations overheard *en famille* I understand that for an overnight stop a Fraulein is considered the best bet, and that few second cousins would make the journey from Pontefract or Slough. He also feels sure that every unaccompanied female tourist has saved through smog and rain in order to be swept off her feet for a fortnight.

This seems to be because few Italian men have ever got shot of Rudolph Valentino; Hollywood landed them with the Latin Lover image and by now it's a matter of national prestige to keep it up twenty-four hours on the trot. In a hot climate this can be wearing, which is why so many keep slipping home to Mama between times

for a vinegar soaked cloth to cool their aching brow, or a cup of nerve restoring camomile tea. They shatter easily, these pulsating lovers, and behind the scenes few can summon the strength to shell their own peanuts unaided.

Of course, your actual genuine Latin Lover should come from the smouldering south. The heat there is very debilitating so like a lot that smoulders he may fail to ignite. But he looks very fetching as he glides sinuous and cat-like across the landscape—that is when he is over four feet ten high, which down there isn't all that often. His eyes as moist as a licked humbug. His trousers so tight that every time he sits down his blood is cut off from the knees. He stalks his prey, and unlike his sophisticated Roman counterpart he often seems to find the foreign variety very confusing indeed.

British women on coach tours, when stalked by some hot-eyed-nature-boy, seem to follow one of two courses. They either run like the clappers back to the bus, or stop dead, with such unmistakable intent that the hunter, reared among the home birds, gets confused at making a kill so early in the game. Not that he complains; by the next season he is meeting the bus, or the boat at Capri, with such heart quickening greetings as " 'Awright, you 'an me Baby, Miss?"

While living in Italy I once met a girl from Blackpool who had fallen for such sweet-talk while on a luxury coach tour of Sicily. Pausing only to collect her superannuation, income-tax rebate and cash her insurance policies—for a dowry is a must in the tempestuous, headstrong love life of Sicilians—she had returned to marry her Latin Lover. The first few heady weeks went by. Then her Sicilian, who like most Italian men carried a purse, began allocating each day her small housekeeping allowance for which he expected an item by item account each romantic evening. The only doctor he allowed her to consult was eighty-two, and even in his youth would never have been hanged for his beauty. Her mother or sister-in-law sat with her every morning and evening when her husband went fishing, and in the afternoon he left her the nets to mend.

I don't say they all turn out this way, but when all's said and done there is a lot to be said for a two weeks' coach tour of the Lake District.

PURITAN BACKLASH

Very soon the pendulum is likely to swing away from permissiveness. PUNCH is horrified to provide some extracts from a new wave encyclopedia which show the completeness of the reaction.

Charles II: One of the kindest of British monarchs. No trouble was too great to bestow on even such humble subjects as an orange girl at the theatre. Not all the objects of his interest were of lowly birth and his court was, indeed, noted for its duchesses.

Chastity, Girdle of: Award given to nuns for exceptional purity.

Chatterley: The Chatterley family are the centre of a society novel by D. H. Lawrence. Sir Clifford had been wounded in the war and his wife nursed him devotedly on their Nottinghamshire estate. Lady Chatterley was much beloved by the servants, especially the gamekeeper, Mellors, who would wheel the invalid round the countryside and always did what he could to make up to his mistress for her rather lonely life. A real character, he liked to pick wildflowers for Lady Chatterley to use for decoration and did a great deal to make time pass quickly for her. It was a similar relationship to that of Mr. Pickwick and Sam Weller, though Mellors was less gay and amusing, if deeper.

Cleopatra: Patriotic and beautiful queen of Egypt. She married first Julius Caesar and then Mark Antony. When he was defeated in battle and fell on his sword, she felt that a wife's place was by her husband's side, in the next world as in this, and, very reprehensibly, followed his example and committed suicide.

Decameron: Book of tales by Boccaccio, supposed to be told by a group of friends escaping from the plague in Florence. They de with pirates, trickery and practic jokes. The emphasis is on go manners.

Desdemona: In Shakespear tragedy, Othello, a general Venice, is wrongly persuaded an evil subordinate, Iago, th his wife, Desdemona, is betrayi his plans to the enemy a executes her himself. The plot supposed to have been reveal when she dropped a handkerchi prepared by Iago, with a plan the Venetian forts embroider on it.

Dilke, Sir Charles: Victori politician who fell from pow because he refused to give eviden against a friend.

Eden: On being created in t Garden of Eden, Adam's first a was to sew himself a long rol with under drawers, from f leaves. Immediately on her arriv Eve did likewise. She was ju beginning to sew for the anima when the expulsion from Parad occurred and henceforward t beasts went naked.

Gloucester: Cathedral city. S of famous limerick:
There was a Young Lady Gloucester
Whose parents both feared th had lost her.
They found on the grass
A ring made of brass
From the nose of a bull that h tossed her.

Goat, The: Nickname of the wa time premier Lloyd George. S called by politicians because of surefooted agility in handli tricky problems.

Hamilton, Lady: Nelson's second wife, the widow of an Ambassador and scholar. Emma Hamilton played a leading part in the Admiral's career, giving him encouragement in many ways and providing the great sailor with the domestic life he needed. She frequently accompanied him to sea and was at his side when he died with the words, "Kiss me, Emma."

Héloise and Abélard: Héloise was the pretty niece of a Cannon of Paris. She fell in love with her tutor, the brilliant young philosopher Abélard, and he with her. Because it was not considered right for the clergy to marry, they had to remain just good friends. Unhappily the Canon became jealous of the friendship and hired ruffians who tried Abélard's Christian charity severely. However, they did not impair his intellectual brilliance and all turned out for the best, with both of the friends at the head of religious institutions, Abélard a famous author and Héloise one of his most loyal readers.

Hill, Fanny: Heroine of an eighteenth-century novel. Reflected in her artless prattle we see the life of the period close to, its commerce, houses, tables and beds. Fanny had a great love of fun and she is the ancestress of all the lively girls we meet in the pages of Scott, Jane Austen and Thackeray. Generous, enthusiastic and accomplished, she shows the century at its most attractive.

Juan, Don: Spanish grandee and traveller. Many well known plays and operas have been written about this lively character. He married the daughter of the Governor of Ulloa. When his father-in-law died, a statue of him was erected. On Don Juan's Silver Wedding anniversary, the guests assembled at a great banquet. What was their surprise to hear a knocking and see the statue enter and sit down at the feast:

the Governor's affection had extended beyond the grave!

Nell, Eskimo: Heroine of ballad celebrating her exploits cf. *Barbara Frietchie, Clementine, The Lady of Shalott.*

Rabelais: French comic novelist and leading figure in history of medicine and science. His work is largely concerned with eating and drinking.

Spanish Fly: The drug cantharis, said in legend to unite lovers.

Stopes, Dr. Marie: Pioneer of action to preserve world food resources.

Ward, Stephen: Osteopath.

Wife-swapping: Old English game in which players exchange their wives, who have to cook a meal for their new "husbands". Often the game ends with all returning happily to their lawful mates.

Wilde, Oscar: Wit, poet and dramatist. Towards the end of his life he fell foul of the tyrannical Marquess of Queensberry whose son, Lord Alfred Douglas, Wilde had tried to protect from his bullying father. The Marquess made many unkind remarks about Wilde, who had to sue him for libel to stop his cruel tongue. Unhappily, Wilde's enemies, including some politicians jealous of his popularity, took revenge by accusing him of stealing from a number of young men whom he had befriended. Wilde was convicted and sent to prison, where he wrote a poem which made it famous. Indeed, without Wilde's ballad would anybody ever have heard of Reading Gaol? So some good came from the sad episode after all.

Zeus: Chief of the Greek Gods. He enjoyed playing pranks on girls, using his magic powers to disguise himself as a bull or a swan or a shower of gold. However, sooner or later the maidens usually found him out.